D1456627

EUROPE AND DEVELOPING COUNTRIES IN THE GLOBALISED INFORMATION ECONOMY

The rapid development of new technology is accelerating the pace at which different regions and countries of the world are becoming interdependent. The convergence of computer and telecommunications technologies, in particular, is making it increasingly easy for services as well as goods to be produced in a cost-effective way at a location that is distant from the market. For example, on-line interactive communication facilities between Europe and India are making it possible for European companies to out-source software service work to India, where there is an abundance of low-wage knowledge workers. Similarly, advances in digital technology make it possible for learners in locations like Brazil to access educational material from Europe and other industrially advanced regions.

This volume explores the challenges and the opportunities created by the rapid growth of 'telematics'. European firms benefit through lower labour costs and from access to big new markets in the fields of education and training. At the same time European governments are concerned about jobs disappearing. For the developing world, there is the bright prospect of new jobs and novel means of education. However, how secure will these new jobs be? Will a more highly educated workforce lead to a brain drain?

Swasti Mitter is Deputy Director of the United Nations University Institute for New Technologies in Maastricht, The Netherlands. Her previous publications include *Women Encounter Technology* (Routledge, 1995).

Maria-Inês Bastos was a Research Fellow at the United Nations University Institute for New Technology in Maastricht, The Netherlands, from 1991–1997. She is now teaching at the University of Brasília. Her previous publications include *The Politics of Technology in Latin America* (Routledge, 1996).

UNU/INTECH STUDIES IN NEW TECHNOLOGY AND DEVELOPMENT

Series editors: Charles Cooper and Swasti Mitter

The books in this series reflect the research initiatives at the United Nations University Institute for New Technologies (UNU/INTECH) based in Maastricht, The Netherlands. The institute is primarily a research centre within the UN system and evaluates the social, political and economic environment in which new technologies are adopted and adapted in the developing world. The books in the series explore the role that technology policies can play in bridging the economic gap between nations, as well as between groups within nations. The authors and contributors are leading scholars in the field of technology and development; their work focuses on:

- the social and economic implications of new technologies;
- processes of diffusion of such technologies to the developing world;
- the impact of such technologies on income, employment and environment;
- the political dynamics of technological transfer.

The series is a pioneering attempt at placing technology policies at the heart of national and international strategies for development. This is likely to prove crucial in the globalised market, for the competitiveness and sustainable growth of poorer nations.

EUROPE AND DEVELOPING COUNTRIES IN THE GLOBALISED INFORMATION ECONOMY

Employment and distance education

DISCARDED

Edited by Swasti Mitter and Maria-Inês Bastos

London and New York

The United Nations University

INTECH
Institute for New Technologies

Published in association with the UNU Press

First published 1999
by Routledge
11 New Fetter Lane, London EC4P 4EE

Simultaneously published in the USA and Canada
by Routledge
29 West 35th Street, New York, NY 10001

Routledge is an imprint of the Taylor and Francis Group

© 1999 UNU/INTECH

Typeset in Times by
J&L Composition Ltd, Filey, North Yorkshire
Printed and bound in Great Britain by
Biddles Ltd, Guildford and King's Lynn

All rights reserved. No part of this book may be reprinted or
reproduced or utilised in any form or by any electronic,
mechanical, or other means, now known or hereafter
invented, including photocopying and recording, or in any
information storage or retrieval system, without permission in
writing from the publishers.

British Library Cataloguing in Publication Data
A catalogue record for this book is available
from the British Library

Library of Congress Cataloging in Publication Data
Europe and developing countries in the globalised information
economy: employment and distance education/edited by
Swasti Mitter and Maria-Inês Bastos.
      p.   cm. – (UNU/INTECH studies in new
      technology and development; 9)
'A collection of papers . . . presented at the workshop . . . held
in Maastricht on 17–19 October, 1996'–Introd.
Includes bibliographical references.
1. Telecommunication–European Union countries–Congresses.
2. Telecommunication–Developing countries–Congresses.
3. Electronic commerce–European Union countries–Congresses.
4. Electronic commerce–Developing countries–Congresses.
5. Contracting out–European Union countries–Congresses.
6. Labor supply–Developing countries–Congresses.
7. Offshore assembly industry–Developing countries–Congresses.
8. Distance education–European Union countries–Congresses.
9. Distance education–Developing countries–Congresses.
I. Mitter, Swasti, 1939– . II. Bastos, Maria-Inês. III. Series.
      HE8084.E96   1999
      384'.094–dc21   98–44184
                                                      CIP

ISBN 0 415 19704 X

CONTENTS

vii

CONTENTS

CONTENTS

TABLES

FIGURES

CONTRIBUTORS

N. P. Basrur has a B.Tech. degree in Electrical Engineering (Electronics) (1973) and M.Tech. degree in Computer Science (1975) from the Indian Institute of Technology, Madras, India. Mr Basrur has been with Tata Consultancy Services, the leading software consultancy firm in India, from 1975 till date. He currently oversees business development and project management activities in select areas like migration, re-engineering, databases and software tools technology for clients in Continental Europe and Japan. During his association with TCS, he has been involved in a number of migration and development projects successfully executed by TCS as team member, project leader and manager. He has also been responsible for development of initial quality standards, services and products marketing, training and a number of consultancy assignments in TCS.

Maria-Inês Bastos graduated with a degree in Sociology and received her master's degree in Political Science in Brazil. After working for the Brazilian government and teaching at the University of Brasília, she received her D.Phil. in Development Studies from the University of Sussex. She worked as a researcher at the Brazilian Council for the Development of Science and Technology and as a legislative adviser for the Brazilian senate in science and technology policy. From 1991 to 1997 she had a research fellowship position at UNU/INTECH where she was also the Dean of Students. She has published on politics of science and technology policy, on information technology policy and on applications of information technology to education in developing countries.

Claus Berg had taught physics/chemistry and computer science for twelve years in 'Folkeskolen', the public primary and lower secondary education in Denmark. He was one of the first teachers in his country integrating computer mediated collaborative network projects into the curriculum. He has been involved in the KIDLINK project since 1991. He was a co-founder of the KIDLINK Society and a member of its

Board of Directors for two years. Currently he is a chief adviser in the Ministry of Education in Denmark, responsible for the establishment of the Sectornet, the high speed Internet connections for all Danish schools. Claus Berg is managing the development of pedagogical contents in the Danish Schoolnet, and is also involved in the upcoming European Schoolnet EUN, planned to be launched in the spring of 1998.

Fabio José Chacón Duque has a Ph.D. degree in Higher Education from Pennsylvania State University (USA). He has been active in the area of distance education in Venezuela since the early 1970s when he participated in the organisation of the Centre of Educational Television. He headed training divisions at various public organisations and coordinated training programmes at the Audiovisual Department of the Open National University of Venezuela. He is currently the Director of the Graduate School at the Open National University of Venezuela. Fabio Chacón has published extensively in the area of distance education, particularly in quality assessment and design of teaching materials.

Seema Chawla is an Assistant Professor of Economics at the University of Delhi, India. She is currently pursuing the UNU/INTECH-MERIT Ph.D. programme. Her research involves exploring various issues related to the evolution of software technology and its implications for the international division of labour.

Andrew Davies is a Research Fellow in the Complex Product Systems Innovation Centre at the Science Policy Research Unit, University of Sussex. Previously he worked as a consultant in Intercai, Telematics Consultants, Utrecht, and before that as a Research Fellow in the Department of Science and Technology Dynamics, University of Amsterdam. He has acted as a consultant to several telecommunications projects for the OECD, the EC, the Rathenau Institute (The Netherlands), the South African government and the Swiss Research Council. Current research interests are in corporate strategy, innovation management and government policies for infrastructural systems such as telecommunications and air traffic control systems.

Abdelkader Djeflat trained as an economist at the University of Algiers and in the UK at the University of Bath, where he took his Ph.D. He has been a Full Professor at the University of Oran in Algeria since 1990 and Associate Professor at the University of Lille in the north of France where he also holds the post of Visiting Research Fellow. As Research Director at the Centre for Applied Economics (CREA) in Algeria, he started the first research unit on science and technology for development of the country. He was a founding member and coordinator of the first network of researchers and practitioners on science and technology in the Maghreb called MAGHTECH. His publications include five books and several other articles. Professor Djeflat has also conducted extensive consultancy work for several international agencies, both in the UN system and outside.

Ümit Efendioglu is a Ph.D. candidate in the joint UNU/INTECH-MERIT Ph.D. programme of the University of Maastricht in the Netherlands. Since the commencement of her Ph.D. programme, she has also been working with Professor Swasti Mitter at UNU/INTECH in the field of relocation of information processing work.

Arlete Azevedo de Paula Guibert graduated in Pedagogy at the Catholic University of São Paulo (Brazil) and received a master's degree in Education from Indiana University (USA). She has large teaching experience in general didactic and methodology and practice of teaching at the Catholic University of São Paulo and the Teacher's College in São Bernardo do Campo (Brazil). She was the Head of the Audiovisual Division at the Regional Centre of Educational Research 'Prof. Queiroz Filho' and of the Didactic Materials Division at the Brazilian Centre for the Development of Human Resources for Vocational Education (CENAFOR). At the time she contributed to this book, she was the Head of the Didactic Resources Division at the National Service of Industrial Apprenticeship (SENAI), Regional Department of São Paulo.

Ursula Huws is the Director of the UK-based social and economic research consultancy, Analytica, and an Associate Fellow of the Institute for Employment Studies. Formerly a senior lecturer in research methodology at the University of North London, she has been researching various aspects of the restructuring of employment, the impact of information technology, and the implications for equality of opportunity, for two decades. She has published and lectured widely and carried out commissioned research for a range of international, national and local government organisations, NGOs and private sector organisations.

David E. Kaplan is currently the Director of the Science and Technology Policy Research Centre (STPRC) at the University of Cape Town. The STPRC is recognised as a national centre and it has made major inputs into government policy in the area of S&T. David Kaplan is the author of two books, a recently published national survey of innovation in the South African manufacturing industry and a wide number of academic publications. His current research concerns focus on the issue of innovation, scientific migration and industrial and technology policy.

Peter E. Kinyanjui is trained in Geography (University of London) and Education (Syracuse University). He pursued a professional career in distance education and international education. He is a citizen of Kenya where he has taught and administered educational programmes in various capacities at the University of Nairobi for over twenty-eight years. He was the Founding Principal of the College of Education and External Studies, University of Nairobi, and a former Director of Higher Education, in the Kenya Ministry of Education. Professor Kinyianjui is currently Head of African Programmes and Training at The Commonwealth of Learning.

Eline De Kleine graduated in Educational Science and Technology at the University of Twente, The Netherlands. She has worked in the design and development of multimedia and hypermedia applications to training, and researched on user interfaces, usability, effectiveness and costs of educational technology for training. She is currently at KPN Research, the R&D branch of the former PTT Telecom of The Netherlands.

Wolfram Laaser has a Ph.D. degree in Economics from the Technical University of Berlin and has lectured in international economics and development policy at the University of Paderborn. He is the coordinator of the didactic sections at the Centre of Distance Study Development of the FernUniversitaet Hagen. He is a member of the editorial boards of the *Journal of Educational Research* (India) and the *Revista Iberoamericana de Educacion Superior a Distancia* (Madrid). He has been directly involved in cooperation for the development of distance education with developing countries, particularly Argentina, Venezuela, Colombia, Brazil, Mexico and Kenya.

Swasti Mitter is the Deputy Director of the United Nations University Institute for New Technologies, based at Maastricht in The Netherlands. Professor Mitter coordinates and conducts research on the implications of globalization, informatics and telematics for women's employment in Europe, as well as in developing countries. She held the Chair of the Gender Advisory Board of the UN Commission on Science and Technology for Development and has worked for many international agencies, including the European Commission, ILO, UNIFEM and UNDP. She has published extensively in the areas of gender, technology and employment.

Geraldine Reardon is a freelance researcher, writer and editor for trade unions and development agencies. Her work concerns issues related to transnational companies, gender and women. She is a founding member of Women Working Worldwide, a voluntary organisation concerned with the working conditions of women internationally.

Ranald Richardson is a Senior Research Associate at the Centre for Urban and Regional Development Studies at the University of Newcastle upon Tyne in the United Kingdom. His main area of research is the impact of information and communications technologies on the organisation of production in the service sector, focusing particularly on work and employment. He is particularly interested in the spatial restructuring of production and in how particular places are differentially affected by technological and organisational change.

Albert Tuijnman received a Ph.D. in Comparative Education from the Institute of International Education. He was Associate Professor at Stockholm University and was with the Faculty of Education, Twente University, before joining the Organisation of Economic Cooperation and Development in 1992. As a Principal Administrator at the OECD, he was responsible for the background report prepared for the 1996 Meeting of the Education Committee at ministerial level on the subject of 'Lifelong Learning for All'. He has served as a Scientific Secretary of the Academia Europaea and Associate Director of the International Academy of Education. He was appointed Honorary Professor at the University of Nottingham in October 1997.

INTRODUCTION

The book is a collection of papers that were presented at the workshop entitled 'Europe and the Developing World in the Global Information Society', held in Maastricht on 17–19 October, 1996.

The workshop was jointly funded by DGV of the European Commission and by UNU/INTECH. The mode of funding itself was significant as it reflected the need for a dialogue between the European Commission (EC) and the United Nations (UN) – two international policymaking bodies with distinct and somewhat different briefs. The principal aim of the EC is to promote the competitiveness of its member countries. The goal of the UN is to assist growth and sustainable development in the developing nations. The workshop provided a forum for exploring whether these distinct objectives could be pursued independently in an increasingly interdependent world.

The concept of an interdependent world has been frequently used in the policymaking documents both of the UN and the EC in the past. The sense of a linked destiny among nations is reflected in the current and somehow indiscriminate use of the term 'globalisation'.

The changing nature of technology has done a considerable amount to account for this new awareness of interdependence. The rapid advances of digital technology, based on the 'ones and zeros' of binary computing, have given rise to the information age, where 'distance' is not a consideration for locating units of production and distribution. Digital technology has made it possible to convert text, sound, graphics and moving images into coded messages which can be combined, stored, manipulated and transmitted quickly, efficiently and in large volumes over wired and wireless networks, without loss of quality, and at a low cost. To quote the *Financial Times Survey on Information Technology* (5 November, 1997, p. 5), the 1990s 'will be remembered as the time when computing, communications and consumer electronics – the three C's – began to merge', opening the way for seamless access to multimedia information and entertainment, and laying the foundation for a new way of organising work, employment and education.

1

Telematics is a short-term way of describing the convergence of computer and telecommunications technologies. One of the major consequences of the telematics revolution is that a number of services, as well as goods, could now be produced in a cost-effective way at a location that is distant from the market (see chapters in this volume by Mitter and Efendioglu, Richardson, and Reardon). Information-intensity in the modes of production has greatly facilitated delocalisation of production units and externalisation of employment. On-line interactive communication facilities between Europe and India, for example, make it possible and profitable for European companies to externalise software service work to India where there is an abundance and surplus of low-wage knowledge workers (see chapter by Basrur and Chawla). Similarly, advances of digital technology make it possible for learners in Brazil, for example, to have on-line access to educational material and to educationalists of Europe and other industrially advanced countries (see chapter by Bastos). It is also digital technology that can offer cost-effective learning opportunities across the individual life-span, at home or at work (see chapter by Tuijnman).

The resultant changes in the pattern of trade in telematics-related goods and services present challenges as well as opportunities, both for the EU and for the developing nations. Europe benefits in corporate efficiency by having access to cheap knowledge workers and to a big market in the field of training and education. At the same time, the EC feels apprehensive about jobs disappearing, particularly in the services sector. The prospect of losing jobs is worrying for a region that is already experiencing a high rate of unemployment and a noticeable decline in manufacturing. For the developing nations, new jobs and novel modes of education mean a bright prospect. Yet, as some of the authors argue, telematics-driven outsourcing may imply the use of the developing world either as a location of footloose information processing work or a poaching ground for knowledge workers (see chapters by Djeflat, Kaplan, and Mitter and Efendioglu). In the field of education and training, on-line interactive education, again, may lead to inappropriate training material and deskilling of the instructors (see chapters by Laaser, Kinyanjui, and Bastos).

The changing nature of work organisation in response to telematics, likewise, poses both opportunities and threats. The case studies of call centres in Europe (see chapters by Reardon and Richardson) exemplify such duality. Call centres refer to a new kind of product site where a set of services are carried out over the telephone, replacing or complementing face-to-face interaction with the customer. These centres can be located at a distance from the main sites. Europe's less favoured regions have benefited from such relocations. Most of the relocated jobs are low grade with little opportunity for career progression. It is arguable as to whether these are the types of jobs that are appropriate for the developing countries to receive, as they are prone to redundancy due to automation (see chapters by Reardon and Richardson) or to technological evolution such as the Internet. Nonetheless, the possibility of outsourcing in some areas cannot be ruled out because of impending skills shortages in Europe (see chapter by Richardson) and because of the need to augment productivity in the corporate sector (see chapter by Reardon). At this stage, it is a matter of conjecture as to whether these jobs will be relocated to the developing world. Cultural, organisational and regulatory factors limit outsourcing across national boundaries (see chapters by Huws, and Mitter and Efendioglu), particularly in teleservices where the accent, the cultural nuances and response provide the key to success (see chapter by Richardson).

Here, we need to assess the impact of such national and transnational relocation of telework (telematics-related distance work) with a gender focus. The consideration of gender assumes significance in this context (see chapter by Reardon). As the experience of the banking sector indicates, those who receive teleservice jobs are generally women. Those who get replaced because of relocation are women as well. The question of gender thus assumes significance in the area of working conditions, remuneration and training for career progression – be that in Europe or in the developing world.

The negative scenarios of the telematics revolution need not be a reality. For the skill requirements of a learning society, capacity building in the developing world may benefit Europe by providing the requisite cognitive skills. It is important and opportune to identify the scope of complementarity rather than to apprehend the threat of competition. In fact, Europe's apprehension regarding the relocation of jobs is fuelled mainly by anecdotes (see chapter by Huws). There is as yet no adequate statistical framework and research methodology to capture the emerging trend or to verify the claim (see chapters by Huws, and Mitter and Efendioglu). In the field of tele-training and tele-education, likewise, there is a need for a correct assessment of the market, a closer vendor–customer interaction (see chapter by Bastos) and for the appropriate technological solution (see chapter by De Kleine). Such an interaction will enrich the information content of educational packages in European countries and will cater to the needs of the market in the developing world.

There is also a special case for in-depth empirical investigation to establish where the comparative advantage of the EU lies. There is a hype about Europe entering a post-industrial society where manufacturing is sure to have a diminished importance. Although the share of the service sector in the trade figures is on the rise, in manufacturing, where there is a high component of research and development (R&D) activities, Europe still has a definite advantage over the developing nations. Whereas the European suppliers in the mass production of mobile handsets, for example, are threatened by new low-cost consumer electronics companies from South-east Asia, Europe has dominance in the area of mobile or cellular phone systems, that encompass the entire range of cellular component technologies. The complex product systems (COPs), that such an architectural design implies, lends a steady and stable market for Europe in the world economy (see chapter by Davies) and in particular in the developing world (see chapter by Kaplan).

The workshop, and the book, have focused on specific areas of the information economy: trade, work and education. These are the factors that affect employment, human resource development and export potentials of trading partners. The papers, written by authors from diverse backgrounds, urge us to evaluate the extent and impact of telematics-driven globalisation. Not all the authors in this book are academics. We deliberately solicited contributions from practitioners, and from representatives of corporate organisations and trade unions. The style of delivery and the mode of writing reflect this diversity. We believe that the plurality of inputs has enriched the message of the workshop and the content of the book.

We have attempted, both in the workshop and in the book, to give a voice both to Europe and to the developing world. Points of view as expressed by contributors from Europe were confirmed or refuted by the participants from the developing parts of the world. The points and counterpoints thus presented have been crucial in identifying areas where policy interventions could lead to 'cooperative competition' between the EU and the developing world.

The counterpoints emphasise the strategies that the developing world needs to adopt, in order to make an entry into the world market for knowledge-based production (see chapter by Basrur and Chawla). Contributors from Africa emphatically raise concerns over the 'brain drain' in cognitive skills which benefits Europe at the expense of the poorer nations (see chapters by Djeflat and Kaplan). Contributors from Latin American countries show how the region is eagerly exploring various communication technologies for education and training in the effort to better prepare the countries' human resources (see chapters by Guibert and Chacón). The developing world now looks towards greater cooperation and foreign direct investment in the area of telematics from Europe, which would ensure a large and growing offshore market for the European Union. This cooperation is considered critical for revitalisation of education and for helping developing countries to find technological solutions that better suit their budgets and expertise (see chapter by Kinyanjui).

Given the limited resources and time, we had to decide on a select number of developing countries. The criteria for selection were the stage of development in telematic infrastructure and the extent of trading links between these countries and Europe. Understandably, the emerging dynamic economies of South and South-east Asia, Latin America, the Maghreb countries and South Africa featured mainly in the dialogue.

The major objective of the workshop was to explore the possibility of cooperation between the EU and the developing world in the belief that social cohesion of the EU is inextricably linked with the growth, prosperity and capacity building of its trading partners in the developing world. The presentations, as documented in this book, recommended the following areas of policy intervention:

- In formulating appropriate research methodologies and statistical classification to capture the nascent trends.
- In soliciting participation from all the stakeholders – corporate sector, trade unions, NGOs, as well as the governmental bodies – in formulating a research agenda.
- In initiating and sustaining a dialogue between the EU and the UN to counteract the negative and to strengthen the beneficial consequences of the emerging trends in trade, employment and education.
- In giving special consideration towards traditionally disadvantaged groups, such as women and older workers, in social benefits and training programmes, be that in Europe or in the developing world.
- In establishing links between scientists and technologists from the European Union and from the developing nations for identifying respective comparative advantages for a mutually beneficial trade.

These interventions may represent modest but crucial steps in altering the current vision of globalisation as the battleground of competing nations. In addition, these will place the wellbeing of people as the central focus in the information society.

Part I

INFORMATION REVOLUTION AND THE NEW MODES OF EMPLOYMENT AND WORK ORGANISATION

1

IS ASIA THE DESTINATION FOR 'RUNAWAY' INFORMATION PROCESSING WORK? IMPLICATIONS FOR TRADE AND EMPLOYMENT

Swasti Mitter and Ümit Efendioglu

The context

The news of Swissair, British Airways or TSB Lloyds Bank (UK) relocating a large part of their current and future information processing work to Bangalore, Mumbai or Manila contributes to the apprehension of a service sector disappearing from the European Union (EU) and surfacing in the emerging economies, particularly Asia. The emerging economies of Asia, such as Malaysia, India and the Philippines, are reportedly the major recipients of such subcontracted or outsourced jobs from the core industrially advanced countries of the EU. The level of wages in these countries is generally low, in some cases less than one-tenth of those prevailing in the industrially advanced EU countries (see Table 1.1). Despite persistent coverage in the press and in business journals, however, there has been little systematic analysis of the extent of this relocation, and of its implications for current and future trading patterns between the EU and the developing world. This paper aims to fill this gap in a modest and cautious way.

Given the newness of the phenomenon, the paper tentatively outlines:

- The factors – technological, organisational and cultural – that are perceived to promote or inhibit transnational relocation.
- The limitations and relevance of existing trade figures for capturing and quantifying current and future trends.
- The significance of these – albeit imperfect – trade figures in determining the comparative advantage of the EU and its Asian partners.

Table 1.1 Average annual salaries of computer programmers in 1994

Country	$US
India	3,975
Malaysia	14,000*
Hong Kong	34,615
France	45,552
Germany (West)	54,075
UK	31,247
US	46,600

Source: Mansell and Wehn (1997); PIKOM (for Malaysia).

*In 1996, on average, with three years' experience.

Such an exercise, we feel, is important not only on academic grounds, but also for a wider political understanding between the EU and the developing world. The fear of 'runaway service sector jobs' from the EU to low-wage countries, fuelled mainly by the publicity surrounding isolated cases, does little to alleviate tension. A more rigorous approach, in contrast, may help to define the dynamic comparative advantages of the trading partners. In an expanding global tele-economy, we have tried to point out that the rule of the game need not be win or lose.

Definition of information processing work

In this paper we refer to information processing exclusively as a telematics-related activity, whereby either paper-based information is digitised, or digitised information is used to provide inputs into the production process. This is found both in manufacturing (as in the design of automobiles or of software packages) and in services (as in financial accounting or airline reservations). Information processing, defined in this way, covers a much wider range of activities than simple data entry, which in the 1980s received some publicity in relation to its transnational outsourcing.

This earlier data entry work related, for example, to insurance claim forms or airline tickets that were sent offshore by plane or ship so that information from them could be put into computer databases (Pearson and Mitter 1993; Posthuma 1987). Although relocation of such clerical work still persists, its importance, both in teletrade itself and in the discussion surrounding it, has declined for a number of reasons. Historically, with the practice of inputting data directly into computers, the quantitative impor-tance of paper-based information for tabulation has decreased. In addition, straightforward outsourcing has become a less significant subject in policy dialogues. In its place, outsourcing as a part of a transnationally integrated system of production has assumed importance.

The fear of relocation to the developing world now stems not so much from a work organisation that is based on stand-alone computers, but on interactive computer networking. Improvements in telecommunications links have promoted the image – and fear – of virtual enterprise, whereby clients sitting in the industrialised countries could interact on-line with vendors overseas, in essence turning offshore subcontracting units or subsidiaries into a back office. The reality is, however, more mundane. Even in the field of high value-added processing, as in software, the use of fax and e-mail has been reported as being of greater importance than on-line interactive communicating (Mansell and Wehn 1998: 25).

Notwithstanding the mode of communication, one cannot deny that some of the developing world has moved quite successfully from providing services that require a low level of computer literacy (and little interaction between customer and vendor) to providing relatively high value-added and sophisticated information processing. India's achievement in export-oriented software programming work, for example, highlights some openings that emerging economies have managed to secure in complex and sophisticated segments of information processing work.

Factors promoting or inhibiting relocation

The fear of a shrinking number of white-collar jobs in the EU arises partly because of the prospect that the telecommunications revolution presents for relocation of information processing work. The convergence of communications and computer technologies has made it possible, at least potentially, to externalise and delocalise a considerable amount of information processing to home-based teleworkers in Europe at one end of the spectrum, and to the teleoffices of the Science and Technology Parks of Asia at the other. A linked computer network is all that is needed between the main company and its national or international subsidiaries or subcontractors. Increased bandwidth resulting from fibre optic technology has facilitated the effective and speedy transnational transmission of high-volume data and voice calls. Even countries, such as India, that have relatively low-bandwidth infrastructure, can access high-bandwidth traffic through dedicated lines so long as the volume of traffic justifies the cost of obtaining such a line. The use and prevalence of dedicated satellite links likewise facilitate speedy and efficient transnational transmission of information.[1] For local area networks (LAN), the availability of mobile and small-scale satellite technologies, such as that of the very small aperture terminal (VSAT), has opened up novel opportunities for connectivity in the poorer parts of the world (Forge 1995). These technological breakthroughs have, indeed, altered the logic of choosing the site of work. It is not surprising that 'the death of distance' and 'the end of geography' have become catchphrases in policy-oriented research and documentation.

It is not only the technological potential but also the rapidly declining costs of externalising information processing work that have contributed to Europe's apprehension. The reduction in computer costs associated with successive generations of integrated circuits has been dramatic, and understandably has led to the widespread adoption and diffusion of computer technology in production and in distribution in the European Union (see Table 1.2). The increased use of digitised information – the consequence of the use of computers – facilitates outsourcing, especially when the technology moves from the personal computer-centric to the network-centric paradigm. The frequent use of terms such as 'groupware' or 'computer-supported cooperative work' reflects the interests of the corporate world in the use of such a network-centric paradigm.

The potential for transnational outsourcing is also expedited by the falling costs of communications, particularly transnational telephoning. Thanks to fibre optic cables and other sophisticated electronics, the capacity of the main trunk lines has increased much faster than the growth in voice traffic, and the cost per call has tumbled as a consequence. The cost of sending data on-line has also fallen – sending them across the Internet costs no more than a local call. The cost of a transatlantic voice call in 2000 will be 1 per cent of what it was in 1970, and by 2010 it will be three cents an hour, or almost zero (Forge 1995). Protectionism has kept the cost of telephoning high in some areas – it costs more to phone Paris than New York from London. But the trend is downwards everywhere. The World Trade Organisation pact, which was ratified on 15 February 1997 by 68 countries, will further liberalise the telecommunications market, and thereby expedite the trend. The recent ascendancy of call-back services as well as of the Internet has already been exerting downward pressure on phone charges, especially on international ones. By the turn of the century, voice traffic will be more like data traffic on the Internet, where there will be no relation between cost and distance, because of the vast over-capacity of satellite and fibre optic technologies.

The threat of losing office work to offshore countries intensifies even more as the pattern of work organisation alters in Europe, as elsewhere. The dynamics of the ICT-driven corporate world are multifaceted, yet one can postulate that the major feature of the current techno-economic regime is that, in it, ICT allows companies to shift production from traditional centralised modes to decentralised ones (Freeman *et al.* 1995; Sayer and Walker 1992). This shift has been described in the literature as the transition from a Fordist to a post-Fordist type of work organisation. Post-Fordism has two important aspects: externalisation and downsizing. The former takes the form of outsourcing and/or delocalisation. In telematics-related information processing work, it can take place in a more 'centralised' manner in the so-called call centres or teleoffices, or else it can occur in a truly decentralised manner in the form of home-based

Table 1.2 Estimates of increase in ICT capacity and decrease in computer costs

Area of change	(1) Late 1940s–early 1970s	(2) Early 1970s–mid-1990s	(3) Mid-1990s onwards
OECD installed computer base (number of machines)	30,000 (1965)	Millions (1985)	Hundred millions (2005)
Components per micro-electronic circuit	32 (1965)	1 megabit (1987)	256 megabits (late 1990s)
Leading representative computer; instructions per second	10^3 (1955)	10^7 (1989)	10^{10} (2000)
Cost: computer thousand operations per $US	10^5 (1960s)	10^8 (1980s)	10^{10} (2005)

Source: Freeman and Soete (1994).

teleworking (Huws 1995). The downsizing element of post-Fordism, on the other hand, relates to the new management philosophy, which favours a small core team in the company and peripheral/marginal workers elsewhere (Mitter 1997). This new philosophy, called 'lean management', welcomes national and transnational telematics-assisted distant working as a tool for efficient work organisation.

The potential for transnational outsourcing is enhanced with the increasing importance of information processing, not only in the services sector but also in manufacturing. In fact, as the information and knowledge intensity of industrial activities expands, the traditional boundaries between manufacturing and services activities become less clear. Some of the traditional services, with the use of ICT, have now become tangible, resembling manufacturing products. Software packages for finance and accounting, or library services on CD-ROM, are prime examples of the 'materialisation' of personal services (Gates 1996; Quah 1997). This phenomenon has been counterbalanced by a rising proportion of information processing work in manufacturing, a trend that has lowered the importance of 'manual' work in the value-added component of manufactured products. Fifty per cent of the value of a car now is in its 'information' content – in its conception, design, operation of assembly, marketing and sales (Charpentier 1994). As the World Economy Survey stresses: 'over three-quarters of the value of a typical "manufactured" product is already contributed by service activities such as design, sales, and advertising', which have high information content (*Economist*, September 28–October 4, 1996: 48).

Information-intensive inputs in manufacturing contribute to the progressive 'dematerialisation' of parts of the production process, making these amenable to digitisation and hence to national and transnational externalisation. In addition, there has been an ascendancy of the service sector in the total value of GDP in EU countries (Quah 1997).[2] The recent advances in informatics have resulted in an ever-increasing volume of information-intensive services, for example, in finance, commodity trading and airline services.

Advances in technology, coupled with managerial exigencies, definitely justify the logic of transnational relocation. There are, however, countervailing factors that are likely to inhibit it. One of the preconditions of successful outsourcing, for example, is the reliability of telephone lines and of other complementary infrastructures. Chronic power shortages in most parts of India, including Bangalore, seriously hamper the quality and delivery time of information processing work (*Sunday Times of India*, June 1, 1997).

Likewise, connectivity to high-bandwidth telephone lines plays an important role. It is companies such as Tata Consultancy Services (TCS) or Infosys in India, with sufficient clientele abroad, that can afford to lease a dedicated line. Governments in some countries are addressing this problem by direct intervention. In Malaysia, for example, the government is gearing up to providing high-bandwidth fibre optic cable links in Cybercity, named as the Multimedia Super Corridor (*Fortune*, August 18, 1997). Indonesia, too, is trying to emulate the Malaysian model. For most companies in the majority of emerging economies, with the exception of well-established ones, such as TCS, or of subsidiaries of large foreign companies, such as those of Hewlett Packard, it will be difficult to receive a substantial amount of outsourced work solely on the basis of cheapness of knowledge workers.

Managerial considerations also place a brake on transnational networking. These relate mainly to quality control and business coordination. Whereas relocation of 'back office' jobs, such as payroll accounting, airline ticket reservations and simple coding for software programming, may not pose insuperable supervisory problems, more complex and high value-added functions, as in system integration in software, entail project management responsibilities and maintaining complex vendor–customer relations (Millar 1996; Schware 1992). Whether the developing countries in general, and some countries in particular, will continue to receive outsourced work from the EU or the US will thus depend much on their ability to develop the requisite managerial skills, and to establish an image. It is not easy for new entrants – companies or countries – to break into the market, since it takes considerable time to learn the requisite skills and to establish a reputation. The challenges that the emerging economies are going to face in obtaining 'front end' activities are worth monitoring, since the impending automation of a large number of back office functions may render low wages relatively less important a consideration for transnational relocation of information processing work.

In addition, other factors, such as questions of confidentiality and the strategic nature of information, are likely to play paramount roles in certain areas, particularly in finance and in research and development work. The unease among the general public in the UK toward outsourcing of income tax data for processing abroad highlights such barriers.

Limitation and relevance of existing trade figures

It is against this background that we attempt to evaluate the available statistics for the trend in trade in information processing services between the EU and a select number of countries in Asia.

Figures for international trade are generally known to be flawed by the custom of 'transfer pricing'. When a multinational firm designs its product in one country, manufactures it in another, and sells it in a third, this gives the firm opportunities to reduce its overall tax bill on its profits by filling its accounts with artificially inflated prices for components that are imported from subsidiaries in a low-tax country. The practice is far from new, but its scale has increased with the growth in the internationalisation of production. The prevalence of intra-firm creative accounting, however, is not the only factor contributing to the lack of accuracy. Strategic alliances within, as well as across, national boundaries make the calculation of the flow of trade, particularly in services, problematic. As Eurostat warns, the increasing speed of worldwide economic integration and the proliferation of transactions between related companies make it difficult, for example, to distinguish flows between services and direct investment (Eurostat 1996: 11).

The growth of the cybereconomy, in which information processing plays the pivotal role, enhances this complexity. When the flow of information becomes mainly electronic, as with the Internet, the role of traditional intermediaries (such as banks or customs and excise departments), which report the relevant transactions to the national statistical office, declines. Moreover, the Internet also makes it infinitely easier to transfer information services between two countries, for example, from India to Germany, via a third country, for example, the Bahamas. This procedure can substantially reduce a company's tax bills legally (*Economist*, May 31–June 6, 1997: 17). The consequence is an increased discrepancy between the actual and reported trade flows. In the future, the introduction of electronic cash, anonymous and untraceable, will complicate the task even further.

Notwithstanding the complexities in calculating the trade flows, it is still rewarding to go beyond the journalistic documentation and identify trends in trade from published statistics, however imperfect these may be. The task has not been easy. Even for manufactured products, the Standard Industrial Trade Classification (SITC) has not been revised at a sufficiently disaggregated level to accommodate products such as packaged software, which is the key to the information economy.[3] Trade flows in information services, understandably, are even more elusive. The recent revision of the *IMF Balance of Payments Manual* (BPM5) in 1993 has to some extent rectified this, and has included categories and classifications that are particularly relevant to the information economy. On the basis of this classification, in 1996, Eurostat published *Geographical Breakdown of the Current Account, EU, 1992–1994*, which allows us to trace the trade flow between the EU and a select number of Asian countries in the field of information processing. A three-year period is, of course, not long enough to establish a meaningful trend. Also, the statistical categories are still too highly aggregated to focus exclusively on information processing (Eurostat 1996). The figures documented by Eurostat thus need to be interpreted cautiously. Their validity lies precisely in identifying where further disaggregation is necessary, and in locating areas where complementary qualitative research is needed in order to identify the comparative advantage of the partners in trade.

With these objectives in view, we have focused on a category which is listed as 'computer and information services' in the *IMF Balance of Payments Manual* (BPM5), which includes the following:

- Data bases, such as development, storage and on-line time series.
- Data processing – including tabulation, provision of processing services on a time-share or specific (hourly) basis.
- Management of facilities of other data processing on a continuing basis.
- Hardware consultancy.
- Software implementation – including design, development and programming of customised systems.
- Maintenance and repair of computers and peripheral equipment.
- News agency services – including provision of news, photographs and feature articles to the media.
- Direct, non-bulk subscriptions to newspapers and periodicals.

The trade figures in this category include some items, such as hardware consultancy, which are related to, but not exclusively focused on, information processing. These figures, albeit imperfect, reveal an interesting pattern that, in many ways, is contrary to what we were led to believe.

To start with, we focus on trade between India and the EU. This is because India, and in particular cities such as Bangalore and Mumbai, have attracted considerable attention in the public mind. The figures cited from Eurostat (see Figure 1.1) show that, for the EU, the credits or exports (money earned by selling computers and information processing to India) have been consistently higher than the debits or imports (money spent in buying computer and information processing services from India), contributing to a positive trade balance for the EU on this item. One could speculate that the gain that India has made by selling low value-added information processing services – for example, data entry or the coding and testing of software programming – has been outweighed by India's purchase of hardware consultancy, licensing and maintenance agreements for hardware. In fact, as India gears up to supplying services to deal with the 2000 millennium problem[4] and Europe's conversion to the EUR in 1999, hardware consultancy and maintenance agreement fees most probably are rising at a much faster rate than the receipts from software services. India relies mainly on imported hardware platforms from the US and the EU to produce, for the world market, services related to programming and data processing.

At this point it becomes interesting to analyse the trading pattern between the EU and the first-tier Asian NICs. As Figure 1.2 indicates, the trade balance in the field of computer and information services is consistently negative for the EU *vis-à-vis* the three city-states – Taiwan, Singapore and Hong Kong – and South Korea. Significantly, the wage

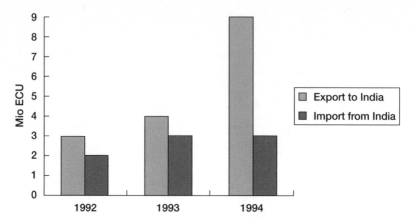

Figure 1.1 Trade between EU and India in computer and information services (in payments).
Source: prepared from Eurostat New Cronos Database on trade in services.

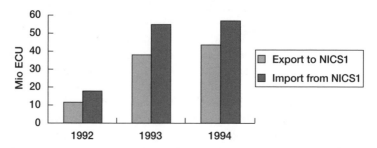

Figure 1.2 Trade between EU and first-tier NICs in computer and information services (in payments).
Source: prepared from Eurostat New Cronos Database on trade in services.

rates in these city-states and in South Korea are much higher than those in India, Thailand, Malaysia or the Philippines (the last three of which constitute the second-tier NICs). One could thus argue, albeit cautiously, that it is the guaranteed quality of infrastructure and the ready availability of skills that are more attractive considerations for the relocation of information processing work than the sheer cheapness of knowledge workers. In contrast with the experience of first-tier NICs, it appears that the second-tier NICs of Asia have paid more to the EU than they have received in the area of 'computer and information processing services' (see Figure 1.3).

Finally, it will be pertinent to place the importance of information processing work in perspective. Compared to total trade figures in services (see Table 1.3) between the EU and Asia, the trade flow in the category has been small. The impact of the telecommunications revolution on regional

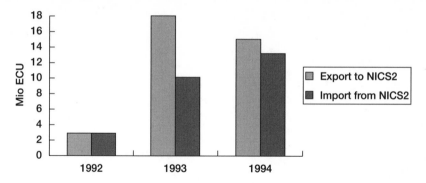

Figure 1.3 Trade between EU and second-tier NICs in computer and information services (in payments).
Source: prepared from Eurostat New Cronos Database on trade in services.

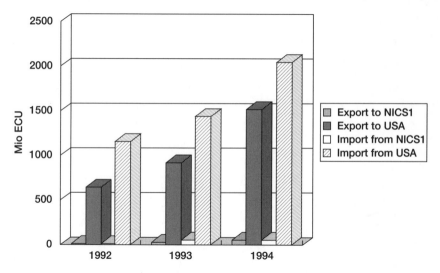

Figure 1.4 Trade in computer and information services in EU (in payments).
Source: prepared from Eurostat New Cronos Database on trade in services.

trade flows has, as yet, not been really revolutionary. One should also note that, in the area of computer and information services, the volume and growth of business between the EU and the US has been spectacularly high compared with that between the EU and the emerging Asian economies of the first-tier NICs (see Figure 1.4).

In terms of strategies, the EU thus needs to be more watchful regarding its competitive advantage *vis-à-vis* the US in retaining or augmenting its share in the global information economy. Trade between the EU and Japan, by contrast, is very small (see Figure 1.5) and could be explained

Table 1.3 Trade in computer and information services in the EU as a percentage of the total trade in services

	Trade in services in EU[a] (I) (in million ECU)			Trade in computer and information services in EU[a] (II) (in million ECU)			Percentage of total trade in services [(II)/(I)] × 100		
	1992	1993	1994	1992	1993	1994	1992	1993	1994
Export to India	1,356	1,198	1,520	3	4	9	0.22	0.33	0.59
Import from India	930	1,076	1,277	2	3	3	0.22	0.28	0.23
Trade balance	426	122	243	1	1	6			
Export to NIC1[b]	7,365	8,971	8,943	11	38	43	0.15	0.42	0.48
Import from NIC1	7,988	9,098	8,787	17	55	56	0.21	0.60	0.64
Trade balance	−623	−127	156	−6	−18	−13			
Export to NIC2[c]	1,925	2,153	2,285	3	18	15	0.16	0.84	0.66
Import from NIC2	2,485	2,879	3,341	3	10	13	0.12	0.35	0.39
Trade balance	−560	−726	−1,055	0	8	3			
Export to USA	66,647	67,796	71,517	648	920	1,501	0.97	1.36	2.10
Import from USA	58,556	60,247	64,045	1,155	1,429	2,034	1.97	2.37	3.18
Trade balance	8,091	7,549	7,472	−507	−509	−533			

Source: Eurostat 1996 and own computations.

Notes
[a] In payments.
[b] First-tier NICs: Singapore, Hong Kong, Taiwan, South Korea.
[c] Second-tier NICs: Thailand, Malaysia, the Philippines.

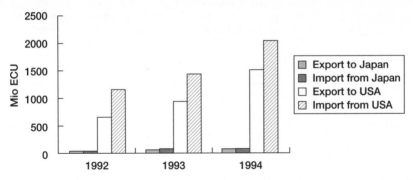

Figure 1.5 EU trade with Japan and USA in computer and information services (in payments).
Source: prepared from Eurostat New Cronos Database on trade in services.

by Japan's tradition of relying on vertical integration of information processing activities within a company, rather than on externalising (Cusumano 1991).

Comparative advantages of the EU and Asia

It is important not to overemphasise the relocation of jobs through tele-trade in information processing services, but the significance of trade in these services should not be underestimated either. As computer-aided technologies spread in both the developed and the developing worlds, the need for and the ease of outsourcing information processing activities, within and across national boundaries, enhance the rate of growth in trade in information services. In the last three years, the growth rate of trade in computer and information services between the EU and a select number of Asian countries has been generally much higher than that in trade, for example, in financial services or transportation (see Table 1.4). The high rate of growth perhaps results from the fact that the trade figures in the initial year were understandably small. Still, one can reasonably expect that the incipient trend is likely to be more pronounced in the coming years.

This possibility does not necessarily bode ill for the EU. With growing shortages of skills in certain key areas – as the millennium problem exemplifies – the corporate sector in the EU stands to benefit from its access to appropriate expertise in the developing world. It was the software crisis in the 1980s, when the demand for software programmes rose faster than the supply of software engineers, that first led to outsourcing of programming work to countries such as India. Certain types of skills, if harnessed from offshore countries, contribute to the productivity of European companies and thus to the creation of sustainable jobs in Europe. The diversity and

21

Table 1.4 Growth rates in different components of trade in services in comparison

	Trade in transportation in EU[a] (million ECU)			Growth rates (%)	
	1992	1993	1994	1993	1994
Export to NIC1[b]	2,397	2,737	3,045	14.18	11.25
Import from NIC1	3,527	3,726	3,463	5.64	−7.06
Export to NIC2[c]	871	805	862	−7.58	7.08
Import from NIC2	1,023	1,236	1,262	20.82	2.10
	Trade in travel in EU[a] (million ECU)			Growth rates (%)	
	1992	1993	1994	1993	1994
Export to NIC1[b]	661	859	930	29.95	8.27
Import from NIC1	837	1,001	1,276	19.59	27.47
Export to NIC2[c]	169	192	228	13.61	18.75
Import from NIC2	720	813	1,023	12.92	25.83
	Trade in financial services in EU[a] (million ECU)			Growth rates (%)	
	1992	1993	1994	1993	1994
Export to NIC1[b]	1,242	1,513	1,164	21.82	−23.07
Import from NIC1	950	1,324	927	39.37	−29.98
Export to NIC2[c]	68	87	107	27.94	22.99
Import from NIC2	13	29	38	123.08	31.03
	Trade in computer and information services in EU[a] (million ECU)			Growth rates (%)	
	1992	1993	1994	1993	1994
Export to NIC1[b]	11	38	43	245.45	13.16
Import from NIC1	17	55	56	223.53	1.82
Export to NIC2[c]	3	18	15	500.00	−16.67
Import from NIC2	3	10	13	233.33	30.00

Source: Eurostat 1996 and own computations.

Notes
[a] In payments.
[b] First-tier NICs: Singapore, Hong Kong, Taiwan, South Korea.
[c] Second-tier NICs: Thailand, Malaysia, the Philippines.

complexity of information processing work, and its fast rate of growth, leave room for both the EU and Asian countries to establish their niche markets to mutual advantage.

In software, the market for solutions to business problems, for example, is large and growing consistently. The world sale of software was already approaching $200 billion per annum in 1992, and has been growing at a rate of between 15 per cent and 20 per cent annually. The potential growth in information processing as inputs into the manufacturing of software packages alone will be substantial. The modular approach to software production makes it possible for European companies to outsource the low value-added side of operations, such as coding and maintenance, to Asia while retaining the high value-added stages, such as requirement definition and system design, in the region. The locational advantage of Europe – in software-related and in other types of information processing – lies in those segments where a deep understanding of the cultural context and business requirements is important.

It is not easy to quantify the overall impact of cross-border relocation of information processing work on the number of jobs lost or gained in the EU. A rough and simple calculation of jobs lost could be based on the total value of imports (money spent on buying computer and information processing services) from Asian countries divided by the annual average wage cost of an information processing worker in Asia. The number of jobs created in Asia to produce the traded services will be a shadow approximation of the number of actual or potential jobs lost in Europe.

Similarly, in the same category, the total value of exports (money earned by selling computer and information processing services) to Asia divided by the annual average wage cost of an information processing worker in the EU will give a rough estimate of the number of jobs gained in the EU. If, for the sake of explication, we assume that the average annual wage of an information processing worker in India is 3,000 ECU, one-tenth of that prevailing in the EU, say 30,000 ECU, the trade figures in Table 1.3 would imply that in 1994 the total number of jobs gained for the EU was 300 (9 million ECU/30,000 ECU). The number of jobs lost, on the other hand, was 1,000 (3 million ECU/3,000 ECU). The exercise indicates that the balance of employment for the EU can be negative even when the balance of trade in computer and information services is positive.

Such a calculation, needless to say, is fraught with problems and needs to be interpreted extremely carefully. To start with, differences in the levels of labour productivity between two regions contribute to the unreliability of such an estimate. A lower level of productivity in India, if that is the case, will mean that the number of jobs lost in the EU would be far less than the number of jobs created to produce similar services in India.

Again, such an exercise is based on the erroneous assumption that the trading relationship between nations is or should be based exclusively on the principle of competition (Krugman 1997: 3–21). Against a background of declining demographic trends in the EU, and skills shortages in an expanding global tele-economy, capacity building in knowledge-intensive occupations in Asia could be of benefit, both to the EU and Asia. For the sake of a better understanding of a mutually beneficial trading relationship, it will be worthwhile to initiate company-level qualitative research. The existing trade figures are not only inadequately disaggregated; the figures cannot, by their very nature, reveal the organisational expediencies and skills requirements that propel the phenomenon of relocation. Yet these are precisely the kind of insights that both the EU and Asian countries need for appropriate policies regarding infrastructure, training and education.

It is not the overall loss of jobs that should be the concern of the EU, as the magnitude is still rather small. Most significantly, such a calculation takes a narrow approach. It does not take into account, for example, the new jobs created in the EU. It is the segments of population that are affected by the relocation that need close attention. In many of the relocated low value-added information processing services, such as data entry, data processing or payroll accounting, women traditionally found jobs. The emerging international division of labour tends to affect them first. The challenge of training these retrenched employees will need innovative planning, for distributive justice and for social cohesion.

The developing countries also need to explore the implications of the emerging international division of labour with circumspection. The efforts of some of the Asian countries to create favourable environments for the location of outsourced information processing work indicate the importance that these countries attach to such developments. High-tech information processing work is perceived as a driving force for modernisation. The Science and Technology Parks now supersede the Export Processing Zones in priorities and in importance. There are eight S&T Parks in India. Malaysia, likewise, takes pride in its multi-billion dollar cybercity, the Multimedia Super Corridor. On the other hand, the infrastructural cost incurred in building up these facilities is high, and imports of hardware and telecommunications equipment, and the servicing costs attached to them, can be substantial (Heeks 1996: 116–17). Then there are national subsidies in the form of tax exemptions of various kinds for export-oriented servicing work.

There are also justifiable concerns about Asia being relegated to the cheap end of information processing work. There are, of course, possibilities of upward trajectories. Taiwan and Singapore, for example, have, with some success, moved to information services that involve project management skills and an understanding of the business context. Most countries in Asia, however, are primarily at the low-skill end of the spectrum. For developing countries, the move from export-oriented manufacturing to the export-oriented services sector has not altered the basic pattern of the international division of labour. *Plus ça change, plus c'est la même chose.*

The optimism for Asia in the information society stems from two universally held – but debatable – assumptions. The first assumption is that a move from manufacturing to service sector activities necessarily represents upward mobility in skills composition and skills acquisition, see for example European Commission (1996: 63). In the case of a shift from craft and related workers to managers and professionals, this assumption may indeed hold true, but it is not empirically correct in the case of a shift to clerks. The clerical key-stroke operations that many data-processing activities require demand no more than elementary computer literacy and communications skills.

The second assumption is that in the information society, where the production process is increasingly being 'dematerialised', a pool of knowledge-workers alone ensures a competitive edge in information processing services. The reality is somewhat different. It is the access to R&D and hardware that gives a country the advantage of being the first mover. In this respect, the EU, along with other OECD nations, still enjoys a favourable advantage over its Asian trading partners.

It is against this background that the comparative advantages of the emerging economies and the vision of their 'leapfrogging' need to be evaluated with caution. In his much-acclaimed and well-argued paper in the *Financial Times* of January 10, 1995, Juggy Pandit questions the conventional thinking on the evolution of world trade and competitiveness. The conventional thinking, he argues, envisages a continuum of economic activity through which economies evolve, ranging from basic agriculture at one end to highly skilled services at the other. But as he indicates, 'The reality is more complex. India is well placed to be an exporter of certain highly skilled [information processing] services . . . [while it] shows little sign of becoming a significant exporter of manufactured goods to the west [after] liberalisation'.

Some questions still remain. Will the Asian trading partners of the EU retain and enhance their share of the world market in information processing? Will they be able to transcend their position, which, in many ways, to borrow Ronald Richardson's phrase (p. 93 this volume, is still the 'information age analogue of traditional industrial branch plants'?

Notes

1 Links to customers are made via satellite for data with a local teleport, mostly in science parks, offering high-quality, high-speed direct links. In India, a dedicated organisation, SATCOMM, provides this type of data communication facility.
2 One could argue that the observation that manufacturing is losing its importance in relation to services in terms of its contribution to both economic growth and employment growth should be interpreted carefully. Although this trend is

clearly observable in relevant figures and statistics in the EU, one should be cautious in interpreting these trends, as there have been major changes in statistical calculations in the past few decades that render data comparability and hence such inferences highly questionable. There have been, for instance, significant advances in the measurement of services such that items previously classified as part of manufacturing are now counted as part of services, which naturally decreases the amount of total manufacturing output. This is primarily because of the increased volume of outsourcing of IT and other services to external subcontractors, nationally. As the report by the Foundation of Manufacturing and Industry states (Spiller 1997), in the UK, because service activities previously undertaken within manufacturing are now performed in the commercial service sector, the growth in manufacturing output has been underestimated by one-third between 1979 and 1994.

3 SITC Revision 3, the final amendment to the classification, which was launched in 1985, includes software under the heading of 'recorded media, not elsewhere specified' with the code 898.79, without specifying software separately. This heading of SITC, Revision 3, corresponds to the code 8524.90 in the Headings of the Harmonised Commodity Description and Coding System (HS). Only very recently has the UN Statistical Office in Geneva started to compile data on packaged software based on the latest HS classification from 1996 where a specific item of software is available with the code number 8524.91. These figures, however, have not been made public yet.

4 The origin of the 'millennium bug' lies in the cost of computer memory at a time when many programmes were written on mainframe computers using languages such as Cobol or Assembler. Developers saved space by storing the year as two digits rather than four. Many ageing programmes, which assume correctly that 97 means 1997, will become confused after the turn of the millennium and wrongly identify 01 as equivalent to 1901 rather than 2001. This legacy problem, although straightforward, is costly to correct. In the UK alone, 300,000 additional staff will be needed, according to Taskforce 2000, an agency backed by the Confederation of British Industry. Thus a considerable amount of work is being sent to contractors in developing countries, such as India, where wage rates are lower.

References

Charpentier, M. (1994) 'Networked Europe – the new opportunities', keynote speech given by the Director General DGXIII – Telecommunications Information Market and Exploitation of Research, European Commission. *Telework'94: New Ways to Work: Proceedings of the European Assembly on Teleworking and New Ways of Working*, Berlin, November 1994.

Cusumano, M. A. (1991) *Japan's Software Factories: A Challenge to US Management*, Oxford: Oxford University Press.

Economist (1997) 'Taxes slip through the net', May 31–June 6, 1997: 17.

European Commission (1996) *Employment in Europe*, Brussels and Luxembourg: European Commission.

Eurostat (1996) *Geographical Breakdown of the Current Account, EU, 1992–94*, Luxembourg and Brussels: Eurostat.

Freeman, C. and Soete, L. (1994) *Work for All or Mass Unemployment? Computerised Technical Change into the 21st Century*, London: Pinter.

Freeman, C., Soete, L. and Efendioglu, U. (1995) 'Diffusion and employment effects of information and communication technology', *International Labour Review*, 134, 4–5: 587–603.

Forge, S. (1995) *Consequences of Current Telecommunication Trends on the Competitiveness of Developing Countries*, a report prepared for InfoDev, The World Bank, Washington, DC, by Simon Forge, Cambridge Strategic Management Group. Boston, London, and Paris. Section 1. Mimeo.

Fortune (1997) 'Malaysia: Building a field of dreams', August 18, 1997: 52–6.

Gates, B. (1996) *The Road Ahead*, Chapter 6: 'The Content Resolution', New York: Penguin Books.

Heeks, R. (1996) *India's Software Industry: State Policy, Liberalisation, and Industrial Development*, New Delhi and London: Sage.

Huws, U. (1995) *Teleworking Research Feasibility Study, Part 2, On-site Teleworking*, London: Analytica Social and Economic Research Ltd.

Krugman, P. (1997) *Pop Internationalism*, Cambridge, MA: MIT Press.

Mansell, R. and Wehn, U. (eds) (1998) *Knowledge Societies: Information Technology for Sustainable Development*, for the United Nations Commission on Science and Technology for Development, Oxford: Oxford University Press.

Millar, J. (1996) *Interactive Learning in Situation Software Practice: Factors Mediating the New Production of Knowledge during CASE Technology Interchange*, D.Phil. Thesis, Science Policy Research Unit (SPRU), University of Sussex.

Mitter, S. (1997) 'Innovations in work organisation and technology', in Eugenia Date-Bah (ed.), *Promoting Gender Equality at Work*, Geneva: ILO.

Pandit, S. K. (1995) 'Wired to the rest of the world', *Financial Times*, January 10, 1997.

Pearson, R. and Mitter, S. (1993) 'Employment and working conditions of low-skilled information processing workers in less developed countries', *International Labour Review*, 132, 1: 49–64.

Posthuma, A. (1987) *The Internationalisation of Clerical Work: a study of offshore services in the Caribbean*, SPRU Occasional Paper, No. 24, University of Sussex, UK.

Quah, D. T. (1997) 'Increasingly weightless economies', *Bank of England Quarterly Bulletin*, 37, 1: 49–55.

Sayer, A. and Walker, R. (1992) *The New Social Economy: Reworking the Division of Labour*, Cambridge, MA, and Oxford, UK: Blackwell, 191–223.

Schware, R. (1992) 'Software industry entry strategies for developing countries', *World Development*, 20, 2: 143–64.

Spiller, J. (1997) *A Restatement of the Slow Growth of UK Manufacturing, 1979–1994*, London: The Foundation for Manufacturing and Industry.

Sunday Times of India (1997) June 1, 1997, and quoted in the publicity brochure of the West Bengal Development Corporation Ltd.

2

BEYOND ANECDOTES: ON QUANTIFYING THE GLOBALISATION OF INFORMATION PROCESSING WORK

Ursula Huws

Introduction

At the recent colloquium in Dublin organised by the European Commission to launch its Green Paper on the Information Society (European Commission DGV 1996), one of the main criticisms the very diverse conference participants aimed at the Paper was that it took insufficient account of globalisation. Indeed, *globalisation* has become one of the most fashionable catch-phrases used to describe current trends in the restructuring of capital and of labour markets throughout the world, whether by policymakers, academic researchers, employers, trade unions, or non-governmental organisations (NGOs). However, the word is rarely defined precisely, and one suspects that it carries quite different meanings for different users.

Because of this lack of any stable and universally agreed-upon definition of the term, it is impossible to estimate the extent to which globalisation is actually taking place. We observe, however, that the word is generally used to describe a process that has developed fairly recently, and is critically dependent on, if not driven by, the combined use of new information and communications technologies. We are frequently presented with dramatic illustrations of this process, but rarely with evidence of how typical these may be.

This presentation will attempt to summarise some of these different meanings, not so much to arrive at an encompassing and conclusive definition as to identify indicators for some, if not all, of its dimensions. This should make it possible to design systematic research programmes that will enable policymakers and other social and economic agents to monitor trends and design appropriate strategies. Without such research, we operate in an empirical vacuum in which assertion and counter-assertion, opinion and counter-opinion, dramatic success story and dramatic horror story compete to influence policy.

One of the problems facing the researcher in this field is that no firm conceptual framework has yet been developed within which to analyse and quantify trends in the relocation of information-related employment. At least three intellectual disciplines are involved, each with important insights to offer.

Economics offers us the basic tools with which to assess general economic trends, and to monitor such factors as trade, investment, productivity, and profitability. However, economics has yet to develop reliable models that would enable us to predict with any degree of accuracy where particular industries will locate. The tools of economics also present us with difficulties in measuring value added to information processing activities. In the case of a factory producing physical goods, for instance, it is relatively easy to measure inputs and outputs in order to assess what value has been added at a particular location. Such measurement is much more difficult in the case of activities involving interactive communications between partners on multiple sites.

Organisational theory provides helpful insights into the dynamics of change, but fails to offer methods for quantification. By focusing on what happens *within* organisations, it also tends to overlook the relationships *between* organisations, which are particularly important for our purposes.

Probably the richest information on these changes comes from the work of geographers, much of it informed by postmodernist thought. This work has provided a wealth of case-study information whose analysis has produced a range of *post hoc* explanations of the decisions as to location of firms using advanced communications networks. It has also afforded some interesting theoretical discussions of the process of globalisation. However, economic geography too has thus far failed to offer a framework that would make it possible to quantify and monitor trends and to develop predictive models. It remains essentially descriptive, illustrating how particular companies have relocated, but failing to explain why others have not, or to provide us with reliable information about the extent of such relocation.

I will begin by summarising some of the main aspects of globalisation as it is currently understood. These aspects are closely interconnected, but only by disentangling their interrelationships are we likely to be able to develop methodologies for measuring the globalisation of employment.

Concentration of ownership

The growing concentration of economic power in the hands of an ever-decreasing number of multinational or transnational corporations (MNCs or TNCs) is often taken as an important indicator of globalisation. It has been estimated that more than a quarter of the world's economic activity is now controlled by the 200 largest corporations, and that this concentration is accelerating (Barnet 1994: 754). The turnover of some of these companies is larger than the GDP of many nation states. It is often argued that they have reached a position of economic dominance that puts them outside the control of, and beyond allegiance to, any individual government.

Such a concentration of power is, of course, a legitimate subject for concern. Nevertheless, as recent research by Paul Hirst and Grahame Thompson (Hirst and Thompson 1996) has demonstrated, it is possible to exaggerate the extent to which such corporations can be said to be truly transnational. After carrying out a comprehensive analysis of data from company annual reports, these authors concluded that most multinational corporations are still firmly placed within their individual 'home' economies, and rely on them for their core market. This holds true across a range of different indicators, including distribution of sales, distribution of assets, distribution of subsidiaries and affiliates, and distribution of gross profits. Some of their results are summarised in Tables 2.1–2.4.

Such data are a useful corrective to crude models, which perceive TNCs as entirely free-floating organisations, lacking anchors in any single local economy. Nevertheless, it is possible that they fail to capture the true extent of the global hegemonic power of these corporations, underestimating the importance of strategic alliances between corporations, for which no good economic indicators yet exist. Increasingly, instead of expanding by means of takeovers or mergers, companies use such alliances as a fast and low-risk strategy to gain access to new markets, protect existing markets, pool resources in the research and development of new products, and target market niches. The development of the Single European Market has undoubtedly encouraged the development of such alliances. Their growth, in combination with the growth of outsourcing, has served to blur the boundaries of the traditional corporation; its scope can no longer be measured simply by the numbers of workers it employs or the size and location of its subsidiaries. Nor is it always possible to allocate the sales of a given product or service directly to a single corporation.

These interacting processes can be seen at work in the restructuring of the airline industry. The OECD estimates that by the end of the century this industry will be dominated by five companies: two US-based, one Europe-based, and two Asia-based (International Transport Workers' Federation 1993: 33). This process has come about not only through mergers and takeovers (though there have been a number of these, many following from the privatisation of formerly state-owned airlines). A range of strategic alliances between airlines has also been important, such as those between Air France and Lufthansa; between SAS, Swissair, and Austrian Airlines; and between Delta Airlines, Swissair, and Singapore

Table 2.1 Percentage distribution of sales by region and country of headquarters

Country	Manufacturing MNCs	Service MNCs
US	70	93
Japan	64	89
UK	66	74
Germany	72	n.a.

Source: Hirst and Thompson 1996.

Table 2.2 Percentage distribution of assets by region and country of headquarters

Country	Manufacturing MNCs	Service MNCs
US	67	81
Japan	52	77

Source: Hirst and Thompson 1996.

Table 2.3 Percentage distribution of subsidiaries and affiliates by region and country of headquarters

Country	Manufacturing MNCs	Service MNCs
US (subsidiaries/affiliates in US/Canada)	74	64
UK (subsidiaries/affiliates in Europe)	62	42
Germany (subsidiaries/affiliates in Europe)	68	54

Source: Hirst and Thompson 1996.

Table 2.4 Percentage distribution of gross profits by region and country of headquarters

Country	Manufacturing MNCs
US	69
UK	67
Canada	80

Source: Hirst and Thompson 1996.

Airlines. Described by one commentator as 'more like casual dating than marriages', these alliances have covered the sharing of technical data, joint participation in frequent flyer programmes, shared ticket sales and check-in facilities, and so-called 'seamless travel' (International Transport Workers' Federation 1993: 31). Similar alliances, made possible only by the sharing of data enabled by the new information and communications technologies, can be found in many other industries, including pharmaceuticals, vehicle manufacture, and financial services (Dunning 1993).

Growth in international trade

Another measure of the growing internationalisation of the world economy is the long period of growth in international trade. Here, too, we are indebted to Hirst and Thompson for some interesting analysis, which modifies significantly the received wisdom that all world economies are becoming increasingly open to foreign goods and that we are, in effect, inhabiting a global market. Their analysis shows that if we look at the volume of international trade (exports and imports combined) in relation to GDP, there was in fact proportionally *less* international trade in most developed countries in 1973 than there was in 1913, as can be seen in Table 2.5.

There has been considerable growth since 1973, as can be seen from Table 2.6; but this has not – with the arguable exception of Europe – been of the dramatic order sometimes claimed by the proponents of the 'globalisation' thesis, at least on the basis of these figures. It should be noted that these analyses are likely to underestimate some types of trade, such as the transfer of information or other services between branches of MNCs. They also fail to take into account some of the changes in what is being traded, notably the growth in trade in services. A recent report by the OECD (OECD 1996) estimates that more than half of total GDP in the rich economies is now knowledge-based, including industries such as telecommunications, computers, software, pharmaceuticals, education, and television; but, as has been pointed out by *The Economist*, precisely these

Table 2.5 Ratio of trade to GDP at current prices, 1913 and 1973

Country	1913	1973
France	35.4	29.0
Germany	35.1	35.2
Japan	31.4	18.3
Netherlands	103.6	80.1
UK	44.7	39.3
US	11.2	10.5

Source: Hirst and Thompson 1996.

Table 2.6 Trade openness (% of GDP) 1970s–1980s

Region/country	1970–79	1980–89
North America	17.8	21.9
Western Europe	48.7	56.9
Japan	22.9	23.9

Source: Hirst and Thompson 1996.

sectors are the most difficult to measure, making it difficult to analyse their relationship to overall economic growth (*The Economist* 1996: 43–4).

It is, of course, in the data on trade in services that we are most likely to find evidence of growth in the globalisation of employment in the processing of information. Unfortunately, in this area the sources of information are not good. Not only are there difficulties in the monitoring of transactions involving only data (e.g., the transmission of information over the Internet); the data are not available at a sufficiently detailed level of disaggregation to distinguish transactions involving labour (which might be termed *intermediate services*) from those involved in the import or export of final services to the consumer. In contrast with data on trade in commodities, which are broken down to a level where it is possible to distinguish with some precision between the separate components of each product, statistics on trade in services are aggregated into broad groups, making any such distinction impossible.

Growth in the international division of labour

The first systematic study of the development of a new international division of labour by Fröbel, Heinrichs, and Kreye (Fröbel *et al.* 1980) focused mainly on employment in manufacturing industries, such as electronics, textiles, and clothing, carried out in free enterprise or export processing zones in developing countries for employers based in the US, Europe, or Japan. Because these forms of employment were relatively concentrated geographically, it was possible to make some estimate of their extent, and to collect data on, for instance, the demographic composition of the workforce involved (which consisted mainly of very young women) and their wages (low), working hours (long), and conditions (poor). Around the same time, reports began to appear in the trade press of other types of work, involving the processing of routine information, being sent offshore from relatively high-wage regions, such as the US, Australia, and Western Europe, to relatively low-wage areas, such as the Caribbean, India, China, and the Philippines.[1]

There is now considerable documentation on some of the forms which this new international division of labour in services has taken, and, in some cases, on the wages and conditions of the workers involved.[2] It is clear that the types of work involved now extend well beyond routine data entry, which made up the first wave of offshore office work, and include a variety of technical and professional functions ranging from computer programming to engineering to accountancy (Huws 1996). In one of the few attempts to quantify this development, one survey found that over 100 of America's top 500 firms buy software services from firms in India, where programmers are typically paid less than a quarter of the American rate (*The Economist* 1996: 34).

Such findings raise interesting questions for researchers, perhaps the most important of which is not 'Why are 20 per cent of these firms using Indian programming services?' but 'Why are the remaining 80 per cent not doing so?'

It is also clear that this type of employment is extremely unstable, with companies engaged in a constant search for ever-cheaper sources of labour. For instance, companies which previously carried out their data entry in Barbados are now moving to the Dominican Republic; those which set up remote offices in Ireland are now investigating locations such as Portugal; and those which made use of computer programming staff based in Bombay are now recruiting staff in the former Soviet Union (Huws 1996).

Such evidence as we have for these developments is essentially anecdotal. We need to establish what proportions of employers, and employers in what industries, are engaging in these practices; what occupations are involved; and what criteria are used in the choice of location. In doing so, it will be necessary to track movements not only in the direct employ-ment of personnel in other countries, but also in subcontracting.

The growth of outsourcing is also a trend for which case-study evidence abounds, but there is little in the way of concrete information about its extent and prevalence. A recent study by the Institute for Employment Studies (IES) (Reilly and Tamkin 1997) investigated the sorts of activities currently being outsourced by employers in the UK and their reasons for choosing to subcontract these functions. The report concludes that when assessing a transaction's cost/benefit, managers should consider a range of characteristics, including degree of uncertainty, frequency, and the specifi-city of the activity or investment involved. On the basis of such an analysis, outsourcing would be favoured where transactions are non-specific, irrespective of their frequency or uncertainty; while for transactions that are very specific, frequent, and subject to high uncertainty, companies would decide to retain activities in-house.

In practice, however, it seems that although some companies make a rational choice on such a basis – and see outsourcing as a fundamental part of their management philosophy – research suggests that these decisions more frequently do not form part of any coherent resourcing strategy. Rather they are *ad hoc* and opportunist in nature, meant to meet short-term and temporary needs. They tend to be made on grounds of cost reduction and to be driven by the financial function rather than by strategic business or resourcing considerations. The emphasis is often on cost control over the short term, with little attempt to consider longer-term implications. Difficulties that arose in the firms studied included: contrac-tual (legal) difficulties; service difficulties; loss of expertise to manage contractors; difficulties with employees over, e.g., the terms of transfer selection, consultation, and negotiation; unexpected costs; the spawning of a new bureaucracy to monitor contractor performance; inability of managers to adjust; absence of the necessary management skills; and poor communication between the parties. While many of the cases did not involve subcontractors based in other countries, this study serves to illustrate the complexity of the issues involved and the dangers of making oversimplistic generalisations about the scope for introducing 'virtuality'.

Growth in economic migration

The ease with which data can be transmitted over long distances and the speed with which work can be relocated around the globe give rise to vivid images of delocalisation or, to quote the title of a recent British publication, the 'death of distance' (Cairncross 1997). It is important to remind ourselves in this context that not all jobs involve the processing of information. Indeed, some of the most rapidly-expanding occupations involve the face-to-face delivery of physical services (whether in retailing, the serving and preparation of food, cleaning, security services, nursing, or care of children, the sick, or the elderly). In many cases, these jobs also share poor working conditions, low pay, and precariousness with some repetitive and low-skilled jobs in manufacturing and assembly.

As international competition drives wages down toward starvation levels and as unemployment grows in the less developed regions of the world, the conditions are created for a growth in economic migration toward regions where jobs seem more likely to be found. It could be argued that the most significant aspect of the global restructuring of employment – at least in terms of the numbers of people involved – is not so much a move of jobs away from the higher-paid regions as a movement of people toward them. Increasingly, the new divisions between 'haves' and 'have-nots' in the workforce are to be found *within* rather than between countries. Although official statistics cannot take accurate account of undocumented or illegal immigrants, this is an area where reasonably reliable data do exist. It has, for instance, been estimated by the Urban Institute that during the 1980s some 10 million legal and illegal immigrants entered the US (a million more than during the decade 1900–10, the previous record) (Holmes 1995). Here the problem is not so much a lack of data as a failure to relate them to the issues that arise in debates about the information society. In other words, the problem is conceptual rather than empirical.

Globalisation of consumption patterns

A detailed analysis of consumer markets is outside the scope of this presentation. It is, however, worth pointing out that the development of a global division of labour in information processing – even when this involves an apparent one-way flow of jobs out of developed economies such as those of the EU into other, less-developed parts of the world – need not necessarily spell bad news for the 'job-exporting' economies. The economic development that takes place in the 'job-importing' countries, particularly when this involves the growth of relatively high-skilled technical or professional work, creates an expanding market for other goods and services. The rapidly-growing middle classes of India and the Asian 'tiger economies' are undoubtedly creating jobs indirectly in Europe in sectors ranging from financial services to tourism. Any attempt to estimate the full economic impact of these developments must take account of such indirect effects.

Conclusions

We appear to have arrived at a point that might be characterized by Kuhnians as a 'paradigm shift'. After nearly two decades of research by groups and individuals – often underfunded and carried out against the mainstream – a convincing case appears to have been made that 'globalisation' must be taken seriously as a phenomenon. The word now appears daily in the rhetoric of journalists and politicians of virtually all parties; it has become part of the academic curriculum; and both employers and trade unionists are aware that relocation is one of the options of companies seeking to reorganise themselves and remain competitive.

When one has been pushing for a long time against a closed door and it suddenly opens, there is an unfortunate tendency to fall on one's face. Having established the legitimacy of the subject, it is now important not to overstate the case – to keep our footing, so to speak. In other words, the time has come for serious empirical research. I hope that one of the tasks of this conference will be to draw up an agenda for such research. Here are a few preliminary suggestions:

- Lobby national governments and international agencies (such as the OECD, the World Bank, UNCTAD, Eurostat) to collect and make available statistics on trade in services in such a way that they can be disaggregated to make it possible to monitor trends in the import and export of service employment.
- The development of econometric models using these data (in combination with other data, such as employment data) in order to assess trends.
- Employer surveys (large enough for statistical validity at the level of industrial sectors, firm size, and regions) to establish the prevalence and distribution of various forms of outsourcing, relocation of back office functions, and other forms of teleworking on employer premises.
- Follow-up studies to identify the criteria used by employers for deciding which functions to relocate or outsource and which locations to choose.

- Studies to assess the impact of relocated back office functions on local economies.
- Studies designed to identify the relative 'fixedness' or 'footlooseness' of particular occupations, in order to identify which are potential 'exports' and which 'imports' in any given economy, and then to develop appropriate training strategies.

Perhaps more important than any specific study is the development of a dialogue between researchers in different disciplines, and a shared recognition that no discipline has all the answers, and that there is a need to construct a new conceptual framework. We are in poorly charted territory, and only a collective effort will enable us to produce a map. The UNU INTECH and the Information Society Unit of the European Commission's, Directorate-General for Employment, Industrial Relations, and Social Affairs have initiated just such a process and are to be congratulated for organising this conference to develop it further.

Notes

1 Summarised at the time in, *inter alia*, Huws, U. 'The Runaway Office Jobs', *International Labour Reports*, March–April, 1984, and Huws, U. 'The Global Office: Information Technology and the Relocation of White-collar Work' in *Third World Trade and Technology Conference Papers*, Third World Information Network, 1985, and more recently in Huws, U. *Teleworking: an Overview of the Research*, joint publication of the Department of Transport, Department of Trade and Industry, Department of the Environment, Department for Education and Employment and Employment Service, July, 1996.

2 See for instance ILO, *Conditions of Work Digest: Telework*, Volume 9 No 1, ILO, Geneva, 1990: 109; Brain, D. and Page, A. *Research and Technology Development on Telematic Systems for Rural Areas: Review of Current Experiences and Prospects for Teleworking – 1991*, Commission of the European Communities, Directorate General XII, 1992: 73–76; Posthuma, A. *The Internationalisation of Clerical Work: a study of offshore office services in the Caribbean*, SPRU Occasional Paper No 24, University of Sussex, Brighton, 1987; Soares, A. 'The Hard Life of the Unskilled Workers in New Technologies: Data Entry Clerks in Brazil' in Bullinger, H. J. (ed.) *Human Aspects in Computing*, Elsevier Science Publishers, Amsterdam, 1991; Pearson, R. 'Gender and New Technology in the Caribbean: new work for women?', in Momsen, J. (ed.) *Gender Analysis in Development*, Discussion Paper No 5, University of East Anglia, Norwich, 1991; and Pearson, R. and Mitter, S. 'Employment and Working Conditions of Low-skilled Information Processing Workers in Less Developed Countries' in *International Labour Review*, April, 1993.

References

Barnet, R. J. (1994) 'Lords of the Global Economy', *The Nation*, 19 December 1994.

Cairncross, F. (1997) *The Death of Distance: How the Communications Revolution Will Change our Lives*, London: McGraw-Hill.

Dunning, J. H. (1993) *The Globalisation of Business*, London: Routledge.

The Economist (1996) 'Survey: The World Economy', 28 September 1996.

European Commission DGV (1996) *Living and Working in the Information Society: People First*, Bulletin of the European Union, Supplement 3/96, Luxembourg: Office for Official Publications of the European Communities.

Fröbel, F., Heinrichs, J. and Kreye, O. (1980) *The New International Division of Labour*, Cambridge: Cambridge University Press.

Hirst, P. and Thompson, G. (1996) *Globalisation in Question*, Oxford: Polity Press.

Holmes, S. A. (1995) 'Surprising Rise in Immigration Stirs up Debate', *The New York Times*, 30 August 1995.

Huws, U. (1996) *Teleworking: An Overview of the Research*, London: Joint publication of the Department of Transport, Department of Trade and Industry, Department of the Environment, Department for Education and Employment and Employment Service.

International Transport Workers' Federation (1993) *The Globalisation of the Civil Aviation Industry and its Impact on Aviation Workers*, London: ITF.

OECD (1996) *The Knowledge-based Economy*, Paris: OECD.

Reilly, P. and Tamkin, P. (1997) *Outsourcing: A Flexible Option for the Future*, Brighton: Institute for Employment Studies.

3

A non-European counterpoint

TRADE IN SOFTWARE SERVICES: FROM INTERNATIONAL TRADE TO TELETRADE

The case study of Tata Consultancy Services in India

N. P. Basrur and Seema Chawla

In 1992, a team of corporate strategists from Harvard Business School led by economist Michael Porter, the global competitiveness guru, embarked on a study of globally competitive Indian industrial houses. The team after 36 months of research came up with four outstanding Indian corporations; Tata Consultancy Services (TCS) was the only representative from the IT industry. Talking about TCS in an October 1994 interview with Global *magazine, the Porter team volunteered: 'TCS was one of the companies that stood out: we stumbled on to it. TCS has a sharply focused business strategy and a high international orientation. TCS decided to have a global orientation, when it was still an infant' (NASSCOM 1996).*

Manufacturing has long been an activity requiring international co-ordination; now, services are joining the discipline of international business (Aharoni 1993). Intangibility of output, co-production requiring input from both producers and consumers, and simultaneity of production and consumption are the inherent characteristics of services. Of these three characteristics, simultaneity of production and consumption is the one that made services more location-bound than manufacturing. But advances in information technology have changed this limitation. Recent developments in information technology have been particularly useful in moving information-intensive services away from the office both domestically and globally. This has been known as the *outsourcing* of services.

One of the earliest examples of the international trade in services is the outsourcing of data entry jobs. In this practice, the customer mails paper-based data forms or sends scanned images of data forms electronically (by fax, e-mail, etc.) to the vendor for data entry. The vendor keys the data into a computer database and sends this database back to the customer via telecommunications lines or by mailing this database stored onto a magnetic medium. Pacific Data Services has been outsourcing data entry services to firms in China since 1961 (Apte 1990). Data entry has been one of the easiest service activities to be globally disaggregated, since it requires a low level of computer literacy and very little interaction between the customer and the vendor. The outsourcing of data entry services from firms in developed countries to firms in less developed countries has been successful because of the very nature of data entry services, which are highly structured and less communications-intensive.

With advances in telecommunications, semiconductor, and information technology, there is an increasing trend toward the outsourcing of software development services (which may be defined as the writing, design, analysis, and maintenance of software code and instructions necessary to operate programmable computers). Software development services, by their nature, differ from data entry services. Software development is a prime example of service work that requires tight coordination between customer and vendor, since designs often have to be reworked at the time of software writing, and new issues arise as systems become more concrete (Platz 1992; Waltz *et al.* 1993). Also, software development is a communications-intensive process, since software is an intellectual work (Kim *et al.* 1989) and requires constant human interaction across cultures, intellectual paradigms, languages, communication styles, etc. (Meadows 1996).

During the 1960s and 1970s, the international business in software services between developed and developing countries emerged. Due to advances in telecom and semiconductor technology and an explosion in demand for software services coupled with mounting pressures on multi-national corporations (MNCs) and other companies to maintain cost competitiveness, software production started migrating from the US and other industrialized nations to developing nations such as India, China, and Taiwan. Software exports from these countries grew rapidly, and India and China emerged as global players in the software industry.

Taking particularly the case of India, Indian software exports have risen from US$6 million in 1984–5 to over US$735 million in 1995–6, with a growth rate of 61 per cent in 1995 alone. Although the share of Indian software market is less than 2 per cent of world's total software market, it is by far the largest producer of software among the developing countries (Heeks 1996). Exports as a percentage of total industry revenues rose from 34.7 per cent in 1986 to over 60 per cent in 1995. The revenues of the

Information Technology industry in India in 1999 are expected to pass the US$2 billion mark. Approximately 60 per cent of software services from India are exported to the US (NASSCOM 1996). The links between Indian and European/Japanese software industries are small compared to those with the US. In 1995, India exported about 20 per cent of its total software services to Europe while its exports to Japan were just 3 per cent of its total software exports. This is also reflected in software exports by TCS to the US *vis-à-vis* Europe.

However, during the 1970s and 1980s, the majority of the firms in the Indian software industry were acting as service bureaus or subcontractors (known as *body shoppers*: firms that merely send out programmers in response to foreign company requests, and so act as glorified employment agencies) for firms in developed countries (Heeks 1995). During this period, these firms from the developing countries relegated themselves to supplying lower value-added programming services such as coding and testing, and international business in software services was managed more as an international trade than as an integrated international production. International trade in software services was more akin to the form of trade where firms from developing countries such as India, the Philippines and China provided programmers at the client location or acted as service bureaus for firms in developed countries (body shopping).

On the other hand, in integrated international production of software services, multiple teams of intellectual workers in multiple countries enabled by modern telecom infrastructure, collaborate to provide world-class software solutions. (One must distinguish between body shoppers and companies that provide software solutions and software services (Heeks 1996).)

During the 1990s, most of the firms in the Indian software industry are still in the phase where they just supply skilled programmers (bodies) to firms in the developed countries (Heeks 1996). However, a few pioneering Indian firms, led by Tata Consultancy Services (TCS), have changed this paradigm. In the 1990s, several Indian firms have demonstrated their technical and project management skills by successfully completing turnkey projects for large corporations. (Turnkey services include fully implemented custom software or systems integration of packaged and custom software.) Gradually, these firms started assuming overall project management, from requirement analysis and design specifications to maintenance. Since the beginning of the 1990s, TCS has been actively participating in all phases of the software development life cycle (see Table 3.1). It is now capable of executing large and complex offshore software development projects, involving the complete software development life cycle, for its clients overseas. It has proved its capabilities by successfully executing several large and complex software projects worldwide. Thus international business in software services has moved from international trade toward

Table 3.1 The systems development life cycle

Business planning	Systems planning	Technical design	Detailed design	Coding/ testing	Acceptance testing/ implementation	Maintenance
Develop IT strategy	Identify software requirements	Design system architecture	Write program specifications	Write program code	Test with existing systems	Changes
Identify user requirements		Identify programs needed	Identify input/output requirements	Test program	Install system	Fix bugs
				Test system		New requirements

Source: Schware 1989; Yourdon 1992.

integrated production in which firms like TCS are participating in all stages of software development, in close conjunction with their overseas clients. This emerging phenomenon of global disaggregation of software services can be termed *teletrade in software services.*

The aim of this paper is to examine how TCS exploited the opportunities made available by advances in telecommunications and semiconductor technology on an international front. Its intent is to analyse how TCS managed to move away from a stage where it was exporting software services just like a body shopper to a stage where it can be termed an innovator in the arena of software development. By analysing the specifics of production and trade in software services, as well as developments in software technology, the paper aims to point out the potential gains for developing country firms to emerge as global players. It also presents a brief review of the reasons for TCS's location-biased exports to the US.

The first section explains what factors led to the emergence of teletrade in software services. The second section explains how TCS exploited the emergence of teletrade in software services. The third section explains TCS's stronger links with the US *vis-à-vis* other advanced markets, such as Europe and Japan. The fourth section highlights the current position of TCS and its contribution to the Indian software industry. The final section presents conclusions.

Emergence of teletrade in software services

Teletrade in software services can be defined as the trade in software using electronic means within or across national boundaries. In this paper, tele-trade in software services across the national boundaries may be defined as *offshore software development done in one part of the world (generally a developing country) and then transmitted to the client (generally located in a developed country) through high-speed datacom links.*

Software services originated when software began to be provided separately from the hardware on which it ran. The potential market for independent vendors increased substantially after 1968, when US antitrust authorities forced computer giant IBM to stop bundling hardware with software.

The software service industry in its early days was concentrated in developed countries. The lack of processing power in hardware required software to be written in low-level computer languages to increase the speed of execution. As a result, writing software was an activity which required a high degree of skills in programming and understanding of underlying hardware architectures. Over time, and especially during the 1980s, advances in semiconductor technologies led to quantum leaps in processing power. The decreasing price/performance ratio in hardware led to a substantial increase in the number of potential commercial applications. This

43

resulted in an explosion of demand for software services, commonly referred to as the '*Software Crisis*': the difficulty of software design and programming exacerbated by the demand for software programs rising faster than the supply of software engineers. The outpacing of supply led software developers to search for skilled labour outside the major software markets. At this stage, developing countries such as India and China saw this as an opportunity to make a successful entry into the global software industry, based on their comparatively low cost of professional and technical manpower.

Custom software services were originally performed near the end user of software. However, by the early 1990s, advances in three major technologies had enabled software production to be located virtually anywhere in the world.

- The procedures for developing software had been systematized by applying industrial engineering concepts. Writing computer instructions was originally viewed as an art open only to those with advanced technical training. Over time, however, methodologies and tools were invented to take advantage of repeatability in the software development process and in the software code itself. A by-product of this standardisation was that more activities in the software development process could be partitioned and performed by people located in different places.

- Improvements in international voice and data communications allowed software specifications to be easily communicated over long distances. Digital telephone lines and satellite capabilities made it possible to transmit files of computer instructions or to access a computer remotely.

- Advances in semiconductor production and operating systems allowed application software to be developed without specific knowledge of the underlying hardware through 'high-level languages'. This allowed software programmers to develop software independently of hardware.

Thus, of software development life cycle activities (software development process consists of phases like requirements definition, design, coding, testing, acceptance and maintenance, referred to as Software development life cycle), detailed design, coding, and testing could be performed anywhere by the early 1990s. These activities were generic across countries and did not need to be performed in close proximity to the buyer. Business and systems planning and technical design were still performed at the client site, as they required observation of client business practices and significant client involvement. Acceptance testing and implementation occurred at the client site due to extensive user involvement. Maintenance was usually performed at the client site because a quick turnaround time was required (though recent advances in communications were making remote maintenance possible).

Thus, advances in technology led to the possibility of software production being located anywhere in the world. And these advances came when firms were facing acute pressures of competitiveness and were looking for cost-effective solutions for their software needs. All these developments made the outsourcing of software development a viable and cost-effective solution, thus leading to the emergence of teletrade in software services.

The next section describes how TCS exploited the opportunities presented by the disaggregation of software services available on an international front.

Tata Consultancy Services

Tata Consultancy Services (TCS) has emerged as the largest Indian computer software company and the largest exporter of software services in South Asia. It has reached a stage of development where it is directly competing against large software companies in Europe and the US. In spite of its small and less sophisticated domestic market, it had a global orientation since its beginning. It has faced many challenges over the past two decades to stay current with trends in software services, despite India's distance from major markets and lack of an advanced hardware market.

TCS was established in 1968 as a division of Tata Sons Limited (TSL), which was a part of Tata Enterprises, the largest Indian business house. It was formed to act as an internal management consulting group to Tata business houses.

In 1969, TCS purchased four IBM mainframe computers and began performing bulk data processing as a bureau service for businesses and government. Due to the difficulty of obtaining foreign currency for travel, TCS had to rely on hardware vendors to stay current with technology developments.

TCS quickly gained business through word of mouth, and generated a small profit in its first year. However, its growth was constrained by government control of equipment purchases. In these early days TCS often had to create demand for computing services, meeting with hundreds of people to educate them on the benefits of computing.

TCS looks outward: an international orientation

In the early 1970s, TCS signed an agreement with Burroughs, a large US hardware manufacturer, to act as its exclusive market agent in India. In the end, the alliance proved to be more beneficial in generating software sales than hardware sales. Burroughs referred many domestic software projects to TCS, and was the source of TCS's first service exports when, in 1974, TCS sent programmers to the US to develop a system for the Detroit police. This early export activity allowed TCS to meet the foreign exchange requirement to buy more Burroughs equipment. Burroughs provided most of TCS's export business during the next few years. Domestically, TCS received 80 per cent of its external revenues from bureau services, mainly for the government. Growth in private sector software sales was slow, due to the inaccessibility of hardware to Indian firms.

In 1978, Burroughs approached TCS to form a joint venture to manufacture its computers in India. Wanting to remain hardware-independent, TCS declined the offer. In its place Tata Burroughs Ltd was formed as a separate company within Tata Enterprises. Tata Burroughs Ltd not only manufactured hardware but also sold software services, placing it in direct competition with TCS. (Tata Burroughs Ltd later became Tata Unisys Ltd when Burroughs merged with Sperry to become Unisys. Recently, it broke its alliance with Unisys on issues of control and became Tata Infotech Ltd.)

Although initially difficult, the break with Burroughs proved to be fortuitous in the long run. TCS management decided that it must gain experience working on IBM machines, since its Burroughs business would begin to decline. In addition, the break forced TCS to focus on selling its own services outside India rather than simply relying on Burroughs, from whom all its overseas work had previously originated.

In 1979, TCS posted a representative in Tata Enterprises' New York office to begin marketing its services in the US. In its marketing, TCS focused on sending consultants to selected jobs where they could be exposed to new technologies and then brought home to teach others, an approach TCS management referred to as 'bootstrapping' and continued to apply in the 1990s.

During the same period, TCS began a project for a US bank consortium to migrate its software from Burroughs machines to IBM hardware, beginning what would become a substantial migration business for TCS. By the mid-1980s, migration services accounted for a large portion of TCS's international revenues. In expanding into the US, TCS began to compete with major software service companies, such as Computer Sciences Corporation and Cap Gemini.

The 1980s: the period of rapid expansion

In the 1980s, TCS expanded its service line both domestically and internationally to achieve rapid growth. Domestically, economic reforms had lowered the price of computing power, enabling more Indian firms to purchase their own hardware. This reduced their reliance on service bureaus and increased their need for new software. As a result, TCS moved away from bureau services toward providing software development services and packaged software.

By the late 1980s, bureau services had decreased to 20 per cent of TCS's domestic revenues, while software development and packages reached 42 per cent and 38 per cent, respectively. Internationally, the nature of TCS services was also changing. With the deployment of technology occurring much faster outside India, the nature of TCS's domestic and international projects began diverging in the late 1980s. International projects required knowledge of the most recent technologies and familiarity with applying systems strategically, rather than automating existing operations. However, TCS management still emphasized the importance of domestic work in supporting its international efforts. According to a senior TCS executive, domestic experience gave TCS project management skills, which allowed it to move away from body shopping.

The 1990s: from international trade
to integrated production

Until the late 1980s, most of TCS's export revenues came from contract programming and on-site project management. This involved producing software on-site in the high-cost country and 'exporting' the development staff (body shopping). International business in software services was more in the form of international trade. During the 1990s, TCS began delivering more of its international services in an offshore mode. With advances in telecommunications and refinements in its procedures for partitioning work, TCS began performing more of its foreign project work in its Indian facilities.

In the beginning, it performed highly structured, non-communications intense work (i.e., coding) because of clients' fears about the capabilities and infrastructure of TCS in its offshore facilities. As TCS successfully carried out projects and clients' fears were assuaged, clients began considering outsourcing all system life-cycle stages, rather than just coding. This shift was based on improvements in TCS's capability in project management and other high value-added tasks, coupled with its ability to stay abreast of the latest technologies.

Gradually, TCS became the leading Indian firm in developing methodologies and tools, and reduced the amount of work performed on-site in a given foreign project from an average of 80 per cent in the early 1980s to as little as 60 per cent in the early 1990s. According to a rough estimate (based on interviews with a TCS resident manager in the US), TCS now performs 60 per cent of its software services to its global customers in India, while the rest is carried out at a client site generally located in an advanced country. TCS exports in the 1980s consisted mainly of programming and migration services, although TCS began to assume full project management responsibilities and performed front-end activities in some projects.

TCS now works in close collaboration with its clients, taking responsibility for all stages of software development. Generally, it holds a face-to-face meeting early on, in which the objective of the project is determined and its scope is negotiated. Then TCS managers and system analysts generally conduct the analysis of the client's need on-site. Sometimes the client has already done so, and provides TCS with the system specifications. Where possible, TCS engages in analysis (even when specifications already exist) in order to learn about the clients and their needs, and also because those needs may have changed or the client may not be aware of what is technically feasible. After the analyses, TCS generally maintains at least one person on-site with the client. Where work is performed mainly in India, TCS also has client managers and users visit the off-site location in order for them to gain an understanding of the environment in which work will be performed. When a system is finished, the bulk of the work again shifts to the client's location. Systems are well documented, and training is conducted in order to ensure that clients can use and maintain their new systems properly; if desired, TCS can also be contracted to provide ongoing maintenance.

Most of the offshore work done by TCS in India is for clients located in the US. Exports of software services from India in general and from TCS in particular are more inclined toward the US. The detailed analysis of India's smaller links with other advanced markets, such as Europe and Japan, is beyond the scope of this paper. The next section presents some observations explaining TCS's stronger links with the US.

TCS/US links

TCS's stronger links with the US are the result of economic and technological forces. The US is the home of most sophisticated purchasers of software services, as compared to Europe and Japan. It has enjoyed a first-mover advantage in all the software industry's market segments (Steinmuller 1995). Most users had completed automation of basic business functions by the late 1970s. The 1980s was a period of employing software technology strategically to change business processes and gain an advantage over competitors. As a result, the US has been experiencing a software crisis since 1968 in terms of demand for software services rising faster than its supply (Cusumano 1991). European and Japanese computer production and rates of utilisation have historically lagged behind those of the US, leaving their domestic software producers with smaller markets and fewer economies of scale. To solve its software crisis, the US had to look outward to developing countries such as India and China earlier than Europe and Japan.

Technology, too, had played its role in explaining the stronger links between the US and the Indian software industry. As explained earlier, the rapid decline in the price/performance ratio of computing power made it very difficult for major computer manufacturers to pursue vertical integration of hardware and software, especially in the case of packaged software (Mowrey 1995). On the other hand, in Western Europe and Japan the domestic software industry was strongest in the development of custom software solutions (by hardware manufacturers and independent firms), that rely on close familiarity with user needs, and so on more interactions with users. Thus, the evolution of software technology in the US as compared to Europe and Japan had made it easier for US firms to extensively use the concept of outsourcing to developing countries. The concept of follow-the-sun as well as the extensive use of English as a second language gave India a further competitive advantage in trading its software services with the US.

TCS's current position

TCS is an international software consultancy organisation. It has 38 offices worldwide, spanning North and South America, Europe, South-east Asia, Australia, New Zealand, the Middle East, and Africa. With over 29 years of experience in the IT industry, TCS has provided 20,000 person-years of service in systems development involving all major platforms and environments to more than 500 clients worldwide.

Today, TCS comprises 8,000 professionals and is regarded as employer of choice, gaining the best recruits from the most prestigious schools. The firm invests over 8 per cent of its revenues in training, half of which is for training new hires. Each year 6 per cent of its revenues are invested in research and development, focusing on developing software engineering tools and techniques and gaining expertise in advanced technologies. Twelve per cent of TCS's revenues are invested in technical infrastructure – hardware, software, and telecommunications. It has several high-speed datacom links, some of which are used so project teams in India can work directly with clients' machines.

TCS has a tremendous amount of expertise in developing high-quality, cost-effective IT solutions for a number of corporate organisations worldwide. TCS clients include major airlines (Swissair, KLM, Hong Kong, SAS Cargo); financial organisations (American Express, Swiss Securities, Citibank); insurance companies (Fireman's Fund Insurance, Prudential); manufacturing companies (IBM, Hewlett Packard, Tandem, General Electric); communications vendors (Nortel, AT&T, AT&T Paradyne, Philips, British Telecom, Motorola); energy companies (Shell Oil, Southern Gas); and health care and pharmaceutical companies (United Health Care, Aetna, Sandoz, Roche), to name a few.

TCS effectively uses its excellent international infrastructure facilities (ISO-9000 certified), including its vast computing and communications infrastructure, its considerable business expertise, its expertise on a wide range of hardware and software platforms, its investment in training/software research and development, and its commitment to keep abreast of state-of-the-art developments in IT, providing holistic solutions for its clients through the entire software development life cycle, from requirement analyses to production support, maintenance, and enhancements to systems re-engineering.

TCS has alliances with leading international hardware manufacturers such as IBM, Hewlett Packard, and Tandem Corporation. TCS is currently working on the latest products from these vendors, developing and maintaining system software and applications systems for them. In 1996, TCS and Ernst and Young, a Big Six consulting firm, formed a strategic alliance for technical consulting and development.

Apart from these commercial collaborations, TCS has collaborations with the University of Waterloo, the University of Maryland, Syracuse University, and the University of Wisconsin, which will help it to incorporate leading-edge technologies in data communications, networking, information systems, and database management systems.

TCS is the only software house invited to form a partnership with the UNIX systems labs, in recognition to its expertise with UNIX and its commitment to open systems. TCS is the authorised distributor in India for various software vendors, including Oracle, Lotus Corporation, Electronic Data Systems, SAS Institute, and Avalon Software.

In 1993, TCS won the Outstanding Quality Supplier of the Year award from IBM Federal Systems out of 400 suppliers providing services to IBM. TCS commits to the highest quality goals of its clients and has the necessary ability, processes/methodologies, and performance experience to meet them. TCS's ability to balance and manage project development, with workloads at both on-site and offshore (India) facilities, can enable cost savings of up to 40 per cent to 50 per cent to the client.

Conclusions

TCS's example shows that with proper planning, policies, and strategies, firms in developing countries can actively participate in the emerging phenomenon of teletrade in software services. Software development has been identified as an area of significant growth potential for developing countries. The usual argument given is that software is a labour-intensive activity with relatively low rates of technical change and relatively low capital requirements. The present chapter has attempted to demonstrate that firms in developing countries have a huge potential for actively participating in global software services, as exemplified by TCS.

In order to achieve a significant position in global software services, TCS focused on the following aspects:

- It ensured that it had the necessary technical and project management skills to take sole responsibility for executing large software development projects.
- It increased its awareness of the latest technologies and trends, and increased its marketing presence in countries with different cultures.
- It addressed the needs of the buyers, with greater focus on quality and cost of software and the increasing involvement of end users in developing software.

Another important factor contributing to the success of TCS was that it had enjoyed an early mover advantage among the firms from the developing countries in the international software services market. Since the late 1960s, it has fruitfully exploited the niche offered by the international market in a specific segment of software development – mainly application software. Rapid developments in hardware technology during this period widened the gap between hardware and software availability. Further, migration of a variety of computing platforms to IBM platform created enormous opportunities at an international level.

The window of opportunity for developing countries in this human resource based industry is an ongoing one. In the 1990s, extremely rapid developments in hardware technology and the emergence of new computing platforms like Network Computers, Internet, E-Commerce, Java, etc. are exacerbating the skills crisis at an international level. If 'migration and conversion' were the words for the 1980s, fixing the year 2000 problem, Java and Internet technology are the words for the 1990s. Conversion projects emerging from the acceptance of the Euro will perhaps present tremendous opportunities at an international front in the next century.

Firms in developing countries like India are normally faced with the barriers of distance from major advanced markets and a less sophisticated domestic market. In the beginning, they are deficient in marketing, productivity, and quality. On the other hand, they have access to high-quality, cheap labour, which can form a basis for them to enter into the global high-tech software industry, which is human labour- and skill-intensive. One of the ways to become globally competitive, as this chapter shows, is to move through the following three stages:

- Building a reputation by providing cheap programming services on-site at a customer's location.
- Shifting the programming services back home with well-specified programs and systems delivered via telecommunications links to the overseas customer.

- Gradually shifting the focus from low-cost services to high-quality services.

The paper is not advocating a model for developing-country firms to successfully participate in the delivery of high-quality software services. Based on the experience of TCS, firms in developing countries can draw some lessons that might be useful for them in exploiting the opportunities made available to them by the emergence of teletrade in software development.

References

Aharoni, Y. (ed.) (1993) *Coalition and Competition: The Globalisation of Professional Business Services.* New York: Routledge.

Apte, U. (1990) 'Global Outsourcing of Information Systems and Processing Services'. *The Information Society.* V7, 287–303.

Cusumano, M. A. (1991) *Japan's Software Factories: A Challenge to US Management.* New York: Oxford University Press.

Heeks, R. B. (1995) 'From Regulation to Promotion: the State's Changing Nature but Continuing Role in Software Production and Exports. Development Policy and Practice', Working Paper No. 30, Open University, Milton Keynes, UK.

Heeks, R. B (1996) *India's Software Industry: State Policy, Liberalisation and the Industrial Development.* New Delhi: Sage Publications.

Kim, Chai, Westin, Stu, and Dholakia, Nikhilesh (1989) 'Globalization of Software Industry: Trends and Strategies.' *Information and Management,* 17, 197–206.

Meadows, C. J. (1996) 'Globework: Creating Technology with International teams'. Ph.D. dissertation submitted at Graduate School of Business Administration, Harvard University.

Mowrey, D. C. (ed.) (1995) *The International Computer Software Industry,* Oxford: Oxford University Press.

National Association of Software and Service Companies (NASSCOM) (1996) *Software Industry in India.*

Platz, Burckhardt (1992) 'Software Export Industry: Prospectives and Problems', in Cyranek, Gunther and Bhatnagar, S.C. (eds) *Technology Transfer for Development.* New Delhi: Tata McGraw-Hill.

Schware, R. (1989) The World Software Industry and Software Engineering; Opportunities and Constraints for Newly Industrialized Economies. World Bank Technical Paper No. 104, New York: World Bank.

Steinmueller, W. E. (1995) 'The US Software Industry: An Analyses and Interpretative History', in Mowery, C.D. (ed.) *The International Computer Software Industry,* Oxford: Oxford University Press.

Waltz, D. B., Elam, J., and Curtis, B. (1993) 'Inside a Software Design Team: Knowledge Acquisition, Sharing, and Integration', Communications of ACM.

Yourdon, E. (1992), *Decline and Fall of American Programmers.* Englewood Cliffs, NJ: Prentice-Hall.

4

TELEBANKING: BREAKING THE LOGIC OF SPATIAL AND WORK ORGANISATION

Geraldine Reardon

Introduction

This chapter looks at the growth of telebanking in the UK and the consequent reorganisation of work in retail banking. Telebanking, in its various forms, is the public face of a method of the storage and flow of information, organised so that the information can be retrieved and amended from anywhere in the organisation virtually instantaneously. Its aim is not necessarily better service but a different kind of service that produces higher rates of efficiency and productivity.

The short-term motivation of banks to cut branches and develop telephone-based services has been to maximise profits in a period of high demands on bank reserves; third world debt and poor investment strategies; to maintain competitiveness by keeping ahead in a deregulated market of financial products and services; and for some, to create new markets by fostering a commercial identity independent of a branch presence. In the longer term, banks see the introduction of telebanking as a stage in the development of new forms of technology-intensive banking that will place greater emphasis on 'self-clerking' by the customer and eliminate the need for large numbers of permanent staff.

The chapter begins by tracing the growth of telebanking. Conditions that gave rise to First Direct and the motivation for other banks to follow it are reviewed and the changing shape of branches and branch networks are put in the context of technological change. The continuing scepticism of bank customers is raised in querying the commercial limitations of telebanking as it is.

The reorganisation of work through call centres is described in terms of centralising control of work processes, and employment issues are examined in terms of outsourcing of labour and of information and communications technology (ICT) expertise. In conclusion, the future of the industry beyond telebanking is considered.

The growth of telebanking

Telebanking is not an isolated phenomenon but exists within a longer term trend in which UK retail banking organisations are reorganising around ICT. This trend began in 1968 with Barclaycard and the first ATM. Originally merely cash dispensers, ATMs gradually acquired a wider range of basic interactive functions. By the mid-1980s, they had lost their novelty value and the idea that customers did not have to go into a bank to get cash, to make a deposit or to request a statement had taken hold. Customers could do more of the work and branch-based bank employees could do less.

However, progress toward telebanking was not smooth, indeed most of the major high street banks adopted it slowly and reluctantly. Banks usually speak of telebanking in terms of responding to customer preference. While customer dissatisfaction with standard banking practice was a key factor for the first real stand-alone telephone bank, First Direct, telebanking would not have been possible without changes taking place outside the financial services industry. These were a combination of government policies for deregulation combined with rapid development in computer and communications technology.

The era in banking leading up to telephone banking

During the 1960s and 1970s, in an attempt to expand, the major UK clearing banks lent heavily to structurally weak economies and by the 1980s, many of these loans had turned into massive debts. The banks were still highly dependent on their UK retail operations when a second round of losses, due mainly to over-lending in the international property market, occurred in the mid–1980s.

In another attempt to recover, the banks invested heavily in their main source of income, the UK retail branch banks. As branches were expanded, investments were also made in mainframe computers and some 'back room' functions were shifted to data processing centres. This was still a period of job creation: between 1983 and 1989, the number of UK bank employees rose by about 30 per cent to a peak of 355,700. However, by 1993 the banks employed only 300,100, about the same as in 1985 (Bannister and Atkinson 1995). This dramatic decline represents job loss due to branch closures and the shifting of routine branch functions to automated call centres.

But in the background to branch closures was the increasing use of cashpoints – automated teller machines (ATMs) and payment cards. During the same period, 1983 to 1993, the number of ATMs grew from 5,000 to over 14,000 and electronic funds transfer at point of sale (EFTPOS) was firmly established in the retail sales sector. The significance of ATMs to the closure of branches will be returned to.

During the 1980s, the UK government's policies for deregulation created both threats and opportunities for the banking sector. On the one hand, the established terms of reference within financial services were shifted profoundly by the Financial Services Act (1986) and the Building Societies Act (1986), which left banks open to real competition, for which they were unprepared. Previously, retail financial service organisations operated within the security of well-defined and well-protected market segments. The greatest challenge to the major clearing banks was the fast-growing and more flexible building societies. Not only did these smaller organisations hold the larger share of deposits, they were now also able to offer the same standard range of retail banking services, and more profitably than the traditional banks. In addition to a stable customer base from which to expand, building societies had large cash reserves, which the major banks lacked, and they were able to expand their product line, services and presence as full banking organisations. Yet on the other hand, a deregulated market meant that banks had a new opportunity to sell a range of potentially profitable non-core products such as insurance, pensions and mortgages.

At this point, banks were faced with a problem they had unwittingly created by situating ATMs outside the branch and thereby successfully discouraging many of their customers from entering their branch on a regular basis. How could banks compete in this newly deregulated market if they could not communicate directly and regularly with a large proportion of their customers?

Which brings us to a second opportunity, that of the deregulation of British Telecom. As a result of the commercialisation of the UK telecoms industry, by the late 1980s telephones had been installed in the majority of UK households and the telecoms network had been extended and modernised in many parts of the country. New price structures including lower off-peak rates, lower line rentals, the ability to reach distant locations by dialling a local number, and so on, have encouraged a 'telephone culture' that previously did not exist in the UK. Today, more people are used to using the phone for a greater variety of purposes than they were before the 1980s. Between 1972 and 1992, the proportion of UK households with a telephone more than doubled from 42 per cent to 89 per cent, growing to 94.3 per cent by 1995, and more than half of households now have two or more phones (Jones 1995: Tables 33 and 34). In addition, however, during this period of the mid- to late 1980s, a new culture of acquisitiveness, combined with a kind of 'technophilia', emerged in the UK, most evidently among prosperous young people (Central Statistical Office 1995). This fact was central to the marketing strategy of the first stand-alone telebank, First Direct, in 1989.

The real motivation of banks to cut their branch networks and to replace them with telephone-based services was not strictly a commitment to improved customer service, nor a desire to be at the cutting edge of the technological revolution. Rather, it was an attempt to reverse declining profits, due to poor lending and investment decisions; to maintain a competitive position within the newly deregulated industry; and to create new markets in retail banking.

The start of telebanking

Although credited with starting the trend in telebanking, First Direct came after earlier remote banking ventures and no doubt learned from these experiences. In 1985 HOBS (Bank of Scotland) was the first banking service in the UK to link home and business PCs to a Videotext network. Girobank (formerly owned by the Post Office and bought by Alliance & Leicester Building Society in 1988) has operated a telephone service as part of a mix of branch (post office) and postal services since 1968.

However, it was not until the launch of First Direct that the idea caught hold. Reasons for the bank's immediate success are clear: it had a stylish new identity at a time when consumer dissatisfaction with traditional banks was generally high, with perceptions of poor service and high charges; it offered a full banking service but at lower cost and with the added convenience of round the clock service; it carefully targeted its customer base; and, it was based on the telephone at a time when telecoms privatisation had resulted in the successful promotion of the personal use of telephones. Most homes had at least one telephone, which was all the equipment necessary, unlike HOBS which also required a PC and modem. Furthermore, although telephone-based, First Direct's service was still 'person to person' and thereby managed to mimic the personal approach of the branch.

Its target market were people who sought convenience, were financially aware and liked to use the telephone: affluent, educated, 25- to 45-year-old professionals. First Direct understood the relationship between the technology of new telephony – it is easier and cheaper to use – and the expectations of the bank's market: financial services should be provided easily and readily over the telephone. First Direct still rejects 45 per cent of applications (Montalbano 1995), yet has 650,000 customers and adds over 10,000 each month.

Although the first post-deregulation strategy of the major banks was to keep branches open as 'shops' where non-core financial products could be sold, they realised, from the example of First Direct, that many non-core products could be sold more profitably by telephone. Banks gradually added a limited telephone service for branch-based accounts and all have continued to add to these services by extending hours and services available. The industry now predicts that by the year 2000 all banks will operate some kind of 24-hour telebanking service, compared to 60 per cent in 1994 (Chetham 1995: Figure 7.3). Table 4.1 shows that this target has almost been reached.

Table 4.1 Some locations of financial services call centres in the UK

Location	Name of enterprise
Birmingham	Girobank
Bradford	PrimeLine (NatWest)
Colchester	Guardian Direct
Coventry	Barclaycall
	Domestic & General (2 sites)
Edinburgh	Centrebank (Bank of Scotland)
	Direct Banking (Royal Bank of Scotland)
	Girobank
Glasgow	Abbey National
	Abbey National Direct
	Clydesdale Bank
	Direct Line (mortgages)
	TSB Phonebank
	Yorkshire (same site as Clydesdale Bank)
Leeds	First Direct
	Girobank
	Halifax Direct
Merseyside	Girobank (2 sites)
Newport	Hexagon Insurance
	TSB PhoneBank
Norwich	Virgin Direct
Sheffield	Norwich Union Direct (Hill House Hammond)
Skelmersdale	Co-operative Bank (Armchair)
South-east	Abbey National Direct
	Access
	Girobank
	Lloyds
	Norwich Union Healthcare
	Sun Alliance
South-west	Direct Line
	Girobank
Stockport	Co-operative Bank (Armchair)
Swansea	Lloyds TSB
Tyne & Wear	AA Insurance
	Eagle Star Direct
	Northern Rock
	Royal Insurance (The Insurance Service)
	TSB PhoneBank

Stand-alone telephone banks are cheaper to run than branch networks because they have lower overheads. Where banks have added a telephone service onto the existing branch network, they have not cut costs but have added to them. Between 1990 and 1994, operating costs of the major banks rose on average by about 16 per cent (see Table 4.2). To compensate, staff were made redundant and branches were closed by about the same rate. These cuts and closures were and are still not a response to the demands of customers who prefer telephone banking; rather branch closures are a way of keeping costs down while also pursuing a long-term investment strategy for new technology in banking. This can be done more efficiently with a smaller and more closely targeted branch network, than the unfocused branches of the past, which together resembled more a membership organisation than a functional network.

The changing shape of branches and branch networks

Between 1983 and 1993, UK banks closed 18 per cent of their (mainly smaller and unprofitable) branches to concentrate operations in larger branches and centres (Anon (a)1996). Conventional banks continue to add telephone services to the branch service and close or 'down-size' low-profit branches. Branches in areas with a high proportion of high-value accounts are being enhanced and in some cases smaller satellite branches are clustered around one larger branch where a broader range of services are concentrated. This process continues, and according to forecasts (Chetham 1995), nearly 20 per cent of bank and building society branches open at the beginning of this decade will have closed by the middle of the next.

It is apparent that banks are not abandoning their branch networks, but are concentrating on key locations and developing new forms of networks. NatWest, for example, is installing 150,000 information outlets throughout its branch network by 1997 as part of its branch automation programme (*Financial Technology International Bulletin*, April 1996). Similarly, the Royal Bank of Scotland has installed a BT network linking 700 branches. The network, covering the entire country, links branches to the bank's mainframe computer. The system provides branch-to-branch communication so that, for example, a mortgage specialist at one branch can confer with a colleague in another branch via a PC-to-PC video conferencing link with simultaneous on-screen data and graphical information exchange.

In the first half of the 1990s, branches were cut by 12 per cent and staff by 17 per cent, while the number of ATMs grew by 15 per cent (see Table 4.3). The changing profile of services carried out at branches has been gradual, starting with the earlier introduction of ATMs outside the bank premises. Cash-dispensing functions of the branch became more automated throughout the 1980s (as did data storage and processing, which was centralised in mainframe computers).

Table 4.2 Branch outlets and staff levels for UK banks, 1990–94

	Number of branches					
	1990	*1991*	*1992*	*1993*	*1994*	*% change 1990–94*
Barclays	2,586	2,476	2,281	2,119	2,090	−19.18
NatWest	2,805	2,683	2,541	2,545	2,410	−14.08
Lloyds	2,111	1,929	1,884	1,860	1,799	−14.78
Midland	1,957	1,824	1,716	1,713	1,706	−12.83
TSB	1,489	1,399	1,369	1,321	1,235	−17.06
Abbey National	681	683	680	676	675	−0.88
Royal Bank of Scotland	841	805	786	752	732	−12.96
Bank of Scotland	515	502	490	455	430	−16.50
Standard Chartered	9	5	4	4	1	−88.89
Total MBBG[a]	12,994	12,306	11,751	11,445	11,078	−14.75
Clydesdale Bank	350	346	330	314	322	−8.00
The Co-op Bank	109	107	106	109	129	18.35
Yorkshire	255	261	266	270	270	5.88
Girobank[b]	20,871	20,638	20,160	19,958	19,782	−5.22

	Number of staff					
	1990	*1991*	*1992*	*1993*	*1994*	*% change 1990–94*
Barclays	84,700	81,600	76,800	68,700	63,500	−25.03
NatWest	85,900	81,700	75,800	72,200	67,200	−21.77
Lloyds	58,600	52,500	46,500	44,900	43,500	−25.77
Midland	47,100	43,700	42,900	42,400	41,900	−11.04
TSB	23,100	23,100	23,000	23,800	23,400	1.30
Abbey National	14,000	15,000	15,800	16,400	16,400	17.14
Royal Bank of Scotland	21,300	20,800	19,900	18,800	19,700	−7.51
Bank of Scotland	12,500	11,900	11,800	11,400	11,300	−9.60
Standard Chartered	1,700	1,500	1,300	1,300	1,200	−29.41
Clydesdale Bank	7,200	6,700	6,400	6,000	6,000	−16.67
The Co-op Bank	4,500	3,700	3,900	4,000	3,900	−13.33
Yorkshire	6,300	6,600	6,600	6,700	6,800	7.94

	Operating expenses of total MBBG[a] (£m)					
	1990	*1991*	*1992*	*1993*	*1994*	*% change 1990–94*
	16,021	17,143	18,091	18,622	18,620	16.22

Source: 'Annual Abstract of Banking Statistics – May 1995', reproduced in *Personal Finance in the UK, 1996 Market Review*, Key Note Publications, Table 8.12.

Notes
[a] MBBG = major British banking groups.
[b] Number of post offices.

Table 4.3 Size of UK branch/ATM network and staff employed, 1990–95

	1990	1991	1992	1993	1994	1995 est.
ATMs	17,004	17,826	18,349	18,771	19,545	20,103
Branches	20,081	19,264	18,541	18,115	17,663	17,123
Staff	348,800	331,800	313,300	300,100	288,000	245,000

Source: adapted from data compiled in *UK Banking 1995*, Market Assessment Publications Ltd, Table 6.

Banks no longer take branches for granted. For example, in 1994 TSB (which later merged with Lloyds Bank) used a geographical modelling and planning consultant to assess its branch network of 1,350. At the time, TSB said it was not a matter of getting rid of branches to be replaced by telephones and new technology but to reconsider the geographic spread of their business and the investment requirements of each branch (*Financial Technology International Bulletin*, April 1994). Within two years its branch network had been reduced overall to about 1,000, even though new branches were opened.

Increasingly, ATMs are situated away from branches: in 1990 this was just 7.7 per cent but by 1995 it was 13.2 per cent (Anon (b) 1996: Table 7). Without knowing it, customers have been preparing for telebanking for two decades by getting used to a certain amount of self-service, or 'self-clerking' as it is called in the industry.

However, even stand-alone telephone banks need access to an ATM network and branch services. First Direct, for example, relies on the Midland branch network and the Mint ATM network to which Midland subscribes. Girobank uses a combination of the Post Office network, a prepaid envelope system, and the Link ATM network.

Branch and ATM networks have also been instrumental in the strategic expansion of regionally-based telebanks. Research has shown how Bank of Scotland used Centrebank, based in low-cost Edinburgh, to reach the 'lucrative English market'. Conversely, the same low-cost base combined with a good ATM and branch network gave Royal Bank of Scotland an advantage over First Direct in the new Scottish telebanking market.

A new culture of banking?

Research (Richardson and Marshall 1995; Marshall and Richardson 1996) has shown how ICT has resulted in the restructuring of retail banking in Britain, relocating operations away from branches to 'a small number of low cost sites on the edge of cities in the north of the country'. This research focuses on the development of the call centre, where contact with customers is conducted via the telephone and facilitated by a combination of computer-based technology and telecommunications as a replacement of branch functions. Call centres have helped firms to expand their geographical reach and reduce their running costs by locating their processing facilities in lower cost areas for export to wealthier areas. In the case of banks, this breaks the centuries-old logic of the branch which situates the branch in the same location as the customer and which assumes person-to-person service.

The relocation of core banking operations has indeed taken place and the concept of the 'branchless' bank is now accepted in fact, but not necessarily in favour. There is still considerable customer resistance to the idea of the diminution of the role of the branch. This wariness of telephone banking by the banking public is borne out by a market survey, according to which three in five customers regularly visit their branch, other than to use a cashpoint (*Financial Technology International Bulletin*, September 1994). Still another reported that the number of people using telephone banking services (2.5 million) is still only 5.6 per cent of adults in the UK, and of those, the main reason that 86.4 per cent use it is for balance enquiries (Caines 1996: 132).

The fact that First Direct itself has set up a 'field sales force' for extending credit authorisation by means of home visits is a strong indicator that not all transactions can be satisfactorily completed by telephone or that all customers want to enter into serious and binding contracts via a remote service (*Financial Technology International Bulletin*, April 1995). NatWest has opened seven-day branches in large shopping centres, recognising that some customers still perceive the need to talk to someone in person and in a bank (Gosling 1995).

Banks command considerable loyalty and many customers see them as primarily providers of services rather than as sellers of products. Cost savings, such as free chequeing are strong incentives to move to telebanking from a fully branch-based account but if all financial services use the medium of the telephone and charges once again level out, where will the element of competition be, and where will employers look to make further cost savings?

Martin Taylor, CEO of Barclays Bank, said that customers cannot be force-fed with new products or services, and that banks need to foresee their needs (speaking on 'In Business', BBC Radio 4, 19 May 1996). Although customers may not be force-fed telebanking, the alternatives are rapidly diminishing as branches are closed or have their staff and range of services reduced.

Call centres and the reorganisation of work

Call centres were set up to serve customers directly and, at the same time, to carry out many administrative functions. The move to call centres was not a giant leap; they were preceded by centralised data processing centres set up in the late 1960s and 1970s when banks converted their manual information storage and retrieval systems to mainframe computers. In today's banks, such data processing centres also perform some internal routine functions previously carried out at the branch. These centres are linked to branch networks and administrative offices and are generally referred to as 'telecentres' because of their telecommunications links within the bank. Customers usually have no direct telephone contact with telecentres.

Call centres, as direct service providers to customers, provide economies over a traditional network of branches, each performing a complete range of administrative and customer service functions. Through ICT, face-to-face contact with the customer is transformed into a routine standardised format. A high level of standardisation of service processes is combined with a massive store of detailed information on each customer account. This information can be retrieved with a great deal of variation so that the customer can be serviced, and new products and services can be marketed, in a highly personalised way.

Due to advances in digitisation, such enormous quantities of data can be stored on computers that terms like 'data warehousing' and 'data mining' are now part of the jargon. Data warehousing refers to the retrieval and processing of information from various sources. In banking, this would be, for example, information of current account holders, credit card holders, loans and mortgages, all stored on different databases. The information is used to improve marketing and to aid decision-making at customer and at corporate level. Data storage hardware and software has become so sophisticated that searches can be made through millions of documents in seconds and records can be retrieved by searching for key words and concepts.

Automatic call distribution (ACD) technology allows calls from customers to be distributed among the workforce in the most efficient way. The workforce might be distributed over six widely dispersed centres, as in the case of Girobank, but calls can still be switched among them automatically. There is no central operator; callers are arranged in a queue and put through to an 'agent' or 'representative', or to an automated system which operates by responding to the caller's touch-tone device or by voice recognition. Then the call can be forwarded within the company by responding via their touch-tone telephone or by voice to a series of recorded messages.

Similarly, as described by Richardson and Marshall (1995: 5–8) a single 'local' telephone number can be redirected to a number of call centres in various distant destinations, thereby creating a virtual single site, whose location is always local in the mind of the caller, an important factor in maintaining customers and in marketing. These destinations can be changed day-by-day or hour-by-hour and 'by spreading production over several sites firms can also ameliorate problems relating to single-site production including technical problems and industrial action' (Richardson and Marshall 1995: 7). The ability of banks to use UK-based homeworkers or even more distant call centres is greatly enhanced by such technology.

Calls may also be channelled according to their source, and it may be possible, by identifying the incoming telephone number, for the operator to know immediately where the call is coming from. The caller's identity is confirmed by answering a series of questions with previously agreed coded responses, or by tapping in codes on a touch-tone telephone.

As well as receiving telephone calls, call centres may also make calls. The technology for mass telephone marketing has been developed so that a range of numbers can be dialled automatically, stopping at the first one to answer and supplying the operator with the relevant details of the individual or organisation receiving the call.

Together, these technological factors create an organisational and spatial logic that banks and similar service organisations find irresistible. It is not only the economies of production that attract banks to call centres, the potential to sell a wider range of products and services more widely and more precisely targeted with a very high degree of efficiency makes them inevitable.

And as Richardson and Marshall argue, it makes sense to locate these centres 'in a part of the country where production costs are low' (1995: 8). This also applies, of course, to a part of the world where production costs are low. With satellite communications, there are no locational constraints on such mechanisms.

Referring to data from the Centre for Urban and Regional Development Studies, Huws points to the simple model of a single call centre servicing a UK-wide market (Huws 1996: 94–5). With a few exceptions, this is the reality of most financial services organisations today (see Table 4.1). However, if the technology allows calls and information to be transferred among several sites almost as easily as within a single building, other factors, such as availability of qualified staff and other essential resources, might work against the development of single large centres and in favour of a network of small or medium-sized centres.

Further developments

Call centres are not the final stage in the reorganisation of work away from the branches. The development and refinement of ICT is occurring at a rapid rate and users continually conduct trials of the technology, the aim of which is to further automate the processes of servicing and selling.

Voice recognition

After years of development, voice recognition has reached acceptable standards. Abbey National is the first bank to introduce 'an automated 24-hour telephone banking system capable of recognising continuous speech' (*Financial Technology International Bulletin*, September 1995). Access to this facility is arranged, not through a branch, but through an ATM, a service running alongside the bank's telephone distribution network. The automated system is designed to deal with routine transactions, leaving more complex queries to human operators.

Imaging technology

Telephone links to customers are being developed alongside other forms of information and communications technology with the aim of integrating information processing throughout the business. Work-flow systems based on imaging technology, as used by the major banks and insurance companies, are designed for centralised telecentres to move work to staff in a seamless manner. A range of products and services, combined with telemarketing, can be merged electronically within a single call centre or a network of branches and centres. In principle, the call centre operator, on a telephone link to the customer, can use the technology to consult records and suppliers and respond to the customer's request almost immediately.

So far, the limitations of such systems are legion: they are rigid, prone to failure and, especially for products such as term insurance policies, they raise legal problems, but the systems are continually being developed and improved and major banks are integrating imaging technology into their organisational development. NatWest, for example, has developed a work-flow system that includes a number of different work areas: call centres, home loans departments and telemarketing, as well as the telecentres that handle correspondence customer queries. And in 1996, TSB (Trustee Savings Bank) began implementing a multi-million pound work-flow system for use in branches and centralised operations to automate the flow of correspondence relating to all customer transactions across a range of products, including loans, insurance, investments and telebanking (*Financial Technology International Bulletin*, April 1996).

In theory, if the technology is in place, every paper document that comes into a business can be scanned and stored electronically to be retrieved from any point in the network. This means that location is no longer a key factor even in paper-based transactions.

Increasing centralisation

Such investments are not made merely to save paper and processing time, they are part of a longer term strategy to create an information flow accessible from any part of the organisation and to exercise more precise control over the workforce.

One bank, National Australia Bank, is using call centre technology as part of a programme to centralise the operations of two subsidiary banks: Yorkshire Bank and Clydesdale Bank. Starting in July 1996, Yorkshire Bank operates a pilot scheme of ten branches out of the Clydesdale Bank's Telephone Centre based in Glasgow (Keith Brookes, BIFU, pers. comm.).

An intrinsic part of the ACD system is a link to the management system which monitors the content of the calls and the activity of the employee. Employees may be monitored for speed, conformity to the procedure and sales performance and these criteria linked to pay (Richardson and Marshall 1995: 6).

From what has been observed, it is not unreasonable to predict that work processes will continue to be brought under centralised control, but not necessarily in the same location. In the case of banking, the work of telecentres that function only internally and that have no direct contact with customers, as do call centres, will probably be gradually absorbed by call centres as technological advances give rise to even more centralised systems with the ability to combine all administrative, sales and customer service functions.

Employment issues

Negotiating a new culture

The introduction of still newer technologies and systems for processing information and for communicating with customers have created new methods and patterns of work not previously encountered in UK banking. This has enabled new companies, whose work is organised according to the logic of ICT systems, to break with long established practice. For example, in the beginning, First Direct did not want to employ former Midland employees because they wanted to break the old banking culture. A similar recruitment policy was applied when Guardian Direct was set up by Guardian Royal Exchange plc: the preference was for staff who had not worked in the old-style insurance industry. As a result, established terms and conditions of work have had to be renegotiated.

Among the new conditions for which there is no precedent is outsourcing, which has become so widespread that the employees of companies under-taking outsourced work are becoming like a permanently semi-detached workforce.

Outsourcing

Over the past decade, outsourcing has been seen as an effective cost-cutting measure among large employers.

In banking, outsourcing is most likely to be in 'back room' functions such as data processing and in IT departments, although other clerical functions and support services such as cleaning are increasingly included – Barclays Bank are outsourcing their Stationery Services (*BIFU Report*, August–September 1996). Cooperative Bank has outsourced its account opening administration to an agency (Caines 1996: 148). Centralised departments such as telecentres and call centres make outsourcing easier to implement than when work was carried out in a single head office and among the various branches.

Some low-waged economies with a sizeable, educated and skilled work-force specialise in attracting work outsourced from Europe and North America. India has become a specialist in outsourced computer pro-gramme and software design so it was not unusual for the Royal Bank of Scotland to award a programming contract to Tata, the largest software exporter in India.

International outsourcing of information processing has been the subject of considerable research effort but as pointed out by Huws (1996: 108) systematic monitoring has not taken place and as such an informed critical overview of the subject is still lacking. In light of recent developments in UK banking, greater knowledge of this subject is of interest to trade unions in the UK, as well as in the exporting countries.

Homeworking is individualised outsourcing. It is now widespread in Britain and includes large numbers of workers carrying out tasks on a computer, which may be linked to another site, or to a telephone line. (Huws 1994). According to BIFU (Jo Seery, pers. comm.), as a result of the closure of branches and offices, banks and insurance companies are pressuring or forcing employees to work from home, yet many cases do not come to light because of the isolation of homeworkers.

Part-time and temporary workers are employed more often where a 24-hour shift system is in force, which is now the case with the majority of banks (see Table 4.4). BIFU reports that in the whole finance industry, the proportion of part timers, the majority of whom are women, went up from 11 per cent in 1989 to 15 per cent in 1995 (Seery 1996). See also Table 4.5.

IT outsourcing

Many banks have sold or closed their IT departments and outsourced the development and maintenance of their information and communication systems to specialists. The assumption is that IT outsourcing saves money. However, one survey of IT outsourcing in the UK showed that either no costs were saved or that costs increased (*Financial Technology International Bulletin*, January 1994). Furthermore, it could be argued that by out-sourcing this crucial area of work, banks are relinquishing control over vital processes to companies that are commercially powerful in their own

Table 4.4 Selected telephone banking systems

Account	Service	Mode	Opening hours	Comments
Alliance & Leicester (Telecare)	Stand-alone	Person to person/ computer	24 hours 365 days a year	1986 and 1994. Free deposit and cheque cashing facilities at around 2,000 main and sub Post Offices. Plus pre-paid postal facility for deposits
Alliance & Leicester (Alliance Account)	Branch-based	Person to person/ computer	24 hours 365 days a year	1994. Plus pre-paid postal facility for deposits
Bank of Scotland (HOBS)	Stand-alone	Person/computer to computer	24 hours 365 days a year	1985. Mainly for business customers using a PC. Option to access account through a Screenphone, a combined electronic screen and telephone
Bank of Scotland (Banking Direct)	Stand-alone	Person to person	24 hours 365 days a year	Account may be accessed through HOBS, including Screenphone
Bank of Scotland (Phoneline)	Branch-based		24 hours 365 days a year	1993
Barclays (Barclaycall)	Branch-based	Person to person	M–F 7am–11pm W'ends 9am–5pm	1994. Calls charges at local rate. Travellers cheques and foreign currency can also be ordered by phone
Bristol&West (Asset)	Stand-alone telephone-based savings mgnt. service		24 hours 365 days a year	1994
Citibank Current Account	Stand-alone		24 hours 365 days a year	Minimum deposit of £2,000 required to open account. Calls are free of charge

Table 4.4 (cont.)

Account	Service	Mode	Opening hours	Comments
Clydesdale (TeleBank)	Branch-based	Person to computer	24 hours 365 days a year	1988. Combination of voice response and tonepad service
Clydesdale (TeleBank PC)	Stand-alone	Person/computer to computer	24 hours 365 days a year	1987 and 1994. Mainly for business customers using a PC
Co-operative Bank (Armchair Banking)	Branch-based	Person to person	24 hours 365 days a year	Tonepad service available outside working hours (since 1993). 500,000 customers
First Direct Current Account	Stand-alone	Person to person	24 hours 365 days a year	1989. Premier service also available for a £5 monthly charge. Banking representatives handle routine queries, more specialised queries referred to financial services adviser
Save & Prosper (Premier Banking Service)	Stand-alone		24 hours 365 days a year	Free Gold VISA card if balance maintained above £2,500. Minimum deposit of £2,500 to open account
Halifax (Maxim Home Banking)	Branch-based		24 hours	1989. Touch-tone and voice recognition
Lloyds (Lloydsline)	Branch-based		8am–10pm 365 days a year	Subscribers are given a plastic card embossed with a membership number which must be quoted when calling
Nationwide (FlexAccount)	Branch-based	Person/computer to computer	24 hours	1987. Access via touch-tone telephone or tonepad
NatWest (Primeline)	Stand-alone	Person to person	24 hours	1991. Tonepad service available outside of opening hours. Customers are allocated a personal account manager. Minimum income of £18,000 to use the service

NatWest (ActionLine)	Branch-based	Person to computer	24 hours	System uses voice recognition, touch tone or tonepad
NatWest (BusinessLine)	Branch-based for small businesses	Person to computer	24 hours	1992. System uses voice recognition, touch tone or tonepad
NatWest (StudentLine)	Branch-based for students	Person to computer	24 hours	System uses voice recognition, touch tone or tonepad
Royal Bank of Scotland (Direct Banking Service)	Branch-based		24 hours 365 days a year	Security system consists of a combination of four digits and a password
TSB Interest (Phonebank)	Branch-based	Person to computer	24 hours 365 days a year	1994. Calls are free of charge. Account can be opened over the telephone, with completed application form sent to customer for signature

Source: Financial Services Retailing 1995 (1996) Market Assessment Publications Ltd, London. 'Telephone Banking – who's offering what?' Money World UK Ltd, 1996 (www.moneyworld.co.uk). 'More set to join direct banking wire brigade', *The Guardian*, 28 September 1996; Marshall and Richardson (1996).

Notes
Person to person/computer = customer speaks to bank representative or adviser, or customer uses a tonepad, touch-tone phone or voice recognition system to interact with a computer.
Person to computer = customer interacts with a voice recognition system or uses a tonepad, touch-tone phone to interact with a voice response system.
Person to person = customer speaks to bank representative or adviser.
Person/computer to computer = customer interacts with bank's computer through a PC or smartphone.
Tonepad generates the necessary tones where the customer's telephone as yet cannot.

Table 4.5 Employment in UK financial services, 1990–95

Year	Men			Women			Total	% change over previous year
	Full time	Part time	All men	Full time	Part time	All women		
1990	443,963	14,198	458,161	467,242	120,022	587,264	1,045,425	n/a
1991	431,759	15,581	447,340	458,142	118,760	576,902	1,024,242	−2.03%
1992	417,298	17,496	434,794	439,534	117,393	556,927	991,721	−3.18%
1993	409,994	14,570	424,564	419,030	117,389	536,419	960,983	−3.10%
1994	403,980	14,708	418,688	405,828	119,071	524,899	943,581	−1.81%
1995	392,900	16,400	409,300	388,600	122,400	511,000	920,300	2.47%
% change 1990–95	−11.50%	15.51%	−10.66%	−16.83%	1.98%	−12.99%	−11.97%	

Source: Adapted from Central Statistical Office, Earnings and Employment Division, 1 February 1996, as reproduced in BIFU discussion paper: *An Overview of Women in the Finance Sector in the UK*, BIFU Research Department, May 1996.

right whose main interest is the promotion of the technology itself: ICL, IBM, Microsoft, Anderson Consulting, and EDS. The providers of the vital links, that is the cable and satellite companies BT, BSkyB, Videotron and Bell Cablemedia, for example, are also taking the initiative on ventures in on-line banking and insurance.

Core banking functions are now strongly influenced by interests with goals that reach beyond the provision of financial services. Thus, the technology is perhaps given a more central position in the structure and function of banks than it otherwise might have had. Software houses are now among the most powerful actors in the industry because they can decide how networks are structured, how products are sold and how services are performed. This raises a question about how decisions regarding technological developments are made, and by whom.

This is not to say that the major banks of the UK are powerless in this relationship. Quite the contrary, they have contracted out IT functions because the technology has become too specialised a field; and they have entered into commercial arrangements, of differing types, with media and communications companies because that is how they get their products and services into the new markets.

What comes after the telephone?

This chapter has summarised how retail banks in the UK are using information and communications technology to restructure the organisation of their work. Banks do not want to stop at telephone-based services; they want to coordinate the technology to create a seamless flow between the transaction, the administrative process and overall control. Thus, telephone links, either person-to-person or computer-to-computer, are not separate from the processing and storage of the information within the various parts of the organisation. Therefore, it is likely that telecentre functions, such as standard word processed letters and document storage, will be automated a step further and brought within the work of call centres.

Despite apparently widespread customer reluctance to adopt telephone banking enthusiastically, industry forecasters continue to predict extraordinary rises in the use of telephones and personal computers as a substitute for branches. For example, in 1995 UK bankers forecast that 'the number of calls taken through telephone banking is set to rise by 600 per cent by 1997' (*Financial Technology International Bulletin*, March 1995). If this is what the industry is predicting, it is reasonable to assume that the industry also has an interest in seeing the prediction realised, thus making Martin Taylor's claim (see above) that customers cannot be force-fed telephone banking sound a little hollow. Or, perhaps he has another idea in mind: the fully automated branch.

So far, even customers of stand-alone telephone banks, such as First Direct, have needed branches through which they can withdraw and deposit cash. However, research by Coopers & Lybrand predicts that although the number of branches will continue to decline, the number of customers being served by a telephone link will stop growing and instead various forms of ATMs and screen banking provided through kiosks, PCs and TVs will take over (*Financial Technology International Bulletin*, April 1996). Midland Bank, for example, has already introduced a new form of branch: banking 'lobbies' served entirely by machines (*Financial Services Retailing 1995*, Market Assessment Publications Ltd, 1996: 9–10). If more multi-purpose ATMs are installed in locations away from branches (in cash machine lobbies, for example), more customers would become independent of the branch system and not have to rely on the telephone either.

So where does this leave the virtual home bank? A survey of home PC ownership predicts that on-line services will make their biggest impact on transaction businesses, such as banking, finance, insurance and travel (*Financial Times*, 26 June 1996). And yet, a study by BT in 1994 found that most customers were not willing to invest in separate equipment only for home banking, but that they would accept home banking if it were offered as part of a package of services based on the basic provision of entertainment (*Financial Technology International Bulletin*, March 1994). Communications companies such as BT and BSkyB, and software companies like Microsoft want banking and insurance products as another group of services and products to be added to their consumer package. Now that digital TV and televisions with built-in modems are on the market, this customer criterion does not sound far-fetched.

Nevertheless, in the meantime, as product and marketing differences diminish further overall, and as companies within each sector once again begin to resemble each other in the eyes of the consumer, competition will force down charges for services and prices of products until uniformly flat rates for similar services and products emerge in each sector. At this point, the pressure for higher productivity from staff and technology will intensify and the consequences of this will be felt most strongly by employees working in the technology intensive call centres.

After reviewing current trends in technology and reflecting on the apparently powerful impact that ICT has had on recent changes in banking services, it is tempting to go along with the frequently heard proposition that the technology is driving the changes. However, this is too simplistic a position to take for such a complex set of conditions. Banks are driving themselves towards rather than being driven by 'new' technology and they are doing so according to their own rationality in response to internal and external pressures: their own heavy debt burden and the deregulation of the industry, followed by the need to expand and to maintain a competitive position.

These are the factors driving banks towards more intensive ICT systems. However, having said that, the point must be repeated: banks have very close relationships with the suppliers of the technology and these relationships should be closely monitored.

Finally, telebanking is not the aim of the exercise, from the banks' point of view. The target is increased productivity through automation and greater potential for expansion in new markets: new product markets and new geographical markets. Banks frequently say that they are closing or shrinking branches because of the benefits of automation associated with telephone-based banking. In fact, they are not closing branches because of automation, they are closing branches in order to automate, to create an organisation centralised by means of information and communications technology based on targets of high productivity.

References

Anon (a) (1996) *Financial Services Retailing 1995*, London: Market Assessment Publications Ltd.

Anon (b) (1996) *UK Banking 1995*, London: Market Assessment Publications Ltd.

Bannister, N. and Atkinson, D. (1995) *The Guardian*, 21 May.

BIFU Report, various issues, 1995.

Caines, R. (ed.) (1996) *Personal Finance in the UK, 1996 Market Review*, London: Key Note.

Central Statistical Office, *Social Trends 25*, 1995 Edition, HMSO.

Chetham, J. (1995) *The Future of the UK Financial Service Industry*, London: FT Financial Publishing.

Financial Technology International Bulletin, various issues 1994–1996.

Financial Times (1995) 'International Telecommunications Survey', 3 October.

Gosling, P. (1995) 'Cheap labour at the end of a phone line', *The Independent*, 3 July.

Huws, U. (1994) 'Teleworking in Britain', *Employment Gazette*, February.

Huws, U. (1996) *Teleworking: an Overview of the Research*, a report to the Department of Transport, Department of the Environment, Department of Trade and Industry, and Department for Education and Employment, London: Analytica.

Jones, D. (ed.) (1995) *Telecommunications, 1995 Market Report*, London: Key Note.

Marshall, J. N. and Richardson, R. (1996) 'The Impact of "Telemediated" Services on Corporate Structures: The Example of "Branchless" Retail Banking in Britain', *Environment and Planning A*, 1843–58.

Montalbano, W. D. (1995) *Los Angeles Times*, November 16.

Richardson, R. and Marshall, J. Neill (1996) 'The Growth of Telephone Call Centres in Peripheral Areas of Britain: Evidence from Tyne and Wear', *Area*, 28 (3), 308–17.

Seery, J. (1996) *An Overview of Women in the Finance Sector in the UK*, BIFU discussion paper, London: BIFU.

5

CALL CENTRES AND THE PROSPECTS FOR EXPORT-ORIENTED WORK IN THE DEVELOPING WORLD: EVIDENCE FROM WESTERN EUROPE

Ranald Richardson

Introduction

Geographers have long been interested in the tendency of firms to (re)-locate low value-added or mature manufacturing activities in less developed regions of advanced countries in order to take advantage of lower input costs. More recently, interest has grown in the trend toward locating such activities 'offshore', often in less economically developed countries. By contrast it has generally been felt that few service activities could be located in this way, because of the need for the co-presence of the producer and the customer during service transactions. Over the past few years, however, it has become clear that developments in information and communications technologies have the potential to alter this position. Freeman and Soete, for example, suggest that:

> Information technology, almost by definition, will allow for the increased tradability of service activities, particularly those which have been most constrained by the geographical or time proximity of production and consumption. By bringing in a space or *time/storage* dimension, information technology will make possible the separation of production and consumption in an increasing number of such activities.
>
> (Freeman and Soete 1994: 91, italics in original)

Once service production and consumption are separated, firms can, at least in theory, locate their activities at a distance from their core markets, and so take advantage of lower costs and exploit spatial divisions of labour (Freeman and Soete 1994; Richardson and Marshall 1996a). There is now a growing body of case study evidence suggesting that certain kinds of service work are being relocated to cheaper production locations 'offshore' and then 'exported' to richer markets. This is occurring within Europe (Richardson 1997; Richardson and Marshall 1996a), but also between continents (see, for example, Pearson and Mitter 1993; Warf 1995; Wilson 1993; Wilson 1994; Wilson 1995; Grimes 1995). Unfortunately, there is no statistical evidence that would allow us to say how widespread this tendency is, particularly at the international level, though on-going research by the author suggests that it is no longer only the leading-edge companies that are transferring work offshore.

Two sets of service activities have received most attention in terms of international relocation: routine 'back-office' data processing work (see, for example, Pearson and Mitter 1993; Wilson 1993; Wilson 1994) and software production, with locations such as Bangalore and Mumbai in India attracting work from the US and Europe (see, for example, Keen 1991; Grimes 1995; Wilson 1995). This process of sending work offshore is not, however, confined to firms based in the northern hemisphere. Firms within the Pacific Basin are also seeking lower-cost locations for production activities. Wilson (1995), for example, sites the case of Singapore Airlines, which outsources much of its computer software services from Mumbai. These service activities can be carried out either in-house, through firms setting up (or acquiring) direct subsidiaries, or through outsourcing them to third-party firms, which are required to meet standards laid down by contract.

This chapter is concerned with a relatively new set of mobile service activities, namely *teleservices*, which are increasingly carried out in a new kind of production site known as the *call centre*. Teleservices refer to service *functions* carried out over the telephone, replacing or complementing face-to-face interaction with the customer. Call centres are offices, usually fairly large in scale, in which most of the telephone functions of a company (or particular types of telephone functions, such as sales or customer care) are concentrated in order to create economies of scale (Richardson 1995).

After a description of these new activities and their rapid growth in Europe, there is a discussion of the locational requirements of call centres. It is suggested that *some* of Europe's less favoured regions are benefiting from the relocation of these activities. The potential for call centre activities to relocate to developing countries, servicing European markets at a distance, is then discussed. It is pointed out that there may be a number of barriers that will impede this process, though it is suggested that some call centre activities may be so transferred. Finally, consideration is given to the implications of call centre work for economic development.

The emergence and growth of teleservices in Europe

Drivers of teleservice growth

In the 1970s and 1980s business became increasingly aware of the potential of information and communications technologies (ICTs) to enhance the efficiency of their operations while at the same time cutting costs. During this period firms tended to focus on internal, mostly data, communications and on establishing data communications with preferred suppliers and customers (Richardson 1994). By the early 1980s, firms in the US were beginning to explore the potential for ICTs as a means of offering their services to a wider range of customers, both business and consumer (Henley Centre 1994; Henley Centre 1996; Keen 1988; Keen 1991). Since the beginning of the 1990s, a similar trend has emerged in the UK and, albeit more slowly, appears to be emerging in the rest of western Europe.

Several factors have led firms to increase their use of the telephone for customer interface:

- Competitive pressures have led firms to seek new, more cost-effective, service delivery channels.
- Telephony has been transformed through information technology, and the emergence of digital exchanges and 'intelligent networks' have radically transformed its functionality, reliability, and performance.
- Telephony costs have fallen rapidly and new *customer*-oriented services, such as toll-free, local call, and premium services, have been introduced, utilising the intelligence in public networks.
- Telephone penetration is high in the key markets of the advanced industrial economies, and individuals and businesses are therefore familiar and comfortable with it.
- Complex and relatively rich information can be communicated over the telephone and clarification and recapping can take place in *real time*, with follow-up instructions sent by fax or e-mail if necessary (Richardson 1995).

Sectors and activities affected by teleservice growth in Europe

Firms are increasingly using the telephone to interface with customers across a range of activities, but the areas in which the telephone is being most regularly used in a strategic manner are:

- Sales
- Marketing
- Technical support
- Appointment setting
- Lead generation
- Brochure fulfilment
- Market research
- Reservations
- Order taking
- Customer enquiries
- Membership renewal
- 'Customer care'

Most of these activities occur in a range of sectors, including:

- Travel and transport
- Computing (hardware and software)
- Marketing
- Financial services
- Distribution
- Hotels
- Telecommunications
- Retail
- Utilities
- Government services

The rate of teleservice growth in Europe

There are no consistently derived and standardised figures which allow us to state precisely the rate of growth of call centres in Europe, but by drawing on a range of consultancy reports and research by the author, however, we can say something about the order of magnitude of growth, and it is clear that significant growth is occurring. A report by the business consultants Datamonitor (1996) suggests that the call centre market in Europe grew by 40 per cent in 1996, and that this rate of growth is likely to continue until the end of the century. These findings are broadly supported by other consultancy studies (for example, Ovum 1995; Henley Centre 1996; Mitial 1997), and by sectoral and areal studies (Marshall and Richardson 1996; Richardson and Marshall 1996b; see also Reardon in this volume). Growth rates have varied among European countries, with the UK in the forefront and southern countries such as Spain and Italy lagging.

Employment growth in teleservices in Europe

There is no agreed-upon figure for the numbers employed in teleservices, largely because of the paucity of official data in this area. One survey (Henley Centre 1994) calculated that 800,000 people, or around 3 per cent of the UK workforce, were employed in what it termed 'telebusinesses' in 1994. Here, however, we are concerned only with teleservice workers employed in call centres, and a recent study by Datamonitor (1996) suggests a figure for that group of 270,000 in Europe (covering the UK, France, Germany, Benelux, Spain, and Italy); 125,000 of those workers are in the UK. The report anticipates that that figure for Europe will be 670,000 by the year 2001, representing 1 per cent of the total working population. Figure 5.1 shows current workforce.

Teleservices and corporate spatial reorganisation: evidence from Europe

Teleservices and the industrialisation and concentration of customer services

When face-to-face interaction is replaced by the telephone, there is obviously less need for production to be located in physical proximity to the customer. In many cases this means that activities that were previously

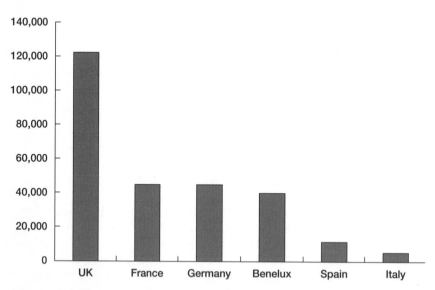

Figure 5.1 Number of agents employed in call centres in selected European countries in 1996.
Source: Datamonitor (1996).

most sensibly carried out in small local offices close to the customer – for example, bank and insurance branches, travel agencies, small sales offices, and local technical support offices – can now be concentrated in large offices, at one or a few sites, covering a national or international territory, where significant cost savings can be made. Similarly, when new firms enter markets or create new markets through the use of teleservices, they tend to establish single/few site operations rather than distributed operations. These new large offices are designed to be ICT-intensive, quasi-Taylorised operations, and can be thought of as 'customer service factories', though in the industry they are known as call centres (Richardson 1995).

Concentration of teleservice operations into call centres presents a number of advantages to firms. These include:

- The reduction of property costs, moving from high-cost sites, rationalising property portfolios, making more cost-effective use of space, and reducing space management costs.
- Reducing unit capital costs by using technology more intensively (indeed, office technologies such as automated call distribution and power dialling systems are being designed specifically for these large-scale operations).
- Management and supervisory costs can be reduced; once again, expensive and sophisticated office technologies can assist in this process.
- Most importantly, technology-intensive large sites present labour cost savings through economies of scale.
- Standardisation of product and service; better management control of the process, through training and building a shared culture.
- Creating a critical mass of knowledge, leading to complementarities and synergies within the workforce.

Further economies of scale can be gained through outsourcing call centre work, and there are now a significant number of firms emerging to serve this market. At present, however, it is estimated that only about 10 per cent of agent positions in Europe are outsourced, and, although the absolute numbers are anticipated to grow to around 62,000 (from about 30,000), the percentage figure is likely to remain the same (Datamonitor 1996). One factor that potentially limits the growth of outsourcing in call centre work is the desire of many firms to keep control of the client interface. This will be discussed below in relation to call centre work going offshore.

Teleservices and the changing location of customer services

The growth of the telephone as a method of conducting business with the customer opens up new locational possibilities for firms engaged in teleservices. In addition, the industrialisation and routinisation of the work process that are also features of much teleservice activity provide the opportunity to move work to areas where supplies of less skilled, lower-paid workers are located, perhaps at the same time side-stepping problems such as trade union opposition to restructuring. Many firms will take advantage of these new possibilities. However, the new locational possibilities are not limitless and remain constrained by the uneven availability of factors of production, particularly labour.

The following list illustrates, in broad terms, the key locational attractors considered by firms involved in teleservices when deciding where to locate call centres.

- Advanced telecommunications suitable for data and voice transmission and capable of hosting intelligent network services. Telecommunications costs must also be considered, particularly when call centres can be located in several countries.
- A pool of labour of sufficient quality to carry out the particular tasks required in the locating firm's call centre, bearing in mind that the call centre may have to be manned 24 hours a day.
- An advantageous labour cost/quality ratio.
- Fiscal and grant incentives.
- A living environment able to attract management and other key staff.
- Low occupancy costs (rents, rates, servicing, parking costs, etc.).
- Access to good local public transport and, in some cases, to national and international transport.

Obviously, firms considering where to locate a call centre will have to balance the factors listed above against each other, as it is unlikely that any single location will offer all these advantages. The two principal locational factors are telecommunications infrastructure, without which teleservice firms cannot operate, and an advantageous cost/quality ratio of labour, without which firms will not relocate. Fiscal incentives are usually regarded as an added bonus, though these incentives usually occur where labour is cheaper in any event. Of course, as with all locational decisions, 'rational' economic criteria may be relegated from the forefront of the process. During the course of the research reported here, several examples were found where the locational decision was ultimately based on the living preferences of senior managers or on the accessibility of the site for senior managers from headquarters. Another crucial factor was senior management's demand that a call centre be set up immediately; here the crucial criterion becomes the availability of suitable real estate. Real estate may also be a factor where a firm's existing property portfolio is under-used but has little resale value.

Telecommunications infrastructure and services

The call centre industry's success relies on there being a sophisticated ICT infrastructure, both where the consumer is located and where the call centre is located. In order to create a market for call centres, the consumer must have access to a good publicly switched telecommunications network (PSTN) with the required 'intelligence' to host advanced services, through which he/she can contact call centres at low or no cost (for example, through freephone or local call-rate numbers). The call centre needs to be effectively linked to that PSTN. It can, however, be located in a region that does not have a generally advanced telecommunications network; but to be cost-effective and robust there must be a local digital telephone exchange, and the firm must be able to lease a high-bandwidth line from the telecommunications provider, through which voice and data traffic can be sent speedily. For example, one firm that has located its call centre in rural Scotland to take advantage of lower labour costs 'gathers' calls from customers in London, made via the PSTN, at its London office and switches them to Scotland over leased lines. The firm sends its internal data in the same way. This strategy adds to telecommunications costs, but these costs are more than offset by lower labour costs. As liberalisation of the telecommunications market takes place within Europe, the falling costs of voice and data traffic make this sort of arrangement more feasible on a pan-European basis.

Interviews suggest that a number of telecommunications factors beyond those mentioned above are taken into account. Not surprisingly, given the dominance of US firms, the existence of a competitive environment with the presence of more than one telecommunications supplier is regarded as important. Beyond this, the precise mix that firms require will depend on the nature of the business – for example, the balance between in-bound and out-bound calls, or whether international toll-free numbers are to be offered to customers. Considerations will include the costs of setting up private circuits, line rental, cost of national and international phone calls, and so on.

Labour availability and costs

The availability of advanced telecommunications infrastructure is, then, a crucial locational factor for teleservice firms. Beyond this, it is the traditional locational factors that remain important; and the most important of these is labour.

The precise nature of labour requirements for any particular teleservice operation will depend on the type of activity undertaken and the products and geographical markets served. Call centre agents can be conceptualised as the interface mechanism between a firm's information systems and the customer. For all call centre activities, firms will attempt to standardise information and embed product knowledge in the information system. There are limits to how far this is possible, however, and agents may be required to 'add value' to the information by mentally manipulating, reconfiguring, and customising it to suit a particular customer. Other activities require additional skills, such as selling, marketing, and 'customer care' skills. Activities such as technical support, which are most advanced in the IT sector, require higher-order skills, and even within these activities the level of skills will vary depending on the complexity of the product and the sophistication of the customer. For firms wishing to establish internationally oriented call centres, there is a further requirement for a workforce that is multilingual.

A number of points regarding location emerge from the studies upon which this chapter is based. First, call centres in western Europe are mainly, though not exclusively, urban-based. This is due to the fact that telecommunications investment tends to be most advanced in urban areas, and that a larger labour pool is available there. The majority of call centres require a large labour pool for a number of reasons:

- Most call centres need a sufficient number of workers to staff 12, 18, or even 24 hour operations, including 'unsocial' hours, without necessarily paying the extra costs normally associated with such work patterns.
- Many call centres operate four-hour shift patterns, the idea being that lunch hours and tea-breaks are thus not paid for by the employer, and that productivity declines after four hours of intense telephone activity in any case; this requires a bigger pool of labour from which to choose.
- Call centres have relatively strict recruitment criteria, even for lower-level activities, involving telephone and face-to-face interviews and a number of proficiency and psychometric tests.

Call centre growth and export-oriented work: opportunities for less favoured regions in western Europe

As previously indicated, call centre growth in western Europe has been very rapid. The data do not exist to allow us to map in detail how this growth has occurred across space. What is clear, however, is that certain less favoured cities and regions are attracting these activities (Richardson 1994; Richardson 1997; Richardson and Marshall 1996b). At the national level this is probably most striking in the UK, where regional disparities in income are pronounced. Telecommunications infrastructure provision in most parts of the UK is now sufficiently sophisticated to allow call centres to operate. The key question thus becomes the cost of labour. Table 5.1

Table 5.1 Average UK call centre salaries by region (excluding bonus/commission)

	Agent	Team supervisor	Call centre manager
South-east	£10,800	£11,000–£13,500	£15,000–£17,000
South-west	£9,000–£10,000	£11,000–£13,000	£15,000–£17,000
Inner London	£10,000–£12,000	£13,000–£15,000	£16,000–£18,000
Outer London	£8,000–£10,500	£11,000–£13,000	£15,000–£17,000
East Anglia	£9,000	£12,000	£15,000
West Midlands	£8,750	£10,000–£11,000	£14,000
North	£8,500	£10,500–£11,000	£15,000
Wales	£8,500–£9,000	£11,000	£13,000–£14,500
Scotland	£8,000–£9,000	£10,000–£12,000	£14,500
East Midlands	£8,000	£11,000	£13,500–£14,000
National average	£9,150	£11,000	£15,025

Source: Call Centre Europe (1995).

shows the differential costs of call centre staff across the regions of the UK. As can be seen, those areas beyond the core South-east region offer the lowest-cost labour. The partial exception to this is Outer London, an area which has long been the recipient of back-office work from the capital, and which has a ready supply of female clerical-type labour. The lower-salaried regions, as would be expected, tend to be those with fewer alternative job opportunities. As a result, labour turnover is also lower, thus contributing to lower training and recruitment costs. Many of these areas are also able to offer a number of property and labour-related fiscal incentives.

As Figure 5.2 shows, UK banks have chosen to locate telebanking centres in cities in the north of the country (Marshall and Richardson 1996; see also Reardon in this volume). Area studies by the author suggest that these cities and regions are succeeding in attracting a range of call centre activities beyond telebanking (see, for example, Richardson and Marshall 1996b).

Call centres are primarily an urban phenomenon in western Europe, but they do locate in less urbanised areas where adequate telecommunications infrastructure is available. In the Highlands and Islands region of Scotland, for example, which is classified as an Objective 1 region by the European Commission because of its peripherality and low-income status, an advanced network has been installed and the region has attracted a number of call centres by providing a highly educated, low-cost workforce (and, it should be said, considerable financial assistance).

There exists a great variety of call centre activities, ranging from very simple information-giving to relatively complex tasks, such as computer software support. In some sectors there is also a growing trend toward pan-European call centres requiring multilingual staff. These centres tend to be smaller, but the jobs can be more challenging and better rewarded. The

Location of retail banking
teleservice centres

1   Abbey National Direct (Abbey National)
2   Centrebank (Bank of Scotland)
3   Barclaycall (Barclays)
4   Telebank (Clydesdale)
5   Armchair Banking (Co-op Bank)
6   Telecare (Giro (Alliance & Leicester))
7   First Direct (HSBC)
8   Midland Direct (HSBC)
9   Pilot to be named (Lloyds)
10 PrimeTime (National Westminster)
11 Direct Banking (Royal Bank of Scotland)
12 Phone Bank (TSB)

Figure 5.2 The location of high street retail banking call centre operations in the
UK, Summer 1996.

range of locations open to firms operating such centres is obviously more
limited than for those addressing lower-skilled, single-language tasks. In the
UK it is likely that the majority of these centres will locate in or around
London to take advantage of its uniquely cosmopolitan character. Similarly,
in the Netherlands most multilingual centres are located in the Randstadt.

Again, however, less favoured regions have been able to capture some of these activities. In the UK, the cities referred to above in the context of national call centres have had some success in attracting international centres as well. Ireland, which is on the geographical periphery of Europe and is classed as an Objective 1 region by the European Commission, has been particularly successful in attracting (mainly US) call centres operating on a pan-European basis, through a combination of low-cost, highly educated workers (including many multilingual workers), and fiscal incentives. These centres are, however, predominantly located in and around the capital, Dublin (see Figure 5.3).

In considering the prospects for less favoured regions in western Europe benefiting from the growth in call centres, the evidence suggests that this growth has created opportunities for export-oriented employment in *some* less favoured regions. To date this appears to be mainly an urban phenomenon, though the evidence suggests that more advanced rural areas (in terms of education, etc.) can benefit if they have the telecommunications and support infrastructure required. I now turn to

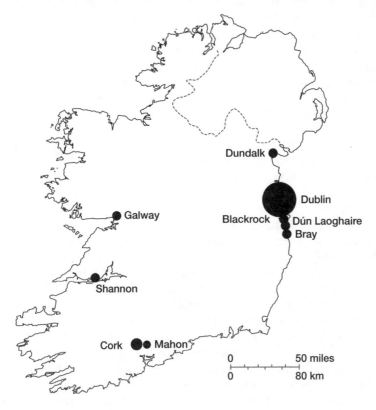

Figure 5.3 The location of internationally-located call centres in Ireland, end 1996.

consider whether the growth of call centres represents an opportunity for developing countries.

Call centre growth and export-oriented work: opportunities for the developing world?

This volume is concerned with the relationship between Europe and the developing world. I will, therefore, concentrate here on the possibilities of call centre activities aimed at European markets creating export-oriented employment growth in the developing world. Before doing so, however, three points need to be made:

1   For the more advanced developing countries, the growth in call centre work may well be internally generated, rather than export-oriented. The evidence from Europe certainly suggests that international trading in teleservices remains relatively limited.
2   Export-oriented call centre activity may well be confined to the global region in which a particular country is situated. Unpublished research by the author suggests that firms are not in favour of a single-site call centre serving the globe, preferring to have at least one centre in each of the three global regions (the US, Europe, and Asia). Examples of inter-regional activity do exist, but they are at the margin.
3   In attempting to forecast call centre trends globally, Europe is probably not the best place to start, since most call centre innovation has tended to emanate from the US.

There are two possibilities for developing countries in creating export-oriented work around call centres. The first is to use this channel to promote the products and services of indigenous firms. This route is more likely to lead to sustainable economic development. It is also, of course, the more difficult to achieve. One example of a firm in a less favoured region in Europe doing this is the leading accountancy software firm in the UK, Sage, a company based in the North-east of England, which has grown into an internationally successful business through selling and supporting products via its call centres. In order to do this, however, a firm must first have a marketable product *and* the capacity to market it. This can be difficult from the periphery of Europe, and it is likely to be even more difficult from outside Europe. If export-oriented call centre activity aimed at European markets is to occur on any scale in developing countries, it is likely that, at least initially, it will be based on attracting inward investment, predicated on a perception by European (or US) firms that their European business and consumer markets can be served from these countries. The next section turns to consider the possibilities for, and barriers to, attracting such investment.

Opportunities for attracting exogenous export-oriented call centre work

There are a number of reasons to suggest that at least some call centre work may follow service operations of the type referred to in the introduction to this chapter offshore:

- Many developing countries represent a cheaper locational option than less favoured regions in Europe.
- Reinforcing the previous point, there are signs of wage inflation and increasing turnover in some successful call centre regions in Europe.
- Call centres with higher skill requirements, such as network software help desk centres, are experiencing skill shortages, and this situation is likely to be exacerbated as economic growth in Europe recovers and skilled workers' expectations increase.
- Many lower-cost regions in Europe appear not to be particularly well placed to attract call centre work, lacking the telecommunications infrastructure and/or the requisite labour skills.
- Many firms that operate call centres have long experience of locating other activities offshore, and are therefore comfortable with the concept.
- Some of these firms have their own global telecommunications networks, which would facilitate the establishment of offshore activities at a minimal cost in terms of telecommunications.
- Outsourcing of call centre work is growing; a number of firms in the developing world have already demonstrated an ability to undertake other forms of outsourced service work.

Barriers to attracting call centre work to developing countries

There are, however, also a number of barriers to call centre work going offshore, and there may also be limits to the number of countries capable of attracting this work. Many of these barriers may be based on misperceptions by European managers, but in questions of locational choices, perceptions are important. These (perceived) barriers can be divided into technological, regulatory, organisational, linguistic, and cultural.

Technology barriers

Much of the service work transferred to developing countries in recent years has not, in fact, required advanced telecommunications. Much of the data sent overseas for processing have been in the form of paper-based records sent by air. Indeed, so far as we can tell, much offshore processing work appears to be concerned with transferring historical data from paper to electronic form. The electronic data can be returned on disk, by air.

Hence air connections have been more important than ICT links. A variation on this practice is to send hard copy by air and to return copy electronically 'across the wire'. More recently, data have been sent offshore in electronic form and, after processing, have been returned electronically. Such transactions require either a cable connection or a satellite link.

Until now most service activities that have gone offshore involve a transaction between the client company and the third-party company (i.e., the company undertaking the outsourced work). But offshore, outsourced, call centre work would involve transactions between the third-party company and the client's customers, either business customers or consumers. As was pointed out earlier, firms can locate in less favoured regions in Europe, regions that do not have an advanced telecommunications infrastructure, and still access the customer so long as there is a digital exchange to switch the traffic and wide-bandwidth leased lines or some other mechanism for accessing calls gathered through the PSTN. On an intercontinental basis it would be possible for customers, say from the UK, to call a UK number; the calls would then be 'gathered', either by the firm itself or within the intelligent network, and transmitted to the location in, say, India. This process could be extended, with calls from European customers from a number of countries being gathered centrally in Europe, then transferred to a developing country. However, the link between that central point and the developing country would have to be a fixed link, that is, a cable link. Satellite would not be generally acceptable, because the 'slap-back' delay associated with satellite telephone calls would be frustrating for customers. Except for companies that already have a leased-line link between Europe and the appropriate developing country, this would be a very expensive option.

Perhaps more importantly, in the customer service environment questions remain over the reliability of long distance electronic links. In processing or software activities, work can continue while a telecommunications problem is being fixed, and the output transmitted later. In a call centre environment, work would come to a halt and the customer be lost.

Regulatory barriers

There are two potential regulatory barriers to call centre work going offshore from Europe. First, there is the question of regulations covering telecommunications. Call centre firms in Europe (particularly US firms) regard a competitive telecommunications environment, with a number of competing suppliers, as important to their locational decisions. Several reports claim that a key element in the UK's rapid growth in teleservices is its competitive telecommunications environment (see, for example, Henley Centre 1996; Datamonitor 1996). Many developing countries remain heavily regulated in this area, and are therefore unlikely to be attractive to teleservice firms. Regulation may also have implications for flow of voice and data traffic and for the cost of communicating data between nation states. In addition, the author has noted a perception in several firms that local telecommunications companies in many developing countries would not have the competencies required to operate the required network.

A second set of regulatory questions concern certain sectors such as banking. For example, in financial services within (a supposedly single-market) Europe, there are key regulatory differences between countries. Even when those regulatory differences decline, their historical legacy and resulting cultural expectations remain to be overcome. So although the financial services industry is the most developed sector in its use of call centres (Datamonitor 1996), there are few examples of cross-border servicing of customers.

Organisational and commercial barriers

One of the principal reasons why service firms go offshore is to speed up the production process. The case of the insurance company processing new policies and claims overnight by sending them across time-zones, thus making it possible to provide the customer with documents the next day, is well documented (see, for example, Wilson 1993). Thus, in addition to potential labour cost savings, exploitation of time-zone differences gives competitive advantage. But despite the fact that many European teleservice firms offer 24-hour-a-day service, the vast majority of calls are still received during traditional office hours, and demand for service outside 8.00 am to 8.00 pm remains limited. Conceivably, call centres in the developing world could act as overflow points for calls received outside traditional European office hours, perhaps acting as a bureau on behalf of a number of European firms. A call centre in a developing country could also adapt its working hours to provide a service that covered European office hours, though there would potentially be cost disadvantages and other disincentives (such as problems of access to public transport) in doing so.

Another potential barrier to work going offshore is managers' perception of loss of control of the production process. This concern is particularly pronounced in the call centre environment, since firms see successful customer relations as a key area in maintaining competitiveness. The majority of firms in Europe still operate their own call centres and see them as a key competitive weapon. This situation may change over time, however, and outsourcing may grow.

Linguistic barriers

Language presents both an opportunity and a barrier for developing countries in attracting call centres. In most areas of customer service, a common language is required. The evidence from Europe suggests that, by and large, customers want agents to be able to speak the customer's own language and to speak it well – they do not want to have to struggle to communicate. In a limited number of areas, for example, where a customer phones a help desk when his/her computer is down, he/she will be prepared to speak in a second language, usually English. In most areas, however, and particularly in sales, a customer will not accept a second language. This is a key reason why the growth in pan-European call centres remains limited. Firms that set up pan-European centres would ideally employ multilingual staff, thus generating economies of scope and scale; but this is not easy to do, given the relatively low wages for these jobs, and many firms end up importing native speakers to overcome this problem. This can be an expensive solution, however, as turnover tends to be high.

This situation may present opportunities for developing countries that have large pools of people who can speak a European language well, perhaps based on former colonial connections and residual educational links. The experience in the UK tends to suggest that customers (on both sides of the Atlantic) are amused by the idea of being answered by someone at a distance. The broader European experience suggests customer resistance to call centre agents who speak the customer's language but are obviously not from the customer's country. For example, it was commonly reported that French customers were not happy dealing with French-speaking Belgians, notwithstanding the geographical proximity of the two countries.

Cultural barriers

Two sets of cultural factors might be important in determining whether to set up a European market-oriented call centre in a developing country: the work/employment culture and the customer-relations/consumer culture. Here I focus on the latter. Cultural differences between countries are much harder to define than linguistic differences, but they may form an important barrier to some forms of call centre activity going offshore. Evidence from Europe suggests that there are significant problems with marketing and selling goods across borders. Many pan-European call centre managers expressed the view that there were cultural nuances which an agent has to understand. Again, this often means using as agents natives of the countries that a firm is targeting. Furthermore, firms went to considerable lengths to keep agents up-to-date with events in the consuming countries, for example, bringing in newspapers and magazines. There is also a perception of cultural differences in the way that consumers from different European countries use the telephone – Germans, for example, being business-like and to the point, Italians being more relaxed and talkative. The perception of managers is that cultural differences across continents will be even greater. One major third-party marketing firm that attempted to serve a South-east Asian market from London found problems coping with the range of attitudes and ways of using the telephone, and in the end decided to establish call centres in Japan and Singapore to service that regional market.

As with the language barrier, cultural barriers are likely to be less pronounced in certain areas of call centre activity, particularly business-to-business operations. For example, the computer industry has its own culture, which transcends local cultures to some extent. Other areas where cultural nuances would have less impact are those such as air travel, where the information exchange is fairly straightforward and the 'language' and procedures have become universal.

Call centres and the economic development of less favoured regions

There are, then, a number of barriers to call centre work being transferred from Europe to the developing world. Nevertheless, with the sector growing so rapidly, countries that can provide the required telecommunications infrastructure, even within a restricted part of their territory, may be able to attract certain call centre activities. This section considers what economic benefits may be derived from attracting export-oriented call centres.

The evidence from Europe's less favoured regions suggests that call centres provide significant benefits in terms of net new jobs. Some city-regions in the UK, for example, claim to have attracted over 10,000 call centre jobs in just a few years, and most of the output of this work is 'exported'. It should be added that regions that fail to attract export-oriented call centres are increasingly likely to import these services over the telephone, thus impacting detrimentally on local employment.

Call centres can also bring new skills to a region. Call centre work offers the opportunity for workers to familiarise themselves with new technologies. However, many of the jobs that call centres bring in are fairly low-skilled. Except for a few activities, agents tend to be overqualified for the mundane tasks they have to handle. The jobs can be boring and repetitive, but at the same time are very pressured. Furthermore, the 'new' skills are fairly basic, and are not of the kind that would permit less favoured regions to 'leap-frog' more developed ones, in the manner suggested by some of the more optimistic commentators on the information society.

One problem with low-skilled work, of course, is that it tends to be the first to be automated. There are already a range of evolving technologies within the call centre environment that are leading to fewer workers being required per unit of output. This is likely to slow the growth in employment, and eventually to result in a decline. Other technologies, such as the Internet, are also likely to have this effect. If call centres can act as a 'point of departure', providing workers with skills that can be upgraded as new technologies eliminate basic call centre jobs, then the employment benefits can be long-term. Otherwise, many call centre employees will find themselves redundant, as did low-skilled industrial workers.

Although the majority of call centres offer what can be seen as low-grade jobs, they may provide wages above the local norm. Certainly, there is evidence in Europe's less favoured regions that these centres provided reasonable incomes in the context of local labour markets. A survey of workers in several call centres in the Highlands and Islands region of Scotland showed that these centres brought genuinely new employment opportunities, not only in terms of numbers of jobs, but also new kinds of jobs, and with better earnings potential (Gillespie *et al.* 1995). Furthermore, sectors such as IT do provide more sophisticated work and higher wages; and given the international nature of IT and the dearth of skills in Europe at present, this is one of the sectors that might transfer work to certain developing countries.

A larger concern is the lack of career structure in call centres, which seldom bring high-level management tasks to a region. Call centres have a flat hierarchical structure, and there is only limited opportunity for promotion beyond supervisory level. Even management and technology support functions tend to be limited, though call centres in developing countries may host more support management, given their distance from their parent/client organisations. On the whole, however, call centre work represents a job rather than a career. There is some evidence from Europe that, in a limited number of sectors (IT again being a case in point, but also in sectors such as chemical and pharmaceuticals), individuals can gain experience that allows them to advance into other parts of a company. Although this is good for the individual, it probably means that the individual's skills are lost to the region, since the higher-order jobs are located elsewhere. The lack of prospects for worker advancement must be a serious concern, given the amount of time, grant aid, and fiscal relief that is likely to have to be provided to attract these firms.

On the plus side, what management there is in these centres may bring with it innovative techniques and practices, either directly or by influencing local third-party firms. And it can be argued that these techniques may contribute to the longer-term economic development of a country or region, though they may also force workers into more intensive and regimented ways of working.

Another potential advantage of attracting call centres is that they bring gains in terms of capital investment, particularly IT investment. It is likely, however, that in order to attract these activities, considerable local (probably public) investment will be required in telecommunications infrastructure. This is likely to mean diverting resources from other areas of investment to create 'hot-spots'; and there may be little overspill to other parts of the territory.

The overarching question, of course, is whether less favoured regions, whether in the north or south, should allow themselves to become so dependent on external capital, whether through direct inward investment or through undertaking externally controlled, outsourced work. In this respect call centres appear to present an information age analogue to the industrial branch plant. Regions that become over-reliant on this form of investment are likely to face the problems that branch plant economies faced in the past, including low growth in support services, a lack of research and development capacity, a concentration of low-skilled jobs and a lack of entrepreurial initiative. Given the short-term benefits on offer from call centres and other low value-added activities, however, it is diffi-cult to see how, on the eve of the 'information age', many less favoured regions will be able to avoid going down the inward investment route and perhaps replicating the mistakes of the industrial age.

References

Datamonitor (1996) *Call Centres in Europe 1996–2001*, London: Datamonitor.

Freeman, C. and Soete, L. (1994) *Work for All or Mass Unemployment?: Compu-terised Technical Change into the 21st Century*, London: Pinter.

Gillespie, A., Richardson, R. and Cornford, J. (1995) *Review of Telework in Britain: Implications for Public Policy*, report prepared for the UK Parliamen-tary Office of Science and Technology.

Grimes, S. (1995) 'Regional Development Aspects of Information Technology in Ireland'. Paper presented to a Workshop on Informatics and Telecom Tectonics: Information Technology, Policy, Telecommunications, and the Meaning of Space, March 20–21, 1995, Michigan State University, East Lansing, Michigan.

Henley Centre (1994) *Teleculture: The Growth and Acceptance of the Use of the Telephone in Sales, Marketing, and Customer Service*, London: Henley Centre.

Henley Centre (1996) *Teleculture Futures: Harnessing Telecommunications to Meet Customer Needs for the 21st Century*, London: Henley Centre.

Keen, P. G. W. (1988) *Competing in Time: Using Telecommunication for Competi-tive Advantage*, Cambridge, MA: Ballinger.

Keen, P. G. W. (1991) *Shaping the Future: Business Design through Information Technology*, Cambridge, MA: Harvard University Press.

Marshall, J. N. and Richardson, R. (1996) 'The impact of "telemediated" services on corporate structures: the example of "branchless" retail banking in Britain', *Environment and Planning A*, 1843–58.

Mitial (1997) 'Telephone Call Centres in the British Isles'. *1996/7 Location Research Monitor*. Wrexham: Mitial Industrial Market Research.

Ovum (1995) *Computer Telephony Integration*, London: Ovum.

Pearson, R. and Mitter, S. (1993) 'Employment and working conditions of low-skilled information-processing workers in less developed countries', *International Labour Review*, 132 (1): 49–64.

Richardson, R. (1994) 'Back-officing front office functions – organisational and locational implications of new telemediated services', in Mansell, R. (ed.), *Management of Information and Communications Technologies: Emerging Patterns of Control*, London: ASLIB.

Richardson, R. (1995) 'The Growth of Teleservices: Opportunities for Less Favoured Regions?' Paper presented to Telecom Portugal Seminar on Tele-working, Oporto, Portugal, 16 October 1995.

Richardson, R. (1997) 'Network Technologies, Organisational Change, and the Location of Employment', in Dumort, A. and Dryden, J. (eds), *The Economics of the Information Society*, Brussels: OECD/EU.

Richardson, R. and Marshall, J. N. (1996a) *The Growth, Location, and Mobility of Services.* Report prepared for Locate in Scotland.

Richardson, R. and Marshall, J. N. (1996b) 'The Growth of Telephone Call Centres in Peripheral Areas of Britain: Evidence from Tyne and Wear', *Area*, 28 (3): 308–17.

Warf, B. (1995) 'Telecommunications and Knowledge Transmission', *Urban Studies*, 32 (2): 361–78.

Wilson, M. I. (1993) *Offshore Relocation of Producer Services: The Irish Back Office.* Paper presented at the Annual Conference of the Association of American Geographers, Florida, March 1993.

Wilson, M. I. (1994) *Jamaica's Back Offices: Direct Dial Dependency?* Paper presented at the Annual Conference of the Association of American Geographers, San Francisco, CA, March 1994.

Wilson, M. I. (1995) *Press 1 for Reservations: Information Technology and the Location of Airline Operations.* Paper presented at the Annual Conference of the Association of American Geographers, Chicago, IL, March 1995.

6

A non-European counterpoint

THE GLOBALISED INFORMATION SOCIETY AND ITS IMPACT ON THE EUROPE–MAGHREB RELATIONSHIP

Abdelkader Djeflat

Introduction

Many people express concern that we are moving toward a world of information haves and have-nots, one where development is no longer measured in calories per head or income per inhabitant, but as megabytes per head and the share of cyberspace we command, either as individuals or collectively as nations and states.

This concern is not remote from the reality and the extent of the changes that are occurring on a daily basis in the world of new information technologies (NIT) (Stern 1995). While some, whom we might call 'NIT optimists', are being carried away by the formidable achievements and undeniable performances and processes currently under way, more and more 'NIT pessimists' are raising their voices to attract attention to some of the dangers, and to try to stop the optimists' increasingly unavoidable and irreversible trajectory.

The arguments this latter group put forward range from the technological to those based on the issue of social disequilibrium, irrespective of the possible political implications. These arguments take on a more specific nature when the developing world is brought into consideration. Indeed, many international gatherings are turning their eyes toward the particular situation in this part of the world. For example, the last G7 Summit concluded that we are moving toward an information society that makes the world a 'planetary village', and stressed the fact that the developing countries must not be left out of this process.

While some are concerned with how to help the less developed countries (LDCs) penetrate this new world of NIT, others express concern that new forms of outsourcing are resulting from NIT, leading to job losses, and that Europe, under the pressure of rising unemployment, should be wary of the way these technologies are moving internationally.

Our objective in this short paper is to examine this argument against some of the hard facts of life from a Maghreb perspective (taking the Maghreb in its restricted sense, i.e., Algeria, Tunisia, and Morocco). But first we shall reflect on some of the conditions that made it possible for the NIT revolution to occur.

The advent of NIT and the issue of outsourcing

NIT in the workplace has generally become a reality (especially in financial and communications services) as a result of three sets of combined factors. The fact that these factors have occurred simultaneously has made the advent of NIT possible.

The first set of factors is a combination of micro-economic considerations (marketing motives, profit motives, and managerial factors); the second set is a combination of changes creating what we might call the 'right environment' (government policy, particularly deregulation, and rapid changes in computer and telecommunications technology); and the third set is one of wider economic factors (tough competition, declining profits). This is the perspective from the supply side.

From a demand point of view, three sets of factors have also occurred, although at a much slower speed: changes in needs (better living conditions, more intellectual activities, greater balance between work and leisure); economic factors (command of a high level of revenue); and technological changes (introduction of electronic equipment in the home, such as games and appliances incorporating more technologically advanced components, such as electronics). There are also cultural factors, which cannot be neglected.

It is through these sets of factors acting simultaneously that NITs appear to have penetrated the productive sphere, spreading rapidly from one sector to another. It is not easy to formulate an explanation of how all these sets of factors were put into play, leading to their rapid adoption by sectors utilising conservative forms of NIT in their businesses – telebanking being one of the best examples.

What might be more easily understandable is the outcome of the massive introduction of these technologies into the workplace, making it possible for traditionally domestic sectors to outsource their activities. Thus, if we take the example of banking, the introduction of call centres has created a new logic of space and organisation (see chapter by Reardon, this volume). Technically, call centres can be located in parts of the world where production costs are lower. Satellite communications contribute to the lowering of locational constraints, and the new developments are making even paper-based transactions free of such constraints.

These are the important factors that liberate telebanking from the need to look for new branches and facilities in order to be able to expand throughout the world, or even at a national level. They include attempts to use this newly acquired flexibility of outsourcing to reduce costs, increase performance, and sharpen competitive edge in a world where technological and innovation-based competition is taking the lead.

This puts low-wage, less developed countries in a position to undertake on a subcontractual basis some of the work currently done in the North. Such job creation in LDCs can be perceived as resulting in job losses in the banking sector in the North, but in fact few of these job losses are a consequence of work being sent to other countries. For example, in recent years many employees have been laid off as a result of the massive introduction of ATMs (automated teller machines).

Those who hold the view that low-wage countries are taking the jobs of high-wage countries offer India as an example of a country that benefits from outsourcing in areas such as data processing, accounting, and software engineering services. According to NIT pessimists, Asia on the whole, apart from Japan and, now, Korea (where comparative advantage in wage costs is disappearing), can receive such outsourcing, leading to massive unemployment in the North.

These examples can, however, be misleading, and they can lead to wrong conclusions and inaccurate generalisations if detailed studies are not conducted and if the differences between countries, and indeed regions, are not properly understood. Job losses in the North have not resulted in equivalent job creation in the developing world. They result from the introduction of NIT itself in the various sectors, and from the constant modification of the labour/capital ratio. In the following section, we shall try to explain this phenomenon with regard to the specific situation of the Maghreb countries.

NIT and outsourcing: the Maghreb perspective

The possibility of developing a local 'insourcing' capacity and gaining the benefits of outsourcing by international banks and production firms is closely linked to the condition and level of local telecommunications facilities, existing infrastructure, and human capacities. The prospect for integrating the countries of the developing world into the NIT revolution depends to a great extent on the density and quality of telecommunications infrastructures in these countries (Béraud 1996).

As we have seen, a combination of several factors was necessary for banks and other companies to undertake outsourcing. Let us examine to what extent this combination of factors is available or can be made available in the Maghreb countries. Studies conducted in the early 1990s give us some statistics regarding the state of the existing telecommunications infrastructures in the three countries of the Maghreb.

In terms of numbers of direct lines, the telecommunications infrastructures of the Maghreb countries are poor compared to those of the EU. While the number of telephone lines in the EU is 40 for every 100 inhabitants, it does not exceed 12 per 100 for the south Mediterranean countries as a whole. The situation in the Maghreb countries taken separately is even worse: in 1992 the proportion of the population with a telephone line was 4.0 per cent for Tunisia, 3.5 per cent for Algeria, and 2.0 per cent for Morocco. Subscribers also endure long delays in getting connected to the network: 6.5 years in the Maghreb countries and more than 50 years in Mauritania (Stern 1995).

Quality of access is also very poor. International telephone lines are often jammed, particularly during working hours. Because there is practically no time difference with Europe, businesses have almost no scope for using a time differential to benefit from relatively less crowded periods on the system. Furthermore, the existing underwater cable between Europe and some countries of the Maghreb is subject to technical problems. Consequently, even in the late 1980s the average rate of successful calls was still around 65 per cent, although there have been slight improvements in recent years.

The number of repairs carried out effectively within 48 hours is relatively low, not exceeding 66 per cent in the late 1980s, improving in Tunisia but deteriorating in Algeria, where delays in completing repairs sometimes exceed one month.

Investment in telecommunications is still fairly low, even during the relative affluence of recent times, ranging from 0.32 per cent of GDP in 1988 for Algeria to 1.0 per cent of GDP in Morocco in 1994. Investment per inhabitant did not exceed US$10 in 1986: US$9.21 in Algeria, US$6.50 in Tunisia, and US$4.32 in Morocco. In comparison, and staying within the developing world framework, Korea and Taiwan invested US$81.80 and US$84.20, respectively, in 1994 (Kavanaugh 1990).

Thus, the 'telephone culture' has still some way to go, particularly when we include the case of rural areas, where the rates of connections are even lower and the waiting time to be connected in small villages can be counted in years. Most telephones are concentrated in a small number of big cities. In the Arab world, there were 43 telephone lines per 1,000 inhabitants, compared to an average of 590 per 1,000 for the advanced industrialised countries, during the period 1986–1988 (Béraud 1996).

The current state of the telephone grid, therefore, presents several difficulties for the introduction of new technology designed for use with telephone lines. In addition, computer technology is equally important for the introduction of NIT, and in spite of improvements in this area, there are still problems and obstacles. A study of the use of microcomputers in Tunisian firms (Ferchiou 1990) shows that the level remains relatively low. In 1986 the ratio of expenditure on computers to GDP was 0.69 per cent, compared to 4.0–5.0 per cent in developed countries, where there were about 3.4 computer units per thousand inhabitants. The number of jobs generated directly by computer usage in Tunisia was estimated in 1986 at 5,300, out of 1.8 million employees, or about 0.3 per cent; in terms of investment, only 0.5 per cent was applied to computer equipment.

Considering these conditions, let us examine whether the three sets of combined factors mentioned earlier can be fulfilled as a minimum basis for introducing NIT technology in the banking system.

First is a set of micro-economic factors (marketing motives, profit motives, and managerial and organisational factors), which exist to varying degrees in the Maghreb countries. They are present in Tunisia and Morocco, where a liberal orientation of the economy and private sector has existed for some years, but much less so in Algeria, where the private sector has been marginalised and the public sector has been the most important agent. Profit motives as a driving force for change are likely to be less important here than in Tunisia and Morocco. Structural adjustment programmes and the economic reforms undertaken since 1988 have brought about some changes, but their effects are slow, and the privatisation programme is still difficult to implement. It will certainly take a few more years to get to the stage of a fully profit-based economy.

This being said, the private sector itself constitutes no guarantee that new technologies will be easily introduced in the workplace. The way it functions at the moment in each of the three countries means that it is relatively slow and hesitant in adopting new technologies, tending to be more rent-seeking than profit-oriented, looking for quick profit activity rather than operating with a long-term perspective.

The second set of factors involves combinations of changes to create what we have called the right environment, in terms of government policy and rapid technological change. Government policies for deregulation are linked to the extent to which the implementation of the structural adjustment programme succeeds or not. The current pace is relatively slow in Algeria, while fairly rapid progress is being made in the other two countries. Again, bureaucracy and resistance to change, even after the issuance of new laws, constitute two major obstacles to deregulation and an adequate policy.

As for technological change, the prospects of locally-initiated technological changes are relatively low in the area of NIT. Although minor technological changes of the incremental type occur sporadically, and there is much talk about computer technology, a change of significant magnitude does not yet exist. So changes in the level of technology in industry must rely heavily on two factors: massive imports of NIT from the international market, and the availability of trained personnel to run the IT system, and to maintain, repair, and modify it as required, as is occurring in India in the Tata Group, for instance. On both grounds, the Maghreb scores relatively low. The level of computer technology has made a great deal of progress in recent years but has a long way to go before reaching that of India or certain other Asian countries.

In the Maghreb, industrial activities currently rely heavily on imported parts being assembled locally, the prospect of manufacturing parts locally being very low. The only remaining possible area of expansion is software production. Yet, this area has also experienced difficulties, despite the massive efforts made in the 1970s to train people in the field. The single most important obstacle here is undoubtedly the brain drain, a phenomenon from which Maghreb countries suffer in general. Relatively well-qualified and experienced people leave the countries of the Maghreb in great numbers, to the benefit of Europe (mainly France) and the US. The region suffers profoundly from this drain of intellectual resources, estimated at 10,000 researchers each year, some of whom have earned good reputations in the wider world of IT through their innovative capability and creativity.

At present, the most crucial problems are the financial crisis, which the region as a whole has been experiencing for several years, and the debt burden. Both problems make it more and more difficult to renew the pool of local skills, as was done in the past. Training facilities are deteriorating in terms of equipment and teaching materials, and teachers themselves are often part of the brain drain.

We will not examine here the third set of factors, those of wider economic import.

This bleak picture brightens a little when we come to the demand side. From a demand point of view, changes seem to have occurred, although at a much slower rate than in Europe. As a result of the geographical proximity of the Maghreb to Europe and the cultural impact of this nearness, the propensity for accepting changes and adopting NIT is very high, particularly in the consumer market. The speed at which the use of satellite dishes for receiving foreign TV channels (especially from France) has spread has been astonishing. This is most evident in Algeria, and increasingly so in Morocco. To varying degrees, changes in needs (better living conditions, more intellectual activities, greater balance between work and leisure), changes in economic factors (command of a high level of revenues, particularly among the middle and upper classes), and technological changes (introduction of electronic equipment in the home in the form of games as well as home appliances incorporating more technologically advanced components, such as electronics) have been seen as basic conditions.

NIT, Europe, and outsourcing to the Maghreb

Outsourcing is not occurring to any significant extent in the Maghreb countries, and we have identified above some of the obstacles that prevent this. However, a close examination of the situation shows that the explanation can be found in factors relating to the general outsourcing phenomenon in Europe as well as to the situation of the Maghreb.

France and the Maghreb

We will examine the case of France and its relationship with the Maghreb countries. It is clear that outsourcing, if it is to occur, is likely to take place first between France and these countries, for colonial, cultural, and geographical reasons, before spreading to other countries in Europe and beyond. As yet, there is no evidence of such outsourcing of computer programming and software design. The reasons for this exist, as we shall see, on both sides.

From the French point of view, the following factors must be taken into consideration:

- A limited culture of outsourcing within French companies.
- The relatively slow rate of adoption of NIT in some sectors, such as banking.
- The preference to employ skilled Maghrebian people directly, in spite of the immigration problem.

A limited experience of outsourcing by some administrative bodies using NIT, such as the legal administration, has been reported but remains relatively small.

From the Maghreb point of view, in addition to the problems mentioned earlier, we can point to one other important factor. This is the attitude of the governments of the Maghreb countries, which are not always in favour of potentially uncontrollable direct information links being established. The information taboo is still strong, and may take some years to disappear completely. Excessive centralisation of power and decision-making is one of the signs of this taboo.

Trends in outsourcing NIT activities in Europe

Studies of the European position regarding the outsourcing of NIT activities indicate that this is not happening to any great extent, particularly when compared with the US (Chrissafis 1994). The computer and telecommunications sector is currently characterised by low demand and tough competition. The market became rapidly internationalised at the end of the 1980s and the beginning of the 1990s, going beyond exports and direct sales to include manufacturing and R&D activities. The implications of this phenomenon are numerous: the first is a new localisation of telecommunications and computer activities under the influence of large companies. These large companies have established a new regional distribution of value-added activities, and have undergone radical technological and organisational changes.

A study by Price Waterhouse, initiated by the European Union, on employment location in Europe, the US, and the Far East in the three main sectors of computer hardware – telecommunications equipment, consumer electronics, and electronic components – produced two interesting results.

First, world employment in these three sectors grew by 20 per cent during the 1980s, rising from 3.0 million in 1980 to 3.6 million in 1991. But this growth was recorded mainly in the Far East (including Japan), which has the highest share of world employment (1.6 million) in this industry.

Second, the activities of national companies tend to orient themselves locally. Thus, R&D employment is located mainly in the region of the company's home base: 85 per cent for European companies and 95 per cent for US and Far Eastern companies. In spite of the internationalisation of technologies, industries, and competition, technology R&D remains to a great extent confined to the national level.

Manufacturing activities are, however, more internationalised in the case of European and American firms: 40 per cent of European employees in European firms and 50 per cent of US employees in US firms are located outside their own regions, while only 10 per cent of Asian employees work outside their regions.

With regard to sales and marketing activities, the study shows complex differences between western and Asian companies. In these activities, both Far Eastern and European companies employ 80 per cent of their employees in their own regions, while US companies employ only 50 per cent of their employees in their region. Consequently, US representatives are more present worldwide than are their European or Far Eastern counterparts.

In terms of the sectoral distribution of employment, computer hardware is the most important area, with 1.4 million employees, followed by electronic components with 1.0 million, telecommunications equipment with 0.7 million, and consumer electronics with 0.5 million.

The location of employment in these four NIT sectors appears to be related to three groups of factors: the organisational structure and strategy of each company; the commercial environment within each region; and the public policies pursued with regard to technology, investment, and market growth. Low wage rates may not necessarily be considered a significant reason for expanding activities to other countries and other regions.

Finally, it should be noted that the study excluded employment in the service sector and in computer software, since these areas include no production activities *per se*. Moreover, these types of activities are mostly carried out by small and medium enterprises (SMEs), which are active in domestic markets but very rarely in international markets.

NIT for the Maghreb: what prospects?

The question of the prospects of NIT in the Maghreb countries cannot be dissociated from other aspects of the relationship between Europe and the Maghreb, and needs to be put within the wider Euro-Mediterranean context. The new dynamic initiated at the Euro-Mediterranean conference in Barcelona in November 1995 mobilised funds and opened up prospects, namely the MEDA programme. NIT must have its fair share of this programme if the 'technology for all' concept developed at the conference is to be applied seriously. Outsourcing and the fears of job losses are, as we have seen, far removed from what some anecdotal reports try to make out.

There is a tremendous potential, and consequently a huge market, to develop European NIT in the Maghreb, not only to improve communications between Europe and the Maghreb, but also to link the countries of the Maghreb among themselves. Currently, intra-regional trade in the Maghreb represents less than 1 per cent of total foreign trade. There is a large scope for this 100 million-strong consumer market, which is at the doorstep of Europe and increasing at a rapid rate. The telecommunications explosion will open new opportunities for investment, and it will require an open dialogue between the various partners of the Mediterranean. The subregion offers great growth potential to EU enterprises, yet the three countries of the Maghreb are lagging badly behind in this field. Only now are they beginning to realise the importance of NIT for their development, and the danger that they will be left behind if significant investments are not made in the services sector.

If left out of the NIT revolution in Europe, the Maghreb will inevitably reduce its demand or reorient it to other sources outside the Mediterranean region, namely the US and Asia. Instead of losing jobs, Europe could, through a massive introduction of NIT investment, contribute to the creation of new jobs both south and north of the Mediterranean.

However, this strategy could not be applied unless some conditions are fulfilled. Local skills need to be developed, both to use the NIT in a highly efficient way and to master them properly. Thus, the need for proper training is important in the Maghreb countries. This implies several actions to be undertaken simultaneously: the upgrading of existing training institutions, the modernisation of training equipment, the introduction of modern pedagogical methods through meaningful involvement of local people in the design of these programmes, and the creation of new institutions to complete the missing links.

A sound basis for technical training and an adequate number of personnel with an appropriate mix of skills are not sufficient, however. There is an urgent need to devise strategies for stabilising this skills base locally in order to curtail the very damaging brain drain. NITs seem to present an important potential in this respect. Some of the reasons put forward by potential candidates for migration to other countries are not only of an economic nature (namely low wages), but are also related to the working environment, which is not at a sufficiently high level and which merely increases their frustration (lack of documentary information, difficult access to data, difficulty in travelling abroad to contact colleagues and undertake proper exchanges, and so on). The Internet could help to overcome the frustrations arising from the lack of documentary information, since through this medium close ties are now more easily established between EU and Maghrebian scientists.

The promotion of EU norms constitutes a key task for Europe and the Maghreb countries, through common research projects and through the access of Maghrebian scientists to European 'know-how'. This is essential if we want a fully functioning connection between the networks and the promotion of relationships between business leaders of the two regions to occur. The adoption of EU standards will provide an opportunity for suppliers of both equipment and software to open new markets and become a real force.

Transfer of know-how, not only of the purely technological sort but also of the legal and regulatory frameworks, can be an important means of strengthening international cooperation. By communicating its experience, the EU could help the Maghreb countries to bring about a transition to a competitive environment for telecommunications. The EU could use its experience in extending telecommunications to other countries, such as Portugal and Corsica (through the STAR and Telematics programmes), to promote more balanced grids in the Maghreb countries, where the rates of urbanisation are relatively high: 50 per cent of the population now live in cities and towns in these countries.

NIT and the Euro-Maghreb cooperation

The Mediterranean countries in general, and the Maghreb countries in particular, have a strategic and economic importance for the EU, for whom peace and stability constitute a priority. Common interests exist: it is in the interest of Maghreb countries to attract foreign investment, and it is in the interest of EU countries to have new business opportunities and to manage adequately the flows of migration. Europe can use two means for this: cooperation and direct investment.

Cooperation

Cooperation can use several means, some of which we list here:

- Arabsat, the Arab League satellite, which appears to be an adequate instrument to use for the promotion of broad-based exchanges between Europe and the Maghreb.
- The financial means to allow Maghreb countries to acquire and use new technologies.
- The introduction of new technologies, such as telematics and electronic exchange.
- The establishment of the means to link the efforts of researchers in science and technology, and in the social sciences related to these issues. In this respect, a network called MAGHTECH (Maghreb Technology), started in 1994, now has more than 120 researchers from the main Maghreb countries and from Europe (France and the UK, in particular). Coordinated by the author, this network reflects the kind of cooperation that can be possible; it was put together with the help of universities in Europe (the Universities of Strathclyde and Lille) and INTECH.

The promotion of European direct investment

NIT creates new barriers of entry through requirements for costly technical infrastructure, and size acquires a more important place than previously – the small size of the local market makes it difficult to undertake major investments to produce NTIC equipment. Thus, the recommendations made by the United Nations Industrial Development Organisation (UNIDO) and the International Union of Telecommunications (IUT) to LDCs are oriented toward integration through services. Services are considered less costly and constitute an easier point of entry in the technological trajectory. Three possibilities exist (Béraud 1996):

- The first is through the acquisition of mature technologies, which are likely to generate learning processes resulting from feedback from the users.
- The second is to mobilise sufficient resources to enter the weakest segment of industries, i.e., at the first or last stage of operation of the technological trajectory, by becoming aligned to world standards.
- The third is through 'leap-frogging' by saving on some stages and avoiding some unnecessary learning processes.

The major constraint for Maghreb countries is still the levelling-off of telecommunications infrastructures, which are currently very poor in

LDCs in general, compared to those of advanced countries. Raising tele-communications infrastructure to the right level requires large investment funds to recapitalise the industry, which is an important supportive component of NIT activities. These funds cannot be mobilised immediately because of the economic crisis and the burden of foreign debt. The World Bank estimates this level of funds to be of the order of US$60 billion. Thus, the only possibility for developing telecommunications technology in these countries is by calling in fresh capital through foreign direct investment. Europe can and must play a prominent role in this respect, not only for the sake of the principle of 'technology for all' but also for wellbeing and security for all, South and North.

References

Béraud, P. (1996) 'Technologies de l'information et développement: les conditions de la mise à niveau des infrastructures de télécommunications', *Informations et Commentaires*, 96: 39–42.

Chrissafis, T. (1994) 'La localisation de l'emploi dans les secteurs de l'informatique et des télécommunications', *I&T Magazine*, 14, Summer 1994: 17–19.

Ferchiou, R. (1990) 'Impact of new information technologies and employment in financial institutions in Tunisia', in *Maghreb et maîtrise technologique: enjeux et perspectives*, Proceedings of the CERP/CEMAT seminar, Tunis, June 1990: 182–208.

Kavanaugh, A. (1990) 'Le rôle de l'autonomie de l'institution dans l'approvisionne-ment des télecommunications: une étude comparative', in *Maghreb et maîtrise technologique: enjeux et perspectives*, Proceedings of the CERP/CEMET seminar, Tunis, June 1990: 83–112.

Stern, A. (1995) 'What co-operation in the Mediterranean Sea?', *I&T Magazine*, 18, October 1995.

7

INNOVATION AND COMPETITIVENESS IN COMPLEX PRODUCT SYSTEMS: THE CASE OF MOBILE PHONE SYSTEMS

Andrew Davies

Introduction

Mobile telephone markets have experienced exponential rates of growth since the introduction of the earliest cellular mobile phone networks in the early 1980s. Between 1994 and 1995, for example, the number of subscribers in the world that were connected to mobile phone networks increased from 34 million to around 55 million. A race for worldwide technological leadership and market dominance is now under way as new competitors challenge the established position of the world's leading manufacturers of mobile handsets and mobile phone systems: Motorola in the US and Ericsson and Nokia in Europe.

Europe's position in each market segment tells quite a different story. In the mobile handset market, the lead of US and European manufacturers over Japan and other East Asian countries is diminishing. As the mobile handset becomes a high-volume commodity good, it is increasingly exposed to intense price competition from consumer electronics manufacturers from the Far East, such as NEC, Mobira, Toshiba, and Samsung.

In the design and production of mobile phone systems, on the other hand, European manufacturers have a lead over the US and are well ahead of East Asia. Ericsson is the world's leading supplier of the entire mobile phone system infrastructure: switches, radio base stations, and network management systems. However, while there are important attempts to explain innovation and competitiveness in the mobile handset industry (Oskarsson and Sjöberg 1994), less attention has been paid to the mobile phone system industry. Unlike handsets, the mobile phone system is not a commodity item assembled from off-the-shelf standardised components.

Competition is intensifying in this market segment as existing suppliers in the US and Europe develop the capabilities to innovate and reduce production costs in the design, development, and installation of these complex systems. As yet, however, there is a noticeable absence of system suppliers from East Asia in this market, and few signs that they are likely to appear in the future.

This chapter argues that Europe's competitive advantage in the global tele-economy lies increasingly in those parts of manufacturing involved in the production of high value-added products, networks, or systems tailored for large users, such as mobile phone systems, rather than low-cost standardised goods for mass consumer markets. This is contrary to the widespread assumption that Europe's high-wage economy is about to lose out to East Asian countries in the manufacturing sector. Focusing on the mobile phone system industry, the chapter explores the reasons why Europe has a lead over the dynamic and emerging East Asian economies in the supply of complex product systems. It also highlights the organisational and management capabilities that currently underpin Europe's advantages in these knowledge-intensive manufacturing sectors.

Mass production vs. complex product systems industries

This section compares two different types of sector – mass production and complex system industries – to explore differences in patterns of innovation and competitiveness. It provides a framework for explaining Europe's success in the design and production of mobile phone systems, an industry that does not fit into conventional categories of analysis.

Mass production and the product life cycle

A widely held assumption among academics, policymakers, and business journalists is that Europe's response to the East Asian challenge has to be informed by a model of innovation that applies to mass production goods, such as cars, semiconductors, and consumer electronics. Product cycle theory helps to explain how the patterns of international trade in mass-produced goods and the location of investment are largely determined by the emergence, growth, and maturation of new technologies and industries (Vernon 1966). Mass-produced goods follow a life cycle from birth, through a period of experimentation with various technical designs supplied by many small manufacturers, to maturity. As mass production industries mature and foreign demand for their products rises, the standardisation of industrial processes makes it possible to shift the location of assembly-line production from advanced industrialised economies to newly developing countries, whose comparative advantage is in their lower wage rates. This shift in the locus of production is occurring in the mobile handset market, where European producers face increasing foreign competition from the Far East.

Established firms in the industrialised world have to acquire the organisational capabilities needed to make the switch from one generation of product and process technology to the next (Utterback 1994) if they are to survive competition from late-comer firms emerging in East Asia. For example, just as the analogue mobile handset market is reaching maturity, the world's three leading suppliers – Motorola, Ericsson of Sweden, and Nokia of Finland – are having to obtain economies of scale in the production of increasingly standardised digital handsets in large volumes at lower unit costs. As maturing digital handset technology comes to resemble a mass-produced product, the three industry leaders face competition from a growing number of companies, including consumer electronic companies from the Far East – such as Japan's NEC, Sony, Panasonic, and Mitsubishi, and Korea's Samsung – that have developed the technical capabilities to enter the market.

A major shakeout is occurring in the digital handset market as prices fall and profit margins are squeezed, in the same way as occurred in the PC clone market over a decade ago (Blau 1996). As the European Union's (EU) 1994 Green Paper on mobile communications explains:

> European companies wishing to compete successfully in this market must reach levels of efficiency in production achieved by Asian manufacturers of high-volume consumer goods. The associated dynamics of manufacturing design and marketing of products with short life-cycles must also be mastered.
>
> (CEC 1994: 158)

Complex product systems (CoPS): a new framework of analysis

An emerging body of literature suggests that Europe may be weak in consumer goods industries relative to East Asian manufacturers, but strong in the design and production of large, engineering-intensive, complex products and systems, such as mobile phone systems and other capital goods (Mowery and Rosenberg 1982; Miller *et al.* 1995; Hobday 1995; Hobday 1996).

While product life cycle is valuable in explaining innovation and competitiveness in mobile phone handset technology, it is unable to explain the pattern of innovation in mobile phone systems. A mobile phone system can be defined as a complex product system (CoPS) (Hobday 1996). CoPS industries supply large, high-cost, engineering-intensive products or systems as single items or in small, tailored batches. Examples include aircraft, air traffic control facilities, business telecommunications networks, electrical power equipment, flight simulators, high-speed trains, intelligent buildings, telecommunications exchanges, turnkey nuclear plants, and other high-technology capital goods.

A CoPS has three distinctive characteristics that may contrasted with mass-produced goods. First, in contrast with highly standardised mass-produced goods, CoPS involve a high degree of customisation in the final product and its key components. Second, close attention has to be paid in CoPS design to the criteria of component and interface compatibility with existing and future component technologies and standards. Third, the introduction of computer technology since the 1970s has fundamentally changed component technologies in CoPS, increasing the complexity of the final product. Embedded software has improved the flexibility and performance of many existing CoPS and made possible the creation of new product generations. For example, the concept of cellular mobile phone technology was only made possible by the introduction of high-capacity, software-controlled switches.

In contrast to high-volume mass production factories, a CoPS is usually designed and made by a project-based unit of production. The initial objective of project management is to obtain an order by selling the idea that the firm is able to produce what the individual customer requires. The sequence begins by obtaining the order, modifying the design to suit the requirements of the customer, producing the required volume of components, and integrating them into a tailor-made system. Users make their requirements known during the whole life cycle of the product, influencing the design, development, manufacturing, and post-production decisions of CoPS suppliers. In mass production, by contrast, product development is undertaken first, then production, followed by marketing to consumer markets (Woodward 1958: 23).

CoPS production takes place in a quite different market and institutional environment than mass production, where a few suppliers sell standardised commodities to mass markets. CoPS industries are usually bilateral oligopolies, with a few large suppliers facing monopsonistic markets, involving a few large customers in each country. Governments are often directly involved as purchasers, users, and regulators of CoPS supply and operation. As a result, the establishment of standards and purchasing decisions in CoPS industries are often highly politicised.

Early research suggests that CoPS industries exhibit a distinctive pattern of product and process innovation (Mowery and Rosenberg 1982), which can be contrasted with the pattern usually depicted in the product life cycle (Miller *et al.* 1995; Hobday 1996). CoPS industries seldom evolve toward the mature stage in the product life cycle, when great progress is made in the ability of firms to manufacture products or systems in large volumes at low unit costs. A CoPS may be assembled using individual, pre-packaged, and increasingly standardised components produced in high volumes, but the design and integration of these components into the final system involves production of a 'one-off' kind to meet the requirements of individual customers. Therefore, it is difficult to measure progress in the way a CoPS is produced in terms of movement along the scale identified by Woodward (1958), from unit production fabricated in stages to high-volume mass production. In other words, the division of labour in CoPS production is limited by the extent of the market.

Henderson and Clark (1990) distinguish between two types of innovation in systems of technology – component and architectural innovation that are relevant to the development of CoPS technologies. Component innovation improves the core design concepts of individual components, but leaves the system architecture unchanged. For example, diesel and petrol engines are different component designs within the internal combustion engine architecture. Architectural innovation changes the ways in which components are linked together, but leaves the components unchanged. Knowledge about components defines the core design concepts, while knowledge about the system architecture defines the configuration of the system.

The organisational capabilities of a firm or business unit come to mirror the architectural arrangement of components in the system they are designing; the architecture shapes organisational learning and the acquisition of core capabilities. Business units become specialised as a result of experience with particular component technologies and design configurations. The importance of interface compatibility between subsystem components places important constraints on the design of the system. Each subsystem has its own core design concepts, and the system as a whole consists of a set of interrelated core designs, each with its own body of knowledge and skills. Different subsystems are typically developed by different organisations or departments with different core capabilities, and the problem of developing compatible technologies is closely related to the issue of communication within and between organisations (Metcalfe and de Liso 1995). The interface problem requires the creation of standards to achieve compatibility between subsystems, while the chosen standard sets limits to the future design process.

Innovation in the mobile phone system

The case of the mobile phone system provides an opportunity to explore some of these issues in relation to one CoPS industry. The purpose here is to examine how the industry has experienced two distinct phases of development – an initial phase when architectural innovation predominates and a later phase when component innovation predominates. In each phase, the pattern of industrial competition and leadership has been altered as a result of the introduction of major innovations.

111

Architectural innovation

The early development of cellular mobile phone system technology occurred in the US. Invented by AT&T's Bell Laboratories in 1947, cellular telephony encountered long delays from its birth to AT&T's initial proposals for cellular systems in the 1960s, and to its implementation in the early 1980s. This period of experimentation with different cellular architectural configurations was influenced by changing regulatory rules, and by technological disputes among leading cellular manufacturers over the 'right' design (Davis 1988). Cellular architecture was introduced to overcome the limitations of existing mobile phone technology. This new technical design represented a complete departure from the core design concepts of existing mobile phone technology. It was made possible by the decision to use microprocessor and large software-controlled switching technologies in the core design of the mobile phone system.

The distributed architecture of computerised switches uses a greater number of channels and makes better use of them through cell splitting. Whereas previous mobile phone systems used a single high-powered transmitter to reach subscribers within a radius of 20–50 miles, cellular systems distribute their channels among small areas, or separate radio cells, throughout the total coverage area of the system. As the subscriber travels from one cell to another, the call in progress is automatically 'handed-off' to the adjacent transmitter and a different channel by software-controlled switching equipment. Small cells within a range of 1–10 miles can be served by low-powered transmitters, and cells only a few miles apart can use the same channels for different calls. The increasing number of frequency channels made available for channel reuse by progressively reducing the size of cells in a given area provided a thousand-fold increase in capacity.

Regulatory involvement and bilateral oligopoly

Cellular technology emerged in the US in a heavily regulated industry, which soon became dominated by two mobile system suppliers: AT&T and Motorola. Despite the obvious superiority of cellular radio over existing mobile technology, the implementation of cellular technology was delayed by changing regulatory rules and market structures. In 1968 the Federal Communications Commission (FCC) initiated an inquiry to make new channels available for the growing mobile phone industry. AT&T responded to the inquiry in December 1971 with a technical description of a cellular radio system. During the inquiry, there was a protracted debate between AT&T and Motorola, the two pioneers of cellular technology, about the technical feasibility of different cellular designs, which led to a delay in FCC rule-making.

In this period of regulatory flux, the FCC tested the viability of cellular standards by requiring that manufacturers conduct developmental trials of alternative cellular concepts. AT&T's trial began in Chicago in January 1979 and operated until October 1983 when it was replaced by a new system for commercial operation. The Chicago trial was configured as a fully operational start-up cellular system consisting of 10 cells and a computer-controlled switch, which served 2,000 mobile units. Meanwhile, Motorola provided the cellular technology used in the American Radio Telephone Systems (ARTS) trial in the Washington and Baltimore area. The ARTS trial commenced in late 1981 and continued until it was converted for commercial use in December 1983. Although each trial used a different configuration of component technologies, the efficient performance and quality of customer service provided by both the AT&T and Motorola systems supported the feasibility of the cellular concept. These trials laid the foundations for technical standards developed by an Electronic Industries Association (EIA) *ad hoc* committee, which dealt with the issue of interface compatibility between the mobile units of competing cellular systems.

After more than a decade of changing rules, cost assumptions, and technical specifications, the FCC adopted the industry standards proposed by the EIA as part of its 1982 order to make commercial cellular service available to the public. The first licence to operate a cellular service was granted to the AMPS Corporation, a subsidiary of AT&T established to design, produce, install, own and operate cellular systems throughout the US. However, the vertically-integrated structure of the AMPS Corporation had to be dismantled as a result of the Justice Department's Modified Final Judgment, which divested the Bell Operating Companies from AT&T as seven regional Bell Operating Companies (BOCs) on 1 January 1984. The AMPS Corporation had to be replaced by subsidiaries of the BOCs, since cellular service was designated a local exchange service. As a result of this legal change in the structure of the cellular equipment industry, AT&T – the company responsible for the invention of cellular technology – was forced to withdraw from the operation of cellular systems. After years of delay characterised by changing regulatory rules, experimental systems and the testing and development trials of alternative architectural configurations, the first commercial cellular system, operated by Ameritech Mobile Communications Inc., began in Chicago on 13 October 1983.

By the end of this experimental period in cellular technology, the US equipment industry responsible for designing and producing cellular phone systems as well as mobile handsets was dominated by two equipment suppliers. By the mid-1980s, AT&T and Motorola each supplied 30 per cent of installed cellular systems. The remaining third of the market was shared by several companies, including Northern Telecom in partnership with General Electric, Nippon Electric Company of Japan, Ericsson of Sweden, Astronet, NovAtel, and CTIE.F. Johnson. Although the US mobile handset market was occupied by more than a dozen manufacturers, Motorola was the only US firm to achieve any success in international trade of these consumer goods. AT&T was excluded by the FCC from the mobile handset market in 1974 to prevent the emergence of a dominant service provider and manufacturer. When the FCC removed this prohibition in 1981, AT&T was too far behind its competitors to catch up.

Component innovation

A period of experimentation in American cellular technology was brought to an end by the rise of a dominant architectural design in the early 1980s. Since then, rival designs in components and their arrangement in new generations of technology could be accommodated by this flexible core design concept. The cellular architectural design incorporates a number of choices about the functions of basic components and their configuration into the system that have not been radically changed in subsequent re-designs over the past two decades.

Cellular phone technology

Cellular mobile phone systems consist of four basic components and an external network to which the mobile system is connected. Figure 7.1 shows how components are joined together by interfaces into a system.

- *Mobile handset.* The mobile handset converts the subscriber's message into an analogue or digital signal to establish radio transmission with the mobile phone network.
- *Radio base station (RBS).* Radio access to the network is established between the handset and the radio base station (RBS) over a designated radio channel. The RBS is a centrally located base transceiver, radiating over a cell area, which establishes an interface between the handset and switching component.
- *Mobile switching centre (MSC).* The mobile switching centre (MSC) monitors and controls the performance of the network and enables calls to be made between any two mobile handsets or between a mobile handset and telephones in the public switched telephone network (PSTN). The MSC subsystem is connected to a subscriber database (home location register) and roaming databases (visitor's location register), which are used to keep track of subscribers.
- *Base station controller (BSC).* Although these functions can be configured in different ways, each cellular system includes its own switching system consisting of several MSCs connected to intermediate distributed switching points, or base station controllers (BSCs).

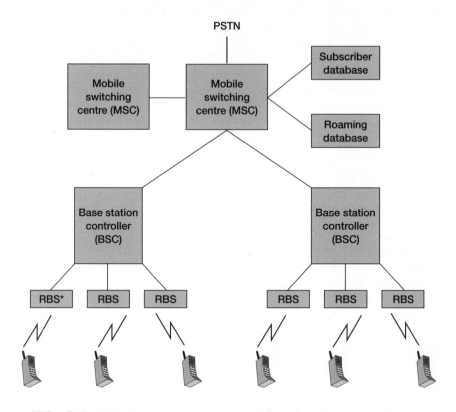

*RBS = Radio base station

Figure 7.1 Cellular system architecture and components.

Generations of cellular systems:
technology, markets, and politics

Once this basic network design was settled, the emergence of different generations of cellular technology and the establishment of international standards has been a highly politicised process, dictated by national and competing industry interests. Since new cellular technologies have to be backward-compatible with existing systems and mobile handsets, every major innovation in cellular components or architecture is more complex and expensive for the system designer. As a result, cellular equipment manufacturers in the US and Europe seek to recover the high R&D costs incurred in cellular development over large international markets. However, cellular suppliers face barriers to entry imposed by the additional costs of developing cellular systems for different international standards. Indeed, rather than develop standards that are compatible with proposed international specifications, some countries have tended to politicise the defining of standards, providing domestic manufacturers with large closed markets for their systems.

Since the 1970s, incremental innovation has refined and extended individual components and the interfaces linking these components. The earliest cellular systems had already reached their capacity by the mid-1980s. They required more spectrum, narrower channels, and even smaller cells than originally envisaged. New component innovations have become available – such as narrowband digital channels, distributed-control architectures, and higher-capacity RBSs that have been incorporated in three successive generations of cellular technology (CEC 1994; Amendola and Ferraiuolo 1995).

The first generation of analogue cellular radio systems used analogue transmission over the air interface between the subscriber handset and the radio base station. (Different generations of cellular systems employ different methods of multiple access, i.e., how large numbers of users share a common pool of radio channels. Traditional analogue cellular systems use frequency division multiple access, or FDMA. FDMA channels are defined by the range of radio frequencies, expressed as a number of kHz, out of the radio spectrum.)

These systems still have the largest installed base of cellular subscribers. The long delay in establishing standards for a commercial analogue cellular service in the US provided opportunities for European and Japanese firms to design and develop analogue cellular systems based on differing technical standards. Ericsson and Nokia benefited in the early 1980s from the rapid take-up of the analogue cellular system called Nordic mobile telephone (NMT) in the Scandinavian markets. (There are three main analogue systems: NMT, developed for Scandinavia in the early 1980s; advanced mobile phone service, or AMPS, used in the US since 1983; and total access communication system, or TACS, which is based on AMPS but uses more efficient management of the radio spectrum, and which has been in use in the UK since 1985.)

The second generation of cellular systems used an all-digital connection over the air interface between the subscriber handset and the radio base station. Rather than introduce more powerful switches or reduce the size of the cells, the preferred option to meet the growing demand for radio telephony was the adoption of digital radio technology. Whereas with analogue transmission a single radio was completely occupied for the duration of the call, digital transmission based on time division multiple access (TDMA) technology allows more efficient use of the available radio spectrum, resulting in a three- to five-fold increase in capacity within the same frequency band. (The multiple access system for digital cellular systems, such as GSM, is known as time division multiple access, or TDMA. TDMA divides a slice of the radio spectrum into time slots, or channels. Only one subscriber at a time is assigned to each channel. No other conversations can access this channel for the duration of the call, or until the original call is handed off to another channel.)

The shift from analogue to digital mobile systems is an example of component innovation. Analogue and GSM systems have similar technical characteristics. They share similar network architectures and the same basic (RBS, BSC, and MSC) components, and are connected to the fixed network in a similar way. MSC equipment is digital in both systems. Although the hardware structure of the MSC technology in each network is similar, each system operates using different application software. The analogue system already contains digital technologies, and the completion of an all-digital connection between handset and network in the GSM system is part of the same path of digital innovation that has occurred in cellular telephony since the early 1970s (Amendola and Ferraiuolo 1995).

US manufacturers lost their leadership position in the supply of digital cellular systems because the federal government was slow to develop technical specifications for digital technology. By contrast, the EU's efforts to develop common standards for a pan-European cellular network began in 1982, when the European Conference of Posts and Telecommunications Administrations (CEPT) established a working party known as Groupe Spéciale Mobile (GSM). The EU pressed ahead with the development of digital standards in 1987 when a Memorandum of Understanding (MoU) was signed by 13 EU signatory countries. The MoU gained the agreement needed to define and implement the pan-European standard, renamed global system of mobile communications (GSM). The first GSM systems entered service in 1992, and by mid-1995 more than 75 networks were in operation in 45 countries. The early adoption of the GSM standard gave Ericsson and Nokia, the major European cellular equipment manufacturers, an early lead over Motorola in the design and development of digital systems. Many European countries mandate the use of GSM, often providing these European manufacturers with closed markets.

The generation of microcellular digital systems currently being introduced uses higher and broader frequency bands, which allow progressive reductions in cell size. Compared to analogue systems, microcellular systems may provide 20 times more capacity. Europe's microcellular network, called the personal communications networks (PCN) service, is based on the digital cellular system (DCS), which operates at 1800 MHz. DCS 1800 is an incremental innovation based on TDMA technology used in GSM systems. It is an application of the GSM standard in the 1800 MHz frequency range. The European Telecommunications Institute (ETSI) decided to base DCS 1800 specifications on the GSM standard to allow operators and manufacturers to exploit the advantages of backward-compatibility when upgrading GSM systems. The first DCS networks came into service in 1993 in the UK, France, Germany, and the Asia/Pacific region.

Competing global standards

In the US, the FCC has not made a ruling on the technologies to be used in the current auctions of personal communications services (PCS) licences. As a result of this liberal approach, cellular operators in the US face a technology choice between adopting well-tested GSM technology or the more advanced code division multiple access (CDMA) technology for microcellular systems. US cellular manufacturers are supporting CDMA technology, which is incompatible with GSM. (The multiple access method used in CDMA is based on unique digital codes, rather than separate RF frequencies (FDMA) or channels (TDMA). These digital codes are used to differentiate subscribers. All users share the same range of radio spectrum. Digital codes are transmitted as data bits along with other signals in a cell area. When the signal is received, the codes that separate the messages of different subscribers are removed from the desired signal.) CDMA was invented by Qualcomm in the US, and is being developed by Motorola, Lucent Technologies, and Nortel. Proponents of CDMA claim that it has potential advantages over GSM in terms of higher capacity, improved voice quality, and lower power consumption.

In the race to establish global standards for third-generation cellular technology, cellular system suppliers have been involved in an intense lobbying war in US, European, and Japanese markets, arguing the merits of their competing CDMA and GSM standards. Ericsson and Nokia claim that CDMA is an unproven technology in comparison to GSM/DCS systems, and requires considerable improvement before it is a commercially viable product for cellular operators. They claim that CDMA is not backward-compatible with the installed base of analogue AMPS systems in the US, and would require the construction of a completely new infrastructure. CDMA technology is being locked out of European markets because EU member states are obliged by law to license GSM and the DCS 1800 systems.

American cellular equipment suppliers have minimised the risks of being locked out of the European market by acquiring and developing design capabilities in GSM technology. In 1994, Motorola was the fourth-largest supplier of GSM infrastructure and had sold base station equipment to operators in Germany, Norway, Portugal, Sweden, and the UK. Nortel has moved into the supply of DCS 1800 systems, combining its knowledge of switching with the base station and radio capabilities of Matra Communications to form Nortel Matra Cellular (CEC 1994: 162). In 1995, Lucent

Technologies, the recently divested manufacturing arm of AT&T, acquired Philips' GSM business.

The leading European manufacturers, on the other hand, have acquired capabilities to enter the US market. Nokia is closely following the evolution of CDMA technology through its membership in the CDMA Development Group. Around half of the American cellular operators to receive PCS licences are adopting CDMA technology, while the others have chosen GSM or a variation of GSM. Several PCS operators, such as Pacific Bell, have purchased Ericsson's PCS 1900 product, based on the GSM platform, for the American market. PCS 1900 technology allows American cellular operators to establish a working system able to generate revenues and build up market share more quickly than a CDMA system.

GSM is currently the dominant worldwide standard for digital technology, with more than 70 countries now offering licences to operate GSM networks. However, the position of the CDMA standard in the battle of global standards was strengthened in 1997 when Japan followed Korea in adopting the CDMA standard in preference to GSM or Japan's own PDC standard, a system confined to Japan.

Competitiveness and industrial leadership in the mobile phone system industry

The cellular phone system industry is a highly oligopolistic. In 1996, three companies – Ericsson, Motorola, and Nokia – accounted for around two-thirds of the world's combined mobile phone system and handset markets (Carnegy 1996). Motorola led the world in the sale of mobile handsets, followed closely by Nokia and Ericsson. Motorola and Nokia experienced a sharp reduction in profitability in the handset market during 1995 and 1996 as price competition intensified. By comparison, Ericsson has been relatively immune to these competitive pressures – in the first half of 1996 the company achieved a 31 per cent increase in profits – because it is less dependent on the sales of handsets, which account for only 14 per cent of Ericsson's sales, compared to 42 per cent for Nokia and 27 per cent for Motorola.

Core capabilities for competitive success

One of the sources of Ericsson's competitiveness lies in the design, production, and installation of digital cellular mobile phone systems, encompassing the entire range of cellular component technologies. Ericsson leads in the world in the sale of all types of mobile phone systems. It has contracts for total GSM solutions, or the supply of major network components, in 34 countries, which amounts to around 50 per cent of the world GSM market.

In 1995, Ericsson's Radio Communications division accounted for more than 50 per cent of the group's sales, compared with less than 10 per cent in the mid-1980s. In September 1995, Ericsson announced plans to restructure its public telecommunications division, where its business is contracting, to accommodate the increasing demand for GSM networks and component equipment. Ericsson is transferring up to 8,000 employees from its public telecommunications to its radio communications business unit.

European manufacturers are now reaping the benefits of sunk costs in organisational learning incurred in the development of GSM technologies during the period of component innovation since the early 1980s. With the exception of Motorola, the top five major GSM system suppliers are European (Ericsson, Nokia, Alcatel, and Siemens). These companies are well positioned to benefit from the growth in world markets for GSM/DCS networks. Although competition is limited in this market, a number of new entrants – including Lucent Technologies, Nortel, Siemens (Germany), and Alcatel (France) – are developing the capabilities to supply cellular systems.

Ericsson is one of the few suppliers with the in-house organisational capabilities to provide a total GSM system, including the design of the base station, switching, and network management systems. The advantage of a single vendor solution is that it is a verified system in which all the components work well together, and can be integrated, tested, and ready for service more rapidly than is possible in multivendor solutions. In Ericsson's single-vendor architecture for GSM and DCS 1800 networks, the main MCS and BSC components are based on a single hardware and software platform: the AXE switch. The processing power of the AXE platform allows Ericsson to build larger, fewer, and more powerful BSCs than companies such as Motorola.

The source of Ericsson's knowledge and skills in cellular technology lies in the company's early development of AXE switching technology in the 1970s, the core design for MSC and BSC components in successive generations of cellular technology (Meurling and Jeans 1985), and in its early involvement in the development of analogue and GSM systems for the Nordic markets in the early 1980s and GSM systems for EU markets in the late 1980s and 1990s.

Ericsson's competitive advantage has been maintained through continuing efforts to control production costs and to innovate in component and system design. Innovation in component technologies has enabled Ericsson to design more standardised, preconfigured GSM component products, as in the RBS, which are manufactured in large batches at lower cost.

However, Ericsson's core capabilities in cellular systems are not confined to conventional manufacturing, but include both the design and development of new generations of cellular technology and the configuration of GSM systems and components to meet the requirements of particular customers.

Project-based activities

The design and integration of cellular systems for customers is carried out by project organisations. These activities are organised in a matrix structure, consisting of product line departments and projects. On the one hand, design activities are organised into organisational nodes, or product line units, such as radio base stations, base station systems, and network management systems, which reflect the internal structure of GSM technologies. On the other hand, Ericsson is involved in three different types of projects, which, for their duration, draw upon the resources of the product lines.

First, large development projects are responsible for major component innovations or architectural refinements in new generations of cellular technology. While key customers are often deeply involved in the design process, large development projects are directed at finding generic solutions for component or architectural designs rather than configuring and installing a network for a particular customer. Each generation of technology reaches a level of maturity when it is surpassed by a new standard, as in the transition from GSM to DCS 1800. Until July 1991, GSM development projects were driven by the evolution of standards dictated by ETSI and the European Commission. Since the first implementation of GSM systems in 1992, development projects have focused on meeting the commercial requirements of GSM customers, such as reductions in cellular operating costs. These projects draw upon Ericsson's design and development activities located in the Radio Communications business unit in Sweden and in design offices throughout Europe.

For example, a recent large development project was responsible for the design and development of the next generation of GSM technology. It was a three-year project that ended in early 1996. Most of the development work was undertaken in Sweden, but the project also involved Ericsson design offices located in eight other European countries. Although substantial innovative efforts were made to improve the MSC, BSC, and network management components, the major component innovation was directed at the development of a new generation of micro base station technology to replace Ericsson's first GSM base station, the RBS 200, developed in 1991. The RBS 200 was expensive to manufacture because it contained a large amount of software processing power, required for signals and data processing. By incorporating custom-designed integrated circuits in the new design, the RBS 2000 operates with greater efficiency and flexibility, since modifications in the base station software can be downloaded from the BSC. In comparison to earlier base station technology, the RBS 2000 is considerably smaller and cheaper to manufacture, and has increased the overall capacity of the GSM system.

Second, mature product line projects are usually smaller projects that are involved in the design, configuration, and integration of an existing cellular technology for specific customers, such as the installation of the TACS analogue system operated by Vodafone in the UK. Ericsson's local companies in the country where the customer is located are responsible for each project. Whereas large development projects are concerned with finding generic solutions, innovation in mature product lines is concerned with local system configurations for a particular customer. However, each of Ericsson's local companies runs a support centre for GSM implementation in each national market. Once the support centre has solved emergent problems with the system in service, a document called a 'trouble report' is sent to Ericsson's central business unit in Sweden. If it is a major problem, Ericsson seeks to find a generic solution for every national market. (On the differences between generic and configurational changes in technology systems, see Fleck (1992).)

Third, Ericsson has recently become involved in the provision of turnkey projects in advanced industrialised countries. Turnkey projects encompass all the activities – network design, cell planning, site selection and acquisition, civil construction, and network installation and testing – required to supply the customer with a system that is ready for service. In turnkey solutions, the customer is no longer involved in systems integration.

Previously, Ericsson had only been involved in turnkey projects in developing countries. The company first became involved in turnkey projects elsewhere in July 1995, when a customer, Mercury Personal Communications, asked Ericsson to help accelerate the rollout of the Mercury One-2-One network, the world's first DCS 1800 system, which entered service in 1993. It was increasing competition from One-2-One's main competitor, the Orange Communications network, based on DCS 1800 technology supplied by Nokia, that was behind Mercury's request for a turnkey solution. At the time, the One-2-One project was the largest of its kind in an industrialised country, and was so important to the group that a new Turnkey Projects unit was established to provide turnkey solutions for the growing number of cellular operators elsewhere in the world that are under commercial pressure to build, expand, and operate their networks as quickly as possible. The Turnkey Projects organisation draws upon in-house systems integration capabilities to design and configure networks, but has had to acquire and develop new project management skills in civil construction and cell planning, as well as using subcontractors for site acquisition, to carry out turnkey solutions.

Conclusions

This paper has treated the mobile phone system as an example of a CoPS industry, which can be contrasted with mass production industries. It has suggested that the competitiveness of European suppliers in the mass production of mobile handsets is now threatened by new, low-cost consumer electronics companies from the Far East. Increasingly, the core capabilities and competitive strengths of Europe's manufacturers lie in CoPS industries, such as cellular systems. Yet, as we have seen in mass production, although the EU currently has a lead in this area, it cannot be taken for granted.

Whereas the product life cycle provides important insights into the development and diffusion of the mobile handset industry, it is less valuable in explaining the dynamics of innovation and competitiveness in the development of mobile phone system technology. While it is difficult to generalise from a particular case, the evolution of the mobile phone system suggests that CoPS industries experience slightly different phases of development than are depicted in product cycle theory. Industrial competition and leadership in the mobile phone system industry is rearranged as firms develop and acquire the organisational capabilities to innovate successfully in different phases of the CoPS product cycle. The early experience in cellular system design captured by the architectural innovators failed to provide leading American suppliers with an unassailable competitive position in the market. In the phase of component innovation of the early 1980s, European suppliers entered the market and challenged the dominance of American cellular system suppliers.

It was the opportunity to develop analogue systems in Scandinavia, Ericsson's and Nokia's home markets in the early 1980s, as well as the EU's efforts to establish the GSM standard as quickly as possible, that provided a favourable institutional environment to help launch European manufacturers in the cellular system market. Ericsson's competitive strength in the cellular system industry originates in the company's early experience with the AXE switch in the 1970s, the software and hardware platform of all major components in Ericsson's cellular systems. Innovation in component design, such as cheaper, more standardised radio base station technology, has helped to bring down the manufacturing costs of components used in GSM/DCS systems. However, the most distinctive feature of the cellular system industry is that the design, production, and integration of these components is for individual customers rather than high-volume markets. As a result, the key organisational capabilities are in the design, systems integration, and project management activities required to configure cellular systems for particular operators.

As cellular system technology matures, the industry is unlikely to follow the pattern of industrial location and international trade often observed in mass production industries. In the early stages of new system generation, refinements and modifications in the design of components may require close communication and interaction with manufacturing plants. Design and production plants are often located in close proximity, since efforts to standardise and pre-configure component design require a detailed technical understanding of how progress can be made in the manufacture of such components at low cost. These knowledge-intensive activities are unlikely to shift to developing countries. In Ericsson, the core design, development, and systems integration activities required to build complex cellular system technologies are spatially concentrated in its headquarters located in Sweden, or dispersed in design offices located in other EU countries.

However, the major cellular system manufacturers are increasingly involved in the supply of turnkey solutions to foreign operators in advanced industrialised nations and developing countries, such as India, China, and South Africa. As these firms export cellular systems technology, they will bring with them the systems integration knowledge and project management skills required to build networks, some of which is transferred to local operators and subcontractors involved in the projects. Moreover, as GSM systems mature, key components, such as the radio base station, are becoming increasingly standardised and produced in higher volume at lower unit costs. As in assembly-line mass production, the supply of these standardised components may shift to the newly industrialising nations of East Asia.

Note

This chapter was prepared as part of the CENTRIM/SPRU Project on Complex Product Systems (EPSRC Technology Management Initiative, GR/K/31756). The author would like to thank Tim Brady, Mike Hobday, and Howard Rush for comments and advice.

References

Amendola, G. and Ferraiuolo, A. (1995) 'Regulating mobile communications', *Telecommunications Policy*, 19, 1: 29–42.

Blau, J. (1996) 'Nokia rebuffs takeover bids', *Communications Week International*, 15 July 1996.

Carnegy, H. (1996) 'Crackling with confidence', *International Telecommunications: Financial Times Survey*, 19 September 1996.

CEC (Commission of the European Communities) (1994) *Towards the Personal Communications Environment: Green Paper on a common approach in the field of mobile and personal communications*, Com (94) 145 final, Brussels.

Davis, J. H. (1988) 'Cellular mobile telephone services', in Guile, B. R. and Quinn,

J. B. (eds), *Managing Innovation: Cases from the Services Industries*, Washington, DC: National Academy Press, 144–64.

Fleck, J. (1992) 'Configurations: crystallising contingency', Edinburgh PICT Working Paper No. 40, March 1992.

Henderson, R. M. and Clark, K. B. (1990) 'Architectural innovation: the reconfiguration of existing product technologies and the failure of established firms', *Administrative Science Quarterly*, 35 (March 1990): 9–30.

Hobday, M. (1995) *Innovation in East Asia: The Challenge to Japan*, London: Edward Elgar Ltd.

Hobday, M. (1996) 'Product complexity, innovation, and industrial organisation', prepared for submission to *Research Policy*.

Metcalfe, J. S. and de Liso, N. (1995) 'Innovation, capabilities, and knowledge: the epistemic connection', University of Manchester, Department of Economics, Mimeo.

Meurling, J. and Jeans, R. (1985) *A Switch in Time: An Engineer's Tale*, Chicago, IL: Telephony Publishing Corporation.

Miller, R., Hobday, M., Leroux-Demers, T. and Olleros, X. (1995) 'Innovation in complex systems industries: the case of flight simulators', *Industrial and Corporate Change*, 4, 2: 363–400.

Mowery, D. C. and Rosenberg, N. (1982) 'Technical change in the commercial aircraft industry, 1925–1975', in Rosenberg, N. (ed.), *Inside the Black Box: Technology and Economics*, Cambridge, UK: Cambridge University Press, 163–77.

Oskarsson, C. and Sjöberg, N. (1994) 'Technology analysis and competitive strategy: the case of mobile telephones', *Technology and Strategic Management*, 6, 1: 3–19.

Utterback, J. M. (1994) *Mastering the Dynamics of Innovation: How Companies Can Seize Opportunities in the Face of Technological Change*, Cambridge, MA: Harvard Business School Press.

Vernon, R. (1966) 'International investment and international trade in the product cycle', *Quarterly Journal of Economics*, 80: 190–207.

Woodward, J. (1958) *Management and Technology*, London: Her Majesty's Stationery Office.

8

A non-European counterpoint

THE SOUTH AFRICAN
MOBILE PHONE SYSTEM

David E. Kaplan

The conference organisers asked me to do two things – to discuss Andrew Davies's paper and, particularly, to examine the South African situation to see how it complements and perhaps 'extends' the paper.

My comments are aimed principally at the second task. I found the paper extremely enlightening and persuasive as to the importance of analysing complex production systems (CPS) and Europe's advantage therein. I think that the South African experience confirms the considerable comparative advantage to Europe in the design and production of complex cellular systems. Let me illustrate this by recounting the experience of cellular telephony in South Africa.

South Africa has a GSM cellular network, initiated in April 1994. It is reputedly the largest GSM system outside Europe, and the fastest-growing, with over 700,000 subscribers. There are two operating consortia, whose leading foreign partners are European (UK) companies, Vodafone and Cable and Wireless. This has been a large and a highly profitable investment.

The two companies have extensive experience with the installation, configuration, and operation of GSM networks. Thus, it would seem that Europe's gains from GSM are not solely trade gains, but also from the investment in establishing and operating GSM systems abroad.

The 700,000-plus cellular subscriber figure compares with some 4.5 million fixed lines. The South African telecommunications industry has always been European-dominated with Siemens and Alcatel as the two main foreign players. The cellular industry is also dominated by European suppliers, even for handsets. The dominant suppliers of equipment and handsets are European companies or the local subsidiaries of European companies – Ericsson, Nokia, Siemens, and Alcatel. Motorola (US) has a limited presence.

How important has the South African market been for European cellular equipment manufacturers? It is difficult to isolate cellular imports from other telecommunications equipment imports. Table 8.1 shows imports of telecommunications equipment by region. The dominance of Europe is evident. Note especially the increases in imports between 1993 and 1994. This is almost all a result of the introduction of cellular telephony. As you can see, it is imports from Europe that have risen massively, by R980 million (at that stage about R4 = US$1) – a 79 per cent increase.

By comparison, exports of telecommunications equipment from South Africa, while growing rapidly, are quite limited – about 12 per cent of imports. As you can see from Table 8.2, Europe is the principal destination. This is a result of exports by European subsidiaries, particularly Siemens (SA) to Germany, where Siemens has not been able to fully meet

Table 8.1 Region of origin of South African imports of telecommunication equipment, 1993 and 1994 (R millions)

Region	1993		1994		1993–94 change	
	Value	% of total	Value	% of total	Value	% of total
AFRICA	2.2	0.3	2.3	0.1	0.1	0.01
Phones, switching and carrier equipment	1.5	0.2	0.4	0.04	–1.1	10.2
Transmission apparatus	0.7	0.4	1.9	0.2	1.2	0.2
EUROPE	553.6	65.8	1,533.2	73.8	979.6	79.2
Phones, switching and carrier equipment	476.0	71.3	794.1	70.2	318.1	68.6
Transmission apparatus	77.6	44.7	739.1	78.1	661.4	85.6
AMERICAS	95.4	11.3	172.3	8.3	76.9	6.2
Phones, switching and carrier equipment	47.7	7.1	79.3	7.0	31.6	6.8
Transmission apparatus	47.7	27.4	93.0	9.8	45.3	5.9
ASIA	181.4	21.6	337.7	16.3	156.3	12.6
Phones, switching and carrier equipment	139.1	20.8	238.8	21.1	99.7	21.5
Transmission apparatus	42.3	24.3	98.9	10.5	56.6	7.34
OCEANIA	9.0	1.1	32.2	1.6	23.2	1.9
Phones, switching and carrier equipment	3.5	0.5	19.0	1.7	15.5	3.3
Transmission apparatus	5.5	3.2	13.2	1.4	7.7	1.0
TOTAL	848.6	100.0	2,034.6	100.0	1,236.0	100.0
Phones, switching and carrier equipment	670.9	100.0	1,135.1	100.0	464.2	100.0
Transmission apparatus	177.7	100.0	949.5	100.0	771.8	100.0

Source: *Customs & Excise Abstract of Monthly Trade Statistics.*

Table 8.2 Exports of telecommunication equipment from South Africa, by region of destination, 1994 (R millions)

Region	Value	% of total
AFRICA	18.5	16.3
Phones, switching and carrier equipment	7.8	13.2
Transmission apparatus	10.7	20.0
EUROPE	71.1	62.5
Phones, switching and carrier equipment	40.2	68.0
Transmission apparatus	29.8	55.6
AMERICAS	6.9	6.0
Phones, switching and carrier equipment	3.5	5.9
Transmission apparatus	3.4	6.3
ASIA	5.7	5.0
Phones, switching and carrier equipment	3.1	5.2
Transmission apparatus	2.6	4.9
OCEANIA	11.6	10.2
Phones, switching and carrier equipment	4.5	7.6
Transmission apparatus	7.1	13.2
TOTAL	112.7	100.0
Phones, switching and carrier equipment	59.1	99.9
Transmission apparatus	53.6	100.0

Source: Commissioner for Customs and Excise, *Foreign Trade Statistics, Calendar Year 1995*, 1: 243–6.

the needs resulting from the modernisation of the network in the former East Germany.

We should also note some export to Africa – this has been increasing very rapidly. Africa currently represents some 3 per cent of the international market for telecommunications equipment. This is generally too small for product development aimed specifically at the African market on the part of the large companies. However, the Chief Executives of both Siemens and Alcatel have declared that they will be utilising their South African subsidiaries to undertake product adaptation and support for the entire African region, for both cellular and fixed line telecommunications.

Andrew Davies's paper is perhaps too overtly focused on the process of innovation, and perhaps under-emphasises the importance of the feedback loops as diffusion proceeds. Interestingly, the European GSM system has undergone quite significant product adaptations in the South African market. Three of these innovations are worth outlining.

Siemens (SA) has developed a digital telephone interface to adapt the GSM network to a fixed line environment. This interface allows the use of the mobile radio network for connection to a two-wire telephone applicator (PABX system or coin-operated public telephone). This has led to the development of containerised public phone shops, designed to provide public telephone services for communities with no fixed line access. These are refurbished 6 × 2 metre freight containers housing up to ten phones. Each has its own radio equipment plus a metering unit.

The GSM telephone interface has also been used for a single telephone unit so that a fixed cellular service can be provided with a pre-paid metering facility. This is for single public telephones – and South Africa has developed the first public telephone utilising GSM.

The spur to both developments was a clause in the licence agreement that required operators to provide a specified number of community telephone services at a tariff less than half the conventional rate. These developments would be easy to deploy elsewhere, particularly in Africa, and there are forecasts of large export sales to the continent.

A further significant innovation was developed by Alcatel Altech Telecommunications (SA). The MPDR-AR multi-point digital radio system was developed to lower costs and to cope with high-capacity community phones. The standard point-to-multi-point (PMP) is limited in the number of high-capacity users it can connect. MPDR can distribute services with a 360 degree coverage that previously would have required more than one point-to-point system (Hodge and Millar 1996).

As Davies has expressed it: this is innovative activity directed at improving the components of the system, but within a basically stable architecture. Nevertheless, these component developments can contribute significantly to improving the system. Further diffusion is likely to result in further improvements to the European GSM system.

Despite its phenomenal growth, GSM cellular telephony is still not accessible to the mass market. Indeed, there are signs that the rate of growth of new cellular subscribers is now starting to tail off – in the US, for example. The real challenge for cellular is whether it can achieve mass penetration ratios that put it on a par with conventional telephony or even television.

In order to do this, the price will have to come down significantly. Market pressures will soon begin to operate so as to require significant cost reductions. This in turn will call into question even the basic architecture, since cost savings via cheapening of individual commodities will not suffice.

Let me recount very briefly the South African story in relation to the other key components of IT – computer hardware and software – highlighting Europe's role.

In terms of hardware, South Africa relies very heavily on imports. As expected, this is overwhelmingly US equipment, with rising imports of equipment from Asia, particularly Taiwan. Europe plays a minor role, although a lot of US equipment is shipped via European subsidiaries.

Accurate software import statistics are not available. (If available, such statistics would not necessarily show country of origin, but if they did,

Europe's prominence would be due to its popularity as a base for distribution to Africa and the Middle East.) The overwhelming proportion (95 per cent) of South African software requirements are met by imports – systems software, in particular. This is dominated by the US companies. Europe's share is about 12 per cent – see Table 8.3. In packaged application solutions, Europe figures more strongly – see Table 8.4. The company with the most significant share is SAP (Germany), which is important in corporate packaged solutions and has 67 per cent of this market. Oracle (US) and Baan (the Netherlands) are the other major players here. This appears to be similar to the Indian case, as outlined by Basrur's and Chawla's contribution to this book. Figures for the rest of the world are not available, but are considered insignificant.

Finally, some concern has been expressed about Europe losing jobs in software and data entry to the developing countries. South Africa is not, at least as yet, a site for such developments. Our exports of software are very small. We have severe limitations in our education and human development resources – particularly at the middle and lower levels. We do have very good high-level training in IT. However, we also have a significant exodus

Table 8.3 South African estimated* imports of systems software and application development tools, by region of origin, 1993–95 (R millions)

Region	1993	1994	1995	CAGR % 1993–95
North America	600	725	880	21
Europe	100	110	120	10
Total	700	835	1,000	20

Source: BMI TechKnowledge, 1996.

*Estimates based on country of origin of specific products.

Table 8.4 South African market of packaged application solutions, by source, and region of origin of imports, 1993–95 (R millions)

Source	1993	1994	1995	CAGR % 1993–95
Locally developed	70	90	110	25
Imported	634	807	1,023	27
Import Origin:				
North America	504	641	814	27
Europe	120	153	193	27
Rest of World	10	13	16	26
Total	704	897	1,133	27

Source: BMI TechKnowledge, 1995.

of highly trained IT professionals. It is people we are exporting and not products. The reasons for this exodus are many, but there does appear to be a mismatch between high-level training and a limited number of opportunities to utilise this training fully locally.

Reference

Hodge, J. and Millar, J. (1996) 'Information Technology in South Africa'. Paper prepared for the UNU/INTECH Workshop on Information Technology and Economic and Social Exclusion in Developing Countries, Maastricht, October 1996.

Part II

LEARNING WITH TELEMATICS IN THE GLOBALISED INFORMATION SOCIETY

9

EUROPE AND DEVELOPING COUNTRIES IN THE EMERGING ON-LINE EDUCATION MARKET

Maria-Inês Bastos

Many people are presently taking post-secondary credit courses and even complete degrees off-campus and entirely on-line. Some of these students are civil servants, managers, and professionals living across the ocean. They are customers within the emerging on-line education and tele-training market, which, together with expert consultancy in new educational applications, is already a promising line of business in many economies and is emerging as one segment of international trade in services.

International trade in on-line education offers many opportunities both for countries with an established capacity in the production and dissemination of knowledge and for those seeking to strengthen their own systems of education and knowledge production. Less favoured regions of Europe, transition economies in Europe, and middle-income developing countries can benefit from domestically developed on-line applications as well as from this new area of international trade to reduce their educational and training deficits, change their educational practices, and upgrade their communications infrastructure. Stronger European participation in on-line education can contribute to increasing the quality of on-line content and to opening channels for international dissemination of rich cultural resources by consolidating alternative forms of expression in various languages other than English. These open channels will help many developing countries to become aware of a richer role they themselves can play in the international on-line education market, allowing them to transcend the narrow role of passive consumers.

In creating or assessing this market in the developing world, Europe needs to take into account the apprehension of the importing nations. International trade in on-line education and tele-training can be perceived as a threat by the importing developing nations for a number of reasons.

First, there is a fear of technological and cultural domination from the developed world, which may offer educational packages that are inappropriate to the needs and capabilities of the developing world. In addition, there is, as yet, little international regulation to protect importing nations against poor quality service and inappropriate content. Assessment of the educational needs of the developing world, as well as the mobilisation of local capability, could pave the way to a novel form of collaboration between Europe and the developing world.

This chapter aims at an exploration of the emerging relationship between industrialised and developing countries in the international on-line education market. Of the triad that dominates the information and communications market, it looks primarily at Europe as the mostly likely challenger of the US and Canada as major players in this segment of the market. As for the vast array of potential world importers, this chapter strives to bring the perspectives of various groups of developing countries to the fore, particularly those of middle-income countries.

The chapter addresses the question of on-line education in the context of the emerging learning economy, where discussion is organised around three issues. The first is an initial appraisal of the emerging international on-line educational market, and of the implications of a strengthened European participation in it. The second issue is that of telecommunications infrastructure and access to computers, lack of which can create barriers to the realisation of the potential of on-line education and tele-training, particularly – but not only – in developing countries. The third issue is the challenge this new area of business and trade represents for developing countries, where on-line applications may divert resources from cheaper and more efficient ways of addressing the educational agenda.

The case for a new mode of learning:
the market for on-line education

As the pace of technological change in the information society increases, the growing knowledge content in production alters skills requirements and puts pressure on learning systems. Product life cycles speed up and processes of production change continuously, so skills learned in vocational centres, at universities, or on the job have to be updated constantly. The usual conception of 'once-and-for-all' schooling is being replaced by the acceptance of a continuous process of learning and of skills improvement, not as an individual option but as the best collective way to face the quick obsolescence of modalities of codified learning. New skills are best acquired 'by doing', and the technological tools that help 'virtually' create a hands-on, a master–apprentice, or a teacher–student interactive environment can be mobilised in favour of continuous learning in enterprises, classrooms, and open environments.

The learning person, young or adult, scientist or engineer, manager or worker, is at the centre of the learning economy and society. The learner is expected and needs to acquire general educational and vocational skills and to keep up with change in order to be able to participate actively in the economy and society. It is not only that the 'knowledge industries' or primary information sector[1] grow and demand higher skilled labour; a host of abilities are now being required of workers, professionals, and managers in practically all areas of manufacturing and services. These include long-established skills that had not previously been mobilised at certain levels of activity, and new abilities demanded by direct and intense involvement with computers in networked working environments.

The new working environment requires from managers and employees the difficult abilities of operating with flexibility of organisation and tasks, and of acting with wider levels of autonomy and within cross-functional processes (Rajan 1996). At the shop-floor, the new environment has pushed for professional profiles in industry that emphasise abstraction, interactivity, speed of response, quality, versatility, and capacity to operate in a virtual team (Lasfargue 1996; Lundvall 1997). Wider dependence on information processing in most working environments requires workers with high levels of adaptability because of the speed of change of operating systems, software, and network arrangements (Mulgan 1996).

Teachers, a key factor in the learning society, have to be adapted to the new demands of students and their learning needs. They are expected to move from a lecturer-centred role into a tutoring one, and to be able to increase attention to individuals at the same time as dealing with students working in groups. Some think that in order to meet the intellectual challenges stemming from change in the role of teachers, it will be necessary to have a complete re-engineering of the teaching profession. Preservice and in-service training will have to develop a teacher's ability to manage complexity, deal with individual learners alone and in groups at different times and locations, and mobilise new resources and tools (Barchechath 1996). Connectivity is reported to enormously help teachers to adapt to these new demands by breaking their isolation, increasing their communications with fellow professionals, making available richer resources for preparation of classes, and opening up the opportunity for on-line in-service courses (Veen 1996).

In brief, skills now required of managers, professionals, and workers range from abstraction, problem-solving, systems thinking, and experimentation to adaptability, versatility, and the ability to manage complexity and to work as a part of a team. In order to acquire these skills and keep up to date in the world of work, cultivated curiosity, a spirit of inquiry, and learning to learn are basic skills that are to be developed by individuals living in a situation of rapid technological change. The quantity of information available on networks requires the development of skills to navigate through information 'as a precondition to knowing' (Delors 1996: 175). Learning was never only about absorbing information, but about having the capacity to cope with the dominance of written language. The abstract working environments in the present and foreseeable future foster more forcefully than ever the need to develop abilities to communicate, to sift and select, to simulate and model (Mulgan 1996). Many of these abilities can be developed directly by learners or by their teachers through on-line education.

Feasibility of on-line education: learning from the developed world

Telematics offers a wealth of possibilities for engaging learners in complex and meaningful tasks; facilitating communication between learners, teachers, and more experienced co-learners; and helping to individualise education and training. It has enlarged the amount of tacit knowledge that can now be codified and transmitted to learners. Multimedia tools can register, store, and transmit more vividly particular aspects of reality that learners could never have experienced unless they were involved in real, 'hands-on' experience or in a master–apprentice relationship.[2]

This is exactly what is at the core of what technology can contribute to widen the opportunities of education and training. However, one has to be aware of the risks of an integrated acquisition of knowledge when delivered piece-meal or in 'infonuggets', as in just-in-time training (Gordon 1997). Codification of tacit knowledge cannot ever be complete, just as 'virtual reality' will always be a simpler, poorer, and incomplete model of the real world. On-line education and just-in-time training represent new opportunities of enriching the learning experience, but they also involve some de-skilling and place some constraints on learners' access to the valuable inputs that the social interaction of classroom or conventional education offers.

On-line education is built mostly on the asynchronous telematics functions of electronic mail and electronic information retrieval and on hypertext mark-up language, the software used for linking chains of content in a web format. These functions and this language support a variety of applications, including bulletin boards, computer conferencing, on-line databases, and visually attractive ways of displaying information and its multiple interconnections. Since the late 1980s, wider diffusion of hypertext mark-up language has led to the explosive growth of the World Wide Web. Web browsers were developed and the web became an attractive tool for production and delivery of on-line education. The web became an obligatory source of information, to be tapped by learners and teachers. Hypertextual teaching aids are being used as a modality of 'automatic' tutoring; complete courses are collaboratively produced with web resources and delivered through the web. In addition to these telematics functions, on-line education is usually supported by printed text and video-recorded material, which has been in much longer use in distance education.

Beyond the basic, asynchronous functions of e-mail, file transfer, and hypertext, there are other sophisticated and technologically demanding telematics applications that are used for on-line education. These include all the synchronous applications for teleconferencing, from audio and audiographics to desktop video and distributed multimedia conferencing. Used in the present mostly as a learning tool for higher-level managers and professional staff, these applications demand a much higher transmission capacity of the telecommunications infrastructure, and require special software and equipment at sending and receiving ends.

Early innovators in the on-line education market

On-line applications in classroom education, a widespread trend in industrialised societies, are here distinguished from on-line education. As opposed to on-line education, classroom applications of asynchronous telematics functions such as e-mail, bulletin boards, and the WWW are not the central mode of learning, which in the school environment continues to be the face-to-face interaction between teacher/instructor and learners. On-line classroom applications have not been subject to organised production nor been explored commercially so far. Classroom education, however, can easily make use of instructional material produced for on-line education, in the same way that conventional education has absorbed much of the material prepared for distance education. In this respect, conventional schools and training institutions may constitute one potential customer for on-line educational materials. Another area of intersection of on-line applications for conventional education and on-line education is that of human resources: skills developed in the creation of on-line classroom applications are a significant asset for the emerging on-line education market.

On-line learning is extensively incorporated in on-campus post-secondary education in Europe. The specialised open universities are using telematics, particularly e-mail, as one component of their multimedia delivery. Only a few European universities are, as of late 1997, offering courses or complete degrees on-line. The Open University (OU) of the UK, the FernUniversität in Germany, and the University of Twente in the Netherlands are early adopters of this system of delivery in Europe. In 1997, the OU is offering four on-line courses at postgraduate level, all in the area of information technology, and two on-line programmes leading to complete Masters degrees, one in Computing for Commerce and Industry and the other in Open and Distance Education.[3] An undergraduate introductory computing on-line course is announced for 1998.

The first on-line courses at FernUniversität were offered in the winter term of 1996/97. This initial offer consisted of 13 courses, all part of the curriculum of electrical engineering.[4] They were based on the traditional paper version enhanced by the integration of animation, simulation environments, on-line literature search and additional help for exams and assignments. All but two courses, 'Introduction to Hypermedia' and 'Software Engineering II', are in the German language. There is also the 'Virtuelle FernUniversität'[5] where registered students find on-line courses in informatics, economics, law and mathematics.

The University of Twente, in the Netherlands, is also an early innovator in on-line education integrated with the dominant on-campus delivery. This dual mode of learning has been put in practice since 1994 when the Faculty of Educational Science and Technology began offering a one-year internationally-oriented Masters programme in Educational and Training Systems Design.[6] This is an on-campus programme, but the six-month minimum specialisation stage can be taken on-line.

Further study of the on-line offering at the OU could shed some light on market prospects from the supply side. The OU has been at the forefront of technological innovation for quality distance education in Europe, its entry into on-line education being an illustration of this trend within the conservative educational environment. The few on-line initiatives at the OU could remain as an area of experimentation or become a decisive step in the globalisation of its services. In any case, the offering at the OU and initiatives such as the one at the University of Twente indicate that two highly prestigious educational institutions are approaching the innovation without haste.

The wider experience with on-line education in the US contrasts strongly with the low rate of diffusion of this innovation in Europe. Many of the top-rated universities in the US, which are also dual-mode institutions (providing on-campus and distance education), offer on-line degrees. In 1993, there were 93 institutions offering on-line post-secondary education. The number of 'cyberschools' grew enormously in four years, reaching 762 in 1997. It has been estimated that 55 per cent of all the 2,215 four-year colleges and universities have courses available off-site (Gubernick and Ebeling 1997). In addition to on-line educational activities within conventional, accredited educational institutions, fully on-line organisations are emerging in the US to offer credit courses and degrees.[7]

The Canadian experience with on-line education is impressive and shows an integrated approach to on-line learning at various levels. The Open Learning Agency[8] is a publicly funded, fully accredited educational institution offering access to education through a variety of technologies and in partnership with other Canadian institutions, particularly the Open University. It offers fully accredited university courses transferable to the Open University; courses leading to professional certificates and diplomas;

interactive courses for students from kindergarten to upper secondary level; on-line internships in the educational use of telecommunications for teachers; and workplace training solutions. The Agency also broadcasts an average of 65.5 hours a week for schools, from kindergarten to post-secondary, teachers, parents, and industry. Since January 1996, it has offered an International Credential Evaluation Service for immigrants and Canadians educated abroad. The Canadian Open Learning Agency is funded by public grants, tuition fees, sales, donations, sponsorship, and partnerships.

Information provided by Gubernick and Ebeling (1997) for the US indicates that on-line education, in addition to the convenience of place and time for learning, may be financially convenient for the student and rewarding for the educational institution. Duke University, the University of Phoenix, and the University of Maine illustrate some of the financial aspects of on-line education.[9] The Fuqua School of Business at Duke University offers an on-line Global Executive MBA[10] taken by a large share (almost half the total students) of learners residing as far away as Switzerland and Hong Kong. They pay US$82,500 in tuition fees for the degree, which is significantly over the US$50,000 for an on-campus MBA. An on-line student at the University of Phoenix[11] pays US$33,150 in tuition fees for a BS degree that can be earned by an on-campus student for US$25,000. At the University of Maine[12] there is no significant differ-ence between tuition fees for on-campus and on-line education; the university charges only an extra US$4/hour for each US$119 credit/hour for on-line education.

An explanation for the differences between on-line and on-campus fees at the same university and between the same on-line degrees offered by various universities will demand further studies to disclose the economics of the production and delivery of on-line education, and reveal the period of amortisation of development costs and profit margins. Based on the little information available about on-line education in the US, it seems that the costs of offering on-line education are much lower than those of conventional on-campus education. According to Gubernick and Ebeling (1997), the costs of offering one credit hour on-line at the University of Phoenix (Arizona) is US$237 as compared to US$486 per hour for conventional on-campus education at Arizona State University. This infor-mation is likely to indicate only the running costs, particularly because most of faculty at the University of Phoenix is part-time, holding full-time jobs in the professions they teach. It is likely that some, if not most, of them have their teaching activities on a 'tele-working' basis. Part-time faculty is less costly to the educational institution than full-time faculty. On-line faculty at Phoenix, with master's or doctoral degrees, research, and publication, earn US$2,000 per course. At Arizona State University full-time faculty earn around thirty times more than on-line faculty at Phoenix.

Development of distance education material is a human-resource inten-sive activity with high initial and maintenance costs. It is not clear how much the development of on-line courses would add to the costs of preparation of multimedia distance education material. In any case, institu-tions with built-in expertise in the production of distance education material may have the advantage of adding only the knowledge of the new media – which is less demanding the more 'user friendly' asynchronous applications become – to be able to compete in the on-line education market. The reverse is not likely to be true: institutions with experience with on-line classroom applications will have to acquire the specialised knowledge of distance education design to be able to enter the on-line education market success-fully. After the production stage, delivery of on-line education will demand faculty for lecturing (text or videoconferencing), tutoring, and marking exams and assignments.

An assessment of the financial implications for learners of a choice between conventional and on-line education would have to consider some other costs besides the gross differences in tuition fees. Conventional on-campus education may charge the learner higher fees, but it offers the rich environment of face-to-face interaction with faculty and fellow students in addition to access to on-line applications. On-line education may cost less, but the learner must provide the necessary hardware and pay for connectivity, unless learning takes place in the working environment and these costs are covered by the employer. However, on-campus learners have to reside away from home, usually entailing high costs of transporta-tion (particularly foreign students) and of temporary residence, and cannot hold a full-time job. On-line learners 'save' transportation and temporary residence costs and can accommodate their education with job commit-ments. Choosing between on-campus and on-line education is not just a financial matter, nor is what is bought precisely the same. Some learners may be in a position where there is no choice, either because of impedi-ments to their mobility or a lack of convenient local offerings. On-line education will cater to this segment of customers.

Telecommunications infrastructure and access to computers: the parameters of the market

Two basic infrastructure elements, at both delivery and receiver ends, have to be present as preconditions for an on-line education market. One is connectivity and has to do with the telecommunications infrastructure; the other is accessibility to computers by individuals in households, offices, and teaching institutions and has to do with the rate of diffusion of the new technology. Skilled professionals in educational software, experienced with the pedagogical use of synchronous and asynchronous on-line tools, are also essential for the production and implementation of on-line education.

It is only for a segment of unknown dimensions of world gross demand for education that these preconditions are met, and which can therefore be considered as a potential market for on-line education.

An approximation of the world gross demand for formal education at all levels can be found in Table 9.1. High adult illiteracy rates in most of the low- and middle-income countries are a hindrance to prospective incorporation of women and larger segments of the total population into learning economies. This is a major educational issue to be tackled with all technical means available.

Distance education can help and has already been mobilised for mass basic education in some of these countries. On-line education can also help, but it is not a solution for mass education. This option for mass education would require not only effective universal access to infrastructure, but also levels of literacy and 'computeracy' that are, by definition, non-existent among the majority of those in need of basic education. The very small enrolment ratios in tertiary education in all but the high-income countries signal an area with prospects for on-line education, particularly in middle-income countries. The dimensions of this prospective market for European

Table 9.1 Male school enrolment as percentage of age group (1980–93) and male and female adult illiteracy (1995) – weighted averages

Groups of countries	Primary[a]		Secondary[b]		Tertiary[c]		Adult illiteracy[d] (1995)	
	1980	1993	1980	1993	1980	1993	Female	Male
Low- and middle-income	**105**	**110**	**45**	**NA**	**8**	**NA**	**39**	**21**
Sub-Saharan Africa	90	78	20	27	1	NA	54	35
East Asia and Pacific	118	120	51	60	3	5	24	9
South Asia	91	110	36	NA	5	NA	64	37
Europe and Central Asia	NA	97	NA	81	31	32	NA	NA
Middle East and North Africa	98	103	52	65	11	14	50	28
Latin America and Caribbean	108	NA	40	NA	14	15	14	12
High-income economies	**103**	**103**	**NA**	**97**	**35**	**56**	**NA**	**NA**
World	104	109	50	NA	13	NA	NA	NA

Source: *World Development Report 1997*, Table 7, p. 227.

Notes
NA = Not available.
[a] Population age 6 to 11. Figures exceeding 100 per cent indicate pupils younger or older than the country's standard primary school age.
[b] Population age 12 to 17. Figures are affected by late entry, repetition, and 'bunching' in final grades.
[c] Population age 20 to 24.
[d] As percentage of population age 15 years and older.

on-line education are not clear, since there are many restrictive conditions to be met for effective demand to emerge. Such conditions go from more general aspects, such as average income levels of learners and levels of proficiency in one of the European languages, to institutional aspects, such as local accreditation of on-line degrees and the infrastructure aspects discussed in this section. An effective market for European on-line education and tele-training services in these countries may not be large, and is perhaps concentrated in a handful of the most industrialised of these countries, which are in need of a quick solution for pressures on the local education system, particularly in relation to specialised technical and post-secondary education. Since the industrialised world meets most of the infrastructure preconditions, it certainly contains the largest part of the emerging on-line education market.

All telematics functions require reliable telecommunications and, in the case of synchronous applications, a highly developed and potent infrastructure for acceptable quality levels of transmission and reception. Bandwidth, the capacity of communications channels to carry a certain volume of information within a certain time, is a very relevant feature for on-line education. High bandwidth (presently measured in megabits per second – Mbit/s – or gigabits per second – Gbit/s)[13] is required for high-volume traffic as well as for accurate and timely transmission of web pages, complex graphic simulation, sound, moving image, and synchronous applications such as video conferencing. International Internet capacity indicates the bandwidth of the backbones, the main communications channels through which international on-line traffic flows. The majority of high international Internet capacity is located in the US, and it is also a link to the US that concentrates the highest capacity available in every country and region in the world.

Table 9.2 illustrates this situation. Presently the on-line world is US-centric. The dominant role the US plays results not only from the initial conditions associated with the origins of the Internet, but also from the deficiencies in infrastructure in other regions of the world that make the US the only available point with the needed capacity for heavy traffic interconnection. In addition, concentration of content in the US explains much of traffic concentration.

International Internet capacity in Europe seems not to favour the region in the emerging on-line education market. The consequences of a relative international on-line insulation of Europe go far beyond the level of lost business opportunities: blocking access to the rich European multicultural heritage and to its social and political experience, contributing to the concentration of power, and hindering the development of quality on-line content.

There are positive indications of coming improvements of Internet infrastructure in Europe with the emergence of large access points in London,

Table 9.2 Bandwidth of regional and intercontinental backbones in selected countries/regions, 1997

Country/Region	Regional backbone	Intercontinental backbone
USA	622 Mbit/s	1.5 Gbit/s
Western Europe	2 Mbit/s (average)	155 Mbit/s (UK)
	155 Mbit/s (Finland, UK)[a]	72 Mbit/s (EUNet/NL)
Russia	?	40 Mbit/s[a]
Japan (KDD)	15 Mbit/s	10 Mbit/s
Australia (Telstra)	2 Mbit/s	10 Mbit/s
Dominican Republic (LIX)	?	155 Mbit/s
India	?	10 Mbit/s
Costa Rica	64 Kbit/s	2 Mbit/s

Source: Evagora 1997a; Evagora 1997b.

Notes
[a] Under construction.
? = Information not provided by source.
EUNet International BV (Amsterdam).
KDD: Kokusai Denshin Denwa Co. Ltd (Tokyo).
LIX: Latin Internet Exchange (Dominican Republic).
Telstra Corp. Ltd (Melbourne).

Helsinki, and Sweden that will distribute international traffic to the region and other parts of the world. This will certainly strengthen Europe's position in the international on-line market, and reflects the improvement of the region's network. The plurality of networks in Europe, and the consequent issues of interoperability, performance, reliability, and functional characteristics, constitute one weak point for the region in this emerging market. Attempts at mobilising synchronous applications for education across national boundaries in Europe have shown the additional difficulties that stem from differences in the existing telecommunications networks (Müller *et al.* 1996).

The first Internet backbone link between Europe and Asia is also on the horizon. In a recent alliance, EUNet (NL) and Asia Internet Holding Co. Ltd (Japan) agreed to establish direct connection between their regional networks and 'jointly develop new products and resell each other's Internet services' (Evagora 1997b). On-line connection with other regions, e.g., Latin America, which have strong historical, cultural, and trade links with Europe, is yet to be on the European agenda, but consumers in that part of the world are likely to welcome the wider choice that European on-line products will bring to the market. The time has come for Europe to consider seriously contributing to the on-line content the international community will be willing to access. On-line education and tele-training could be part of this effort, delivered by a combination of not-for-profit and commercial means.

If infrastructure capacity is improving within the developed world, there is much still to be done in developing countries to allow them to participate in the on-line education market. The development of radio transmission, compression techniques, and satellite communications technologies has removed most obstacles for many in the developing world to access on-line distant sources of knowledge. There are now many options for upgrading the telecommunications infrastructure and circumventing some obstacles of expansion of access through fixed lines. The question that remains – and which is not trivial – is economic, not strictly technological.

World aggregate data on information and communications technology (ICT) diffusion, shown in Table 9.3, indicates the relatively 'parochial' character of the information society and the broader limits of the emerging on-line education market. Telephone line, personal computer, and Internet access, the fundamental components of on-line education, are rare commodities in all but the higher-income countries.

The wider penetration of television sets in households of middle- and lower-income countries makes for a much more powerful communications infrastructure, which, however, is far from allowing interactivity. If the major aim of technology choice for education in developing countries is outreach and economies of scale rather than individualised access and interactivity (Hancock 1993), the level of development of their infrastructures would point to a more systematic and innovative use of mass communications. The penetration of the television network in these countries may be conducive to the development of cable television, at least in the larger urban areas, and may eventually create the option of a cable-based on-line network. Broadcasting of educational programmes on tele-

Table 9.3 Indicators of ICT penetration, 1995

	Low-income countries	Lower middle-income countries	Upper middle-income countries	High-income countries	World
TV receivers (per 100 inhabitants)	12.9	20.4	26.1	61.2	22.8
TV households (% of total households)	47	71	87	90	66
Telephone lines (per 100 inhabitants)	2.0	9.1	14.5	53.2	12.1
Estimated PC (per 100 inhabitants)	0.2	1.1	3.3	20.5	4.2
Estimated users of Internet (per 1 million inhabitants)	17.2	811.6	3,757.5	24,679.5	4,833.8

Source: ITU, *World Telecommunication Development Report 1996/97.*

vision or radio has been a less sophisticated use of television for mass education, which has produced some degree of success as a supporting medium for distance education in many of these countries. Television broadcast is still considered by educational authorities as an alternative for delivery of some levels of education. Recorded programmes on video-cassettes for distance and classroom education offer bright prospects as a massive innovation to education.

Presently, on-line education cannot be taken as a serious technological alternative to mass education anywhere, but particularly in the developing world. It is emerging in industrialised countries as a delivery mode in post-secondary education and very specialised technical training, and is likely to remain so at least until universalisation of access to infrastructure allows it to become an alternative delivery mode of education at other levels. The trajectory of on-line classroom applications can be illustrative in this respect. Having started within small circles of highly specialised research in the late 1960s and early 1970s, such applications soon diffused to post-secondary education in the 1980s and spread out quickly to secondary and primary schools in Europe as well as in other industrialised regions in the early 1990s. Similarly, but with some years lag, on-line classroom applications were introduced in many upper-middle income countries and are now penetrating the educational structure into the upper and lower secondary schools of some developing countries. In some middle- and upper-middle income countries of Latin America and Africa it is already possible to develop on-line cooperating projects with secondary schools in the US, Canada, or Europe. Projects such as 'SchoolNet' in Thailand,[14] 'Smart Schools' in Malaysia, 'Enlaces' (Chile), and 'Escola do Futuro' (School of the Future)[15] in Brazil illustrate the eagerness with which developing countries are willing to explore the educational possibilities of electronic networking and on-line classroom applications (Bastos 1997).

All this effort requires and at the same time justifies investments in telecommunications infrastructure. World telecommunications trade figures, shown in Table 9.4, illustrate the intensity of middle- and lower-income countries' push to overcome deficiencies in their telecommunications infrastructure and to become agents in the world telecommunications market.

Industrialised countries have a long-established telecommunications infrastructure and the average income levels required for massive and quick updating of this infrastructure to the level that is necessary for advanced telematics services. Telecommunications imports from these richer economies have obviously grown at lower rates than in the developing world, where infrastructure has to be built almost from scratch. The rate of growth of imports in low-income developing countries was more than one-and-a-half times larger than the world figure between 1990 and 1995. China accounts for practically all of this growth. The Republic of Korea,

Table 9.4 Telecommunications equipment imports and exports, 1990–95 (US$ millions)

Group of countries (GNP/capita)	Imports					Exports				
	1990	% of total	1995	% of total	Average growth (1990–95)	1990	% of total	1995	Average growth (1990–95)	% of total
Low-income countries (US$725 or less)	1,137.6	4.8	4,606.1	7.6	32.5	142.9	0.6	1,747.2	65.0	3.1
Lower middle-income countries (US$726 to $2,895)	1,714.5	7.2	5,336.4	8.8	25.2	374.7	1.6	1,233.3	24.8	2.2
Upper middle-income countries (US$2,896 to $8,955)	1,992.5	8.4	6,727.1	11.2	22.9	1,366.0	5.7	4,469.3	25.8	7.9
High-income countries (US$8,956 and over)	18,834.9	79.5	43,626.8	72.4	18.3	21,961.1	92.1	48,904.2	17.4	86.8
World	23,679.6	99.9	60,296.4	100.0	20.1	23,844.7	100.0	56,354.1	18.7	100.0

Source: ITU, *World Telecommunication Development Report 1996/97.*

Malaysia, Mexico, Brazil, and South Africa were responsible for the largest rates of growth of telecommunications imports by middle-income countries. Some of these countries have also become significant tele-communications equipment exporters, and will benefit from the increase of world investments in telecommunications infrastructure.

High-income economies, which are also at the centre of the information revolution, have the means and the incentives to become the core of the emerging on-line education market. Compared to this core, the segment of the market constituted by developing economies may be small and constrained by lower average income levels. However, the telecom-munications infrastructure, which has been practically non-existent in these countries, is now being provided at the highest levels of tech-nological development. Many of these countries are leapfrogging from practically no telecommunications to digital exchanges, satellite trans-mission, and mobile communications. With the infrastructure in place, their educational demands and achievements may well position them as participants in the emerging on-line education market. On the other hand, the prospect of access to international opportunities of on-line education and training (accreditation issues apart) is one additional incentive for modernisation of their telecommunications infrastructure.

Concluding remarks: prospects for Europe's new trading lines with developing countries

On-line education is still a non-issue for the majority of developing countries. Some of them are presently considering the utility of on-line classroom applications or even the more general need to introduce computers into education (Bastos 1996). Local debate on such innovations reflects to some extent an older discussion about distance education *vis-à-vis* conventional education. On-line education is likely to find easier acceptance within countries with some tradition of post-secondary distance education. In those countries where distance education is absent or does not confer social status, on-line education may provoke strong resistance within the conventional education system, but may help confer higher social status to distance learners.

Infrastructure conditions for on-line education and for on-line classroom applications are likely to be too restrictive for many low-income developing countries. The potential on-line education market would be restricted to the economic and political elites of these countries, who have access to the best infrastructure there is in their countries, but who also have wide opportunities for on-campus education abroad. Middle- and upper-middle income countries are investing in their telecommunications infrastructure and thus expanding the conditions of connectivity to a larger, but still privileged, part of their population. They may offer better prospects for the emergence of a demand for European on-line education.

There is a positive feedback link between the development of tele-communications infrastructure and economic incentives for the emerging on-line education market. The market can only emerge and prosper with the precondition of an adequate telecommunications infrastructure; the more disseminated on-line education becomes and the higher its demands for bandwidth are, the more they generate market incentives for upgrading the telecommunications infrastructure. Expansion of the European on-line education market can thus contribute to the development of Europe's telecommunications infrastructure, which is one weak point of the region in international competition (EITO 1996). It can likewise indirectly stimulate the development of infrastructure in those developing countries, which will thus have a wider choice of content to tap into in the process of upgrading the general education and vocational skills of their population.

Another condition of effective demand is the language in which on-line education is offered. English is the 'lingua franca' of the on-line world. Presently this is as much an expression of the concentration of content in the US as a requirement for global communications. A stronger European presence in the on-line market will be decisive in widening the spectrum of on-line content to other cultural and linguistic settings. On-line courses offered in English certainly have a wide market, but on-line offerings in French, German, and Spanish will certainly cater to the needs of a broad spectrum of on-line learners. They will also diversify channels for international expression of the rich content of other cultures and societies. From this point of view, a stronger European presence will be one step forward in the globalisation of content of the still parochial on-line world.

The major educational demand in developing countries, mass basic education, cannot be served by on-line education. However, even in this case European on-line education can make an indirect contribution by providing a flexible alternative for some level of pre-service and in-service teacher training, and for the preparation of specialists in distance education. European on-line education will also increase and diversify options of post-secondary education, advanced professional specialisation, and high-level vocational training. Countries where there is a potential market for European on-line education also have fully developed conventional education systems. A careful selection of niches in the offerings of graduate and undergraduate courses, to be filled in by on-line education, would prevent the creation of unnecessary areas of friction with the educational establishment. Partnership between European on-line education institutions and local conventional education ones should be explored for pedagogical support to on-line learners, the logistics of some form of examination, and political and institutional support. Governments in developing countries have an important 'steering' role to play in balancing supply and demand factors in the on-line commerce of education services by promoting partnerships and finding innovative institutional arrangements for certification of on-line credits and degrees, accreditation of on-line education providers, and rating of on-line educational classroom applications.

Governments and professionals of middle-income developing countries are convinced of the need to introduce computers in education, but many are still doubtful in relation to on-line classroom applications and others reject up-front the idea of on-line education. The most well-organised and apparently knowledgeable pressure group in favour of the wider use of on-line classroom applications in developing countries consists of computer scientists in higher education and some educators willing to extend to their schools the same on-line facilities they have been used to in their graduate (or undergraduate) courses. Publishers, broadcasters, service providers, and telecommunications operators in developing countries constitute new and stronger pressure groups for integration of on-line classroom applications. International development agencies play a relevant role now as they did in the past with other technological experiments for education in developing countries. In these countries as well as in the industrialised world, a tension between pedagogical and commercial priorities creates a line of conflict separating educators, scholars, and librarians on one side and tele-communications operators and publishers on the other. On-line education in some countries is likely to deepen these lines of friction. A difficult political challenge to governments is to arbitrate the conflict and promote the establishment of partnerships for the benefit of the many.

What is at stake now for the less-favoured regions of Europe and many developing countries is not whether they should or should not seek integration of on-line applications to education and training, but how to pursue it, with what scope and at what pace. The risks of pushing forward in the information society are high for many developing countries, but the risks of staying behind are certainly higher. Some fear that, in regard to advanced on-line applications, developing regions are once more having to discover a use for the latest gadget advanced countries want to sell. 'I have a bridge; where is the river?' would have said the engineer visiting a developing country in earlier days (Murphy 1993). Now, the engineer would have been replaced by the telecommunications provider or the satellite company and computer manufacturer who, with on-line applications in hand, look for markets in developing countries.

Less favoured regions of Europe and middle-income developing countries certainly have their own priorities in the process of building their learning economies and integrating them into the global, information-richer society. They may perhaps aim at first building their community and regional information roads instead of information superhighways (Theobald 1996). In fact, these internal information roads may constitute a precondition for the effective integration of superhighways. If this is so, on-line classroom applications and on-line education will help them develop the required infrastructure.

Again, as they might have wished to do in the past with iron, they will have to decide when and where to place the electronic bridges. The issue, then, is to be aware of what the local needs and lines of desired development are, what options are available, and then make the decision that makes the best use of the human and financial resources. The size and structure of the market for on-line education in developing countries and Europe's share in it will depend on definitions made within the developing world as to what are their own needs and what they wish and can do about investment in infrastructure. The dynamic element on all this points to a continuous challenge to planners of content, services and infrastructure.

Notes

1 Studies in the economics of knowledge and information introduced in the 1960s the statistical construct of 'knowledge industries', comprising education, communications media, information machines, information services, and other information activities. The same activities have been called, since the late 1970s, primary information sectors because they participate directly in the information market. Information activities that take place as part of the manufacturing process for non-information products have been referred to as 'secondary' information sectors (Foray and Lundvall 1996).

2 The development of computer graphics capabilities and compression techniques have widened the use of image and sound for codifying knowledge. Moving image, sound, and text in CD-ROM have been for some time now an important medium for education and training. Recent developments of digital video disks (DVD), either in DVD-ROM or DVD-Video versions, promise a revolution in the quality of production and reproduction of simultaneous moving image, text, and sound information, but will require computers with high-performance graphics and power to display in full the accuracy of motion and quality video, and a high-bandwidth telecommunications infrastructure for eventual delivery on-line.

3 http://cszw.open.ac.uk/zx

4 http://www.et-online.fernuni-hagen.de/

5 http://www.fernuni-hagen.de/feuvus-f.html

6 http://www.to.utwente.nl/masters/mscgen.htm

7 One such initiative is the Magellan University, which uses video and on-line interaction for learning. It offers non-credit courses, mainly in Calculus and Differential Equations, as well as library and student union services for a flat rate of US$14.95 per month, which would save Magellan-registered students a total of US$165 to US$190 if they were to pay for the services without registering. Magellan plans to offer credit courses in the spring of 1998 and two complete BA degrees, one in Business (majors in General Business and International Business Management) and the other in Liberal Arts (major in History and Culture). See: http://magellan.edu

8 http://www.ola.bc.ca

9 Other universities offering on-line education in the US include: Carnegie

Mellon University (http://www.gsia.cmu.edu); Michigan State University (http://www.msu.edu); New School for Social Research, New York (http://www.dialnsa.edu); California State University at Dominguez Hills (http://www.csudh.edu/dominguezonline); Indiana University System (http://www.extend.indiana.edu); National Technological University (http://www.ntu.edu); New York Institute of Technology (http://www.nyit.edu/olc); Nova Southeastern University (http://www.nova.edu); University of Colorado (http://www.jec.edu); University of Maryland University College (http://umuc.edu); and Washington State University (http://www.eus.wsu.edu/edp). The original list was compiled by Ashlea Ebeling and Scott Bistayi (Gubernick and Ebeling 1997).

10 http://www.fuqua.duke.edu/programs/gemba
11 University of Phoenix Online Campus (http://www.ouphx.edu/online).
12 Education Network of Maine (http://www.enm.maine.edu).
13 Mbit/s (million bits per second); Gbit/s (billion bits per second). Lower bandwidth is measured in Kbit/s (thousand bits per second).
14 See http://k12.nectec.or.th
15 See http://www.futuro.usp.br

References

Barchechath, E. (1996) 'What Change for Teachers?', paper presented to the conference *Lifelong Learning for the Information Society*, Genoa, 24–28 March.

Bastos, M.-I. (1997) 'The World Market for Telematics Applications to Education: Challenges and Opportunities for Industrialised and Developing Countries', Discussion Paper #9705, Maastricht: UNU/INTECH.

Bastos, M.-I. (1996) 'Learning with Telematics: Opportunities and Challenges to Students, Teaching Institutions, Enterprises, and Governments', paper prepared for the International Workshop *Europe and the Developing World in the Globalised Information Society: Employment, Education and Trade Implications*, Maastricht, 17–19 October.

Delors, J. (1996) *Learning: The Treasure Within*. Report to UNESCO of the International Commission on Education for the Twenty-first Century, Paris: UNESCO.

EITO (1996) *European Information Technology Observatory 1996*. Frankfurt/Main, Germany: EITO.

Evagora, A. (1997a) 'World Wide Weight', *tele.com*, September. [http://www.teledotcom/0997/features/tdc0997globe]

Evagora, A. (1997b) 'Un-American Activities', *tele.com*, September. [http://www.teledotcom/0997/features/tdc0997globe]

Foray, D. and Lundvall, B.-Å. (1996) 'The Knowledge-based Economy: From the Economics of Knowledge to the Learning Economy', in *Employment and Growth in the Knowledge-based Economy*, Paris: OECD.

Gordon, J. (1997) 'Infonuggets. The Bite-sized Future of Corporate Training?', *Training Magazine*, July. [http://www.lakewoodpub.com/trg/trgcvrst.html]

Gubernick, L. and Ebeling, A. (1997) 'I Got My Degree through E-mail', *Forbes*, 19 June.

Hancock, A. (1993) *Contemporary Information and Communication Technologies in Education*, Paris: UNESCO.

ITU (1997) *World Telecommunication Development Report 1996/1997*, Geneva: International Telecommunication Union.

ITU and TeleGeography, Inc. (1996) *Direction of Traffic – Trends in International Telephone Tariffs*, Geneva: International Telecommunication Union.

Lasfargue, Y. (1996) 'The Evolution of Industrial Professions in the Information Society: How Can Outcasting Be Avoided?', paper presented to the conference *Lifelong Learning for the Information Society*, Genoa, 24–28 March.

Lundvall, B.-Å. (1997) 'Development Strategies in the Learning Economy', paper presented at the *International Symposium on Innovation and Competitiveness in Newly Industrializing Economies*, Seoul, 26–27 May.

Mulgan, G. (1996) 'Lifelong Learning for the Information Society', paper presented to the conference *Lifelong Learning for the Information Society*, Genoa, 24–28 March.

Müller, K., Lekkou, M. and Weydandt, D. (1996) 'CNCplus – A Multimedia Distance Learning Project bringing Universities and Production Together', paper prepared for the *IEEE Fifth Workshop on Enabling Technologies: Infrastructure for Collaborative Enterprises*, Stanford, CA, 19–21 June.

Murphy, P. (1993) *Education and Development: The Contribution of Distance Education*, Lisbon: ICDE Standing Conference of Presidents.

Rajan, A. (1996) 'New Skills for the New Age Service Organisation', paper presented to the conference *Lifelong Learning for the Information Society*, Genoa, 24–28 March.

Theobald, R. (1996) 'Who Said We Wanted an Information Superhighway?', *Internet Research: Electronic Networking Applications and Policy*, 6, 2/3: 90–92.

Veen, W. (1996) 'Telematics Experiences in European Classrooms: Overview and Evaluation', *Open Praxis*, 1: 7–11.

World Development Report 1997, New York: Oxford University Press for the World Bank.

10

LIFELONG LEARNING POLICIES IN A NEW TECHNOLOGICAL ERA

Albert Tuijnman

Introduction

This chapter reviews the trends and developments that have made lifelong learning a high priority on the policy agendas of governments worldwide. A broad international perspective is taken, with a focus on Organisation for Economic Co-operation and Development (OECD) member countries. First, changes in the technological, economic, and social environment that have increased the premium on adult competencies and skills are reviewed. Second, some of the interfaces between the education and training system and the emerging knowledge economy are described. Third, the case for making lifelong learning a reality for all is presented, in particular as it relates to new technologies. Turning to issues of implementation, the chapter then focuses on three aspects: the foundations for lifelong learning; the role of new learning technologies; and issues in the financing of a coherent framework for lifelong learning. The views expressed in this chapter are those of the author and do not necessarily reflect those of OECD or its member countries.

The technological, economic, and social environment

Adult education and training have become central to the strategic agendas of governments, enterprises, and trade unions. The reason for this is the realisation, now widespread, that countries are confronted by the challenge of managing a fundamental adjustment in the forces and factors of production, brought about by the ongoing shift from an industrial to a post-industrial or knowledge economy.

Vast economic changes have been under way since the mid-1980s, and the social landscape is being altered accordingly, propelled by developments such as the rapid penetration of interconnected information and communications technologies, the deregulation of markets and financial services, the elimination of certain barriers to cross-national trade, and the globalisation and relocation of manufacturing and services. These changes intersect with other factors, such as ageing populations, emerging post-modern values, new attitudes to family, work, and leisure, and rising anxieties over wealth creation and its distribution within and between countries. The new techno-economic situation brings opportunities, but poses numerous dilemmas as well. Uncertainty about the future looms large.

The best way of meeting the challenge of uncertainty is to strengthen the capacity of labour markets, enterprises, and individuals to adjust to change, improve productivity, and capitalise on technological innovation (OECD 1994). Flexibility is the watchword. This depends on many factors – macro-economic, structural, and social – but the capacity to adapt to technological innovation and exploit new opportunities depends first and foremost on the knowledge, skills, and competencies of the adult popula-tion. A sufficiently developed foundation of essential knowledge and skills is a prerequisite for promoting a high-skill, high-wage route to job creation and economic growth.

The emerging knowledge economy accommodates a modest but growing share of the workforce in most OECD countries (Colecchia and Papacon-stantinou 1996). Trend data from the early 1980s to the 1990s show that, in the OECD area overall, employment grew fastest in high-skilled jobs, and grew slowest – or declined – in low-skilled jobs. The upskilling trend is more apparent in manufacturing than in services, while overall the shift to higher-skilled jobs has occurred primarily within industries, rather than between them. Technology is a prime factor behind the changes in the skill mix of labour markets: upskilling has occurred fastest in labour market sectors with higher than average reliance on new information technologies and higher than average expenditures on research and development.

In the new technological era, it is expected that the demand for low-skill workers will be reduced and the demand for high-skill workers increased. This is in part because more highly skilled workers can adapt more easily to new technologies. Another factor is that the skill requirements for many professional, technical, and administrative jobs have risen as a direct con-sequence of the digital revolution. Computer technologies, in particular, have made firms want to recruit more highly skilled workers, because such technologies raise the productivity of highly skilled workers more than low-skill workers. Thus, as labour markets change and firms adjust to the new technological era, many workers are in a position to do well, but others face an increased risk of redundancy or delegation from the core to the periphery of the labour market. While certain, mainly low-skill jobs are made obsolete, new ones are created. These new jobs tend to require more highly skilled people to fill them. With participative, just-in-time, and total quality management strategies, and as work environments themselves become more complex and ill-defined, more is obviously expected of the employed workforce.

The pressure on poorly trained workers on the periphery – especially the unemployed – is mounting likewise. Whereas occupational change opens up new opportunities for literate and skilled individuals, this is not true for those who lack the appropriate skills necessary for work. Poorly trained workers who find it difficult to adapt to new conditions and labour market demands face an increased risk of unemployment and alienation.

The role of education and training in the knowledge economy

Levels of educational attainment in the adult population correlate with the labour force participation rates of both men and women. Education also enhances an individual's position in the labour market: those with less schooling are much more likely to be caught in jobs characterised by frequent turnover, low wages, and high unemployment than better educated workers (OECD 1995). However, the relationship between educational attainment and unemployment is not linear, because the largest difference in experience is usually found between the least-educated and all other groups (OECD 1996a). The risk of unemployment is especially high for young school-leavers; educational attainment conditions that risk. In all OECD countries, individuals without an upper secondary qualification have the highest rates of unemployment. That risk has grown markedly since the late 1970s, concomitant with the rise of the minimum threshold of skills and competencies required in the labour market. Finally, educational attainment is also closely related to earnings from work. Whereas earnings differentials by attainment levels vary in size and in the degree to which they have changed over the past decade, there is a clear tendency in many countries for mean earnings differences to widen persistently from the more to the lesser educationally qualified workers (OECD 1996b). For all of these reasons, a well-educated and trained labour force is crucial to social and economic wellbeing. Developing education and training systems and improving labour force qualifications should be major features of a country's long-term strategic agenda.

Policy problems are encountered, however, because the technology-driven changes that accompany the shift to the global knowledge economy are so profound that national governments can no longer rely on the same range of policy instruments they traditionally used to regulate trade and intervene in human capital formation processes in the industrial welfare state. The new technological era necessitates a new approach not only to trade, monetary, and fiscal policies but also to social and educational policies. The establishment of the World Trade Organisation, the planned

European Monetary Union, and the current discussion about the desirability of creating an Asian Monetary Fund are examples of policy responses at the macro-economic level. The sweeping social and welfare reforms under way in a number of OECD countries are additional indicators of the extent to which the social policy landscape has been altered by globalisation.

Education policy is obviously affected by the new conditions. For example, the policy of gradually expanding enrolments and improving the quality of initial formal education to meet the demand for new skills and competencies generated by the economy, which was common to all industrialised countries, will be found wanting in the new technological era, because of the time lag involved in raising skill levels. In the new scenario in which global capital flows swiftly to places where risks are average but profits high, national governments have fewer intervention options to choose from. What they can and should do, however, is to facilitate and improve the adjustment capacity of all economic actors. There are several ways of doing this (see OECD 1994). Promoting labour market flexibility and improving the knowledge, skills, and competencies of the labour force, as part of a broader strategy for realising lifelong learning for all, are central to all of them (OECD 1996c).

The case for lifelong learning

The education system has always served a variety of social and economic objectives, but their scope and relative importance change with time. The question now is whether the sector is equipped to meet the new demands placed upon it, and whether it can lead, rather than follow, the march into the twenty-first century. This section examines the goals and objectives of education and training systems, argues that a lifelong learning approach provides an appropriate framework for pursuing them, and raises a set of policy issues that deserve urgent consideration.

The goals and objectives for education and training systems include: contributing to personal development and fulfilment; maintaining social cohesion; strengthening democratic traditions and other values; and meeting the requirements of the workplace, leading to higher productivity and economic growth. These objectives are clearly interconnected.

All OECD societies are experiencing an increasing demand for learning opportunities that lead to personal development and the realisation of individual potential. This can be inferred from the increasing participation rates for tertiary and general adult education, and for leisure programmes for older people. Individual expectations are rising, influenced, in part, by the opportunities opened up by the new information and communications technologies, by increases in the standard of living over long periods of time, and by the frequent changes of skills and competencies demanded at work. As populations age and leisure time increases for a large number of people, new and varied demands for personal fulfilment are likely to emerge. Information technologies will have a large role to play in satisfying these demands because they can offer a means of opening up and widening access to learning opportunities that are 'just-in-time', cost-effective, and adaptable to individual needs and interests.

The new demand for learning opportunities by an increasing number of individuals is clearly linked to the social objectives of a pluralistic society that aims to maintain social cohesion. Education has always played a key role in fostering democracy; wider access to learning can play a similar role in strengthening it. Where access to education and training opportunities is restricted to certain groups, the result will be a stratified society, lacking in social cohesion. In the new techno-economic situation, access to learning opportunities is increasingly tied in with the world of work. Since the early 1980s, while the absolute number of participants in general and leisure-related adult education has increased, the share of employer-sponsored and job-related education and training in total provision has increased even more. In 1994, in all six countries for which such data are available (Canada, the Netherlands, Poland, Sweden, Switzerland, and the US), job-related adult education has become more important in terms of the number of people involved and expenditures incurred than general or leisure-related adult education (Bélanger and Tuijnman 1997).

This reinforces the risk, already evident in the social distribution of information technology access and use, that certain groups will be excluded from the emerging learning societies. For the labour force in general, evidence collected in a large international survey of adult literacy proficiency shows that many adults – in some countries up to one-third of the total adult population – perform at either low or intermediate levels, suggesting that they encounter skill deficiencies in daily activities and at work (OECD and Statistics Canada 1995). This points to a large need for adult basic education. Yet workers in manual occupations receive less training than those in non-manual occupations, and professional, managerial, and technical workers receive much more training than clerical and production workers. It is also clear that there is considerable variation across labour market sectors and enterprises of different size, with small and medium-size firms spending at best half as much on training as larger ones. Moreover, the likelihood of participating in employer-sponsored training is directly related to the level of educational attainment, so that those who already have a good initial education tend to be those who benefit most from available learning opportunities.

There is thus a strong complementarity between the personal and social objectives of education and training and the acquisition of skills and competencies needed for the world of work. Only a well-educated and trained population can provide the labour force required for flexible enterprises.

Appropriate matching of worker skills and job requirements is essential for improving productivity and the rate of economic growth. The problem is that the demand for skills and competencies is evolving more rapidly than ever before. Changes in management practices and work organisation, and the twin processes of globalisation and technological innovation, are contributing to changes in the skills profiles required for many jobs. The thrust is not only for a higher level of skill generally, but for different types of skill. As skills become obsolete more rapidly than previously, once-for-all careers will become less and less the norm. Changing conditions thus necessitate a fundamental response in education policy: a shift from the industrial model of mass initial schooling to a post-industrial framework of individual learning pathways across the entire life-span. But government authorities are likely to remain more concerned with the quality of the foundations for lifelong learning than with the development of learning and training markets for adults.

The foundations for lifelong learning

In the perspective of lifelong learning, the foundations assume new importance and meaning, since they are the basis for developing the ability and motivation to learn throughout life. There are several areas of weakness, of which four are particularly noteworthy. First, there are important gaps in the provision of educational services for young children and for those adults who have missed out on their initial schooling. Second, the school organisation, curricula, and teaching and assessment practices are not as conducive as they might be to engaging all students in a broadly-based, full cycle of secondary education. Third, there remains a divide between general and vocational education and the esteem in which each is held. Finally, there are questions about how new technologies are introduced and applied in schools.

Current conditions suggest that the first task is to fill the participation gaps in formal schooling, both quantitatively and qualitatively, for all age groups. Enrolment of young children in pre-school education is presently low in many countries. Enrolment rates continue to rise in Europe, Oceania, and North America, but in some countries the rates are stable at comparatively low levels. For young children in particular, the participation rates are patchy in a number of countries. While there is some controversy as to the appropriate participation rate and age to aim for, a consensus is emerging that the provision for young children should be expanded. In secondary education, retention is still not universal in OECD countries. Another gap is evident for those adults who did not manage to achieve a solid foundation for lifelong learning in their early years. In a majority of countries over half the population aged 25–64 has reached that level, but in some European countries over half the labour force has received little education beyond primary schooling. There also exist large differences between the educational attainments of men and women in several countries.

Important gaps in provision make the process of transition from education to work difficult for several groups. For the young, early school leaving, defined as failing to complete upper secondary education or leaving without a vocational qualification, remains a serious problem. There is a high risk of unemployment for the least qualified, and the disadvantage in earnings becomes cumulative over the life-cycle – with implications for tax revenue forgone. Failure occurs for a number of reasons. Perhaps the school itself is unattractive, lacking a favourable learning ethos. Students may consider schooling irrelevant, may not be motivated, may have been wrongly selected, may experience language difficulties, or achieve little success. Social factors ranging from poverty to poor housing may contribute. Measures to alleviate the problem of early school leaving have included educational guidance and career counselling, diversifying upper secondary options and curricula, giving special help to slow learners, and enlisting a partnership of parents and industry, but problems remain (OECD 1997). Rigidity and lack of attention to individual needs and interests are prime concerns, and it is by addressing these that new learning technologies may offer a means to help break the cycle.

New technologies and lifelong learning

Inherited structures and the organisation of pathways through them vary considerably across countries. A flexible and interconnected framework of learning pathways facilitates the acquisition of new skills and competencies and can help to improve the match of people and jobs. As learning is undertaken increasingly in combination with other activities, such as work, family, and leisure, fulfilment in life will depend critically on the linkages permitted by the arrangements for education and training, as well as on the organisation of labour markets, enterprises, and social and private arrangements, including educational and career guidance.

Closed and unconnected programmes create inefficiency in the system and cause frustration for the individual. Open-ended and interconnected learning pathways, in contrast, invite learners to progress from one type and level of education and training to another, and to move back and forth between, or to combine, learning and work activities. Building a framework that allows for individual switching and stacking of learning pathways will require much in the way of capitalising on the role of new technologies in improving the supply of information about available learning opportunities, improving access and facilitating recruitment, encouraging individualised, 'just-in-time' instruction, building connectivity through programme moduling, and improving the efficiency and quality of learning, for example by means of using advanced, iterative testing and assessment technologies that match instruction programmes to individual learning needs and interests.

New information and communications technologies are linked intricately with the demand, supply, and process of lifelong learning (OECD 1996e; OECD 1996f). First, as was seen in a previous section, such technologies have greatly stimulated and amplified the *need* for lifelong learning. In many jobs, and increasingly in everyday life, citizens require the knowledge, skills, and tools to cope with the complexity of information technologies. Lacking that capacity for many people will mean social exclusion and alienation from both the new techno-economic environment and the learning society. Second, and also suggested above, information and communications technologies might offer a *means* for realising a cost-effective supply of learning opportunities across the individual life-span. Finally, the new technologies exert a major influence on the *content* of much education and learning, as well as on the applied methods of instruction, evaluation, and assessment.

New technologies for learning place an emphasis on the role of the individual. All three issues mentioned above – demand, supply, and the learning process that connects the two – focus attention on the individual's motivation and capacity to learn. For in order to use technologies effectively, prerequisite knowledge, competencies, and skills are often needed. It is for this reason that such technologies may hold more promise for adult education and training than for the foundation learning that goes on in schools.

The role of new technologies in lifelong learning is potentially enormous. But whether this potential can be realised depends on a number of factors. First and foremost, there is the need for a stable technological basis that is widespread, easily accessible, and flexible in use. Access to and use of lifelong learning opportunities depend to an extent on access to information and communications technologies and the prerequisite knowledge and skills to use those technologies. If there is unequal access to such technologies along social or cultural gradients – as is currently the case in all OECD countries – then lifelong learning risks not being for all, but for the already privileged. It will then serve to deepen the already existing disparities in, *inter alia,* life chances, employment opportunities, and income between the knowledge 'haves' and 'have-nots'. Thus technologies and lifelong learning can become the twin driving forces determining who is included in and who excluded from the new techno-economic system.

It is in order to prevent this scenario from happening countries pursuing a strategy for making lifelong learning a reality *for all* will need to pursue simultaneously a strategy for making the information technology infrastructure more widely accessible. This will, no doubt, mean policy intervention not only in the markets for education and lifelong learning but also in those for information technologies. Whether policy intervention in technology and learning markets will be successful in turn hinges on the distribution of the public and private costs and benefits that accrue to both learning and technology.

Financing an expanded vision of learning for all

The contribution of education and training to productivity and economic growth is well documented, and can be expected to increase as the knowledge-base of society rises. There is evidence of a positive and robust correlation between economic growth rates and educational attainment, especially secondary completion. At the level of enterprise, as well, there is evidence to suggest that skills and competencies – and efforts to augment them – improve productivity (OECD 1997). Increased economic dividends thus made available can potentially be used to pursue policies for making learning technologies more widely available, and thus to improve the quality and cost-effectiveness of lifelong learning. Investment in education and training serves to address, simultaneously, a number of social, technological, and economic objectives.

Learning in all its forms represents a substantial investment of public and private funds. As participation expands at all stages and pressures continue to mount on public budgets, however, all partners – governments, employers, individual learners, and other agents – are finding it difficult to maintain their share of the investment costs. Making lifelong learning available to all, which in turn necessitates substantial public and private investment in information and communications technologies, will obviously require additional resources. Questions that must be addressed thus are: What short-term costs are incurred by enlarging programmes of lifelong learning? How may lifelong learning be made affordable for all partners?

There are additional costs if lifelong learning policies are adopted. A part of these costs result from the expansion of early childhood, upper secondary, and tertiary education, and, by implication, the reduced number of drop-outs along the way and the increased number of adults who return. As a broad approximation, if all OECD countries are to realise the enrolment rates achieved in the best performing countries (e.g., 90 per cent for pre-primary and upper secondary education, and 25 per cent for tertiary education for 18–21-year-olds), an enrolment gap of 4 to 85 per cent of 3–6-year-olds will need to be closed in early childhood education, depending on the countries and the structures of their systems. For secondary education as a whole, the enrolment gap ranges from 1 to 12 per cent of the 14–17-year-olds. In tertiary education, Belgium and the US are already beyond the target enrolment rate of 25 per cent of all 18–21-year-olds; in other countries the gap is about 5 per cent. See OECD

(1996c) for further estimates and an explanation of the methodology used in calculating the costs of closing the enrolment gaps.

For most OECD countries, the cost of closing the enrolment gaps in formal education would be in the range of 0.25 to 1 per cent of GDP. The largest share of the increase is associated with the expansion of early childhood education, in part because the enrolment gap is so great. But the really large costs are associated with bringing all adults with low education up to an intermediate skill level, up to 4–5 per cent of GDP in countries such as Germany, the Netherlands, and Sweden. While these figures are rough estimates, they do point to the approximate volume of investment capital that will be needed.

The benefits of lifelong learning are considerable, but raise the question of cost, and in particular, of how and by whom the necessary financial resources are to be created and supplied. Present school systems pay for themselves in terms of the financial and other benefits they make possible (OECD 1996c). For tertiary education, which concerns rising numbers of young adults, this may also be the case to some extent (OECD 1997). From another perspective, the lack of access to lifelong learning in itself imposes large costs for society and the individuals concerned. One approach to finance is to base the allocation of investment costs on the distribution of social and individual rates of return. Education and training make individuals and firms more productive, as is apparent in their earnings. However, determining how the benefits of education are distributed in relation to the amounts invested by government, employers, learners, and other agents has proved to be very difficult (OECD 1996d).

Patterns in rates of return to different forms of learning and different groups of learners offer an inadequate basis for decisions about cost-sharing because the estimates fail to account fully for other factors giving rise to earnings differences, such as cognitive ability, prerequisite skills, and perseverance. Further, the rate of return estimates do not take into account certain externalities that tend to be, on balance, positive – by some estimates, as much as double the monetary returns. In the new technological era characterised by globalisation and restructuring, there appear to be growing constraints on budgets. Hence the challenge is to direct public resources toward those forms of learning and those groups of learners where the social return (including externalities realised by the society as a whole) on the public investment is the greatest. This approach would call for the targeting of public money to foundation learning and adult basic education.

A similar case can be made for increased investment of public resources in the information and communications infrastructure. As with education, however, the problem is that little is known about the precise magnitude of public and private investment, or the distribution of the economic and social returns that accrue from an investment in information and learning technologies.

It has proved difficult to generate additional resources for lifelong learning and infrastructure investment from all of the partners concerned. Lifelong learning will not constitute the most 'productive' investment for all those who participate in its financing. The mix of learning does not at present maximise returns or minimise costs. While educational training costs, like infrastructure investment, are incurred immediately, the returns are spread out over a long time. The resulting pattern of uncertain and more distant returns tends to reduce the attractiveness of investment in learning and learning-related technologies relative to other investments, which may have lower but more certain returns. There is, therefore, a need for devising appropriate incentive structures to encourage all participants to invest more. Where benefits are clearly understood and incentives are in place, the partners may be willing to shoulder larger investments for learning and skill acquisition. What has been lacking is an effective means to encourage, extend, and make full and productive use of such resources across a wide range of learning provision.

Two steps have been taken by countries to increase the cost-effectiveness of provision beyond the stage of foundation learning. One has been to discourage, via regulation or incentive, undue 'switching' and 'stacking' in tertiary education, and by capping the length of diploma and degree courses, which in some countries seems unduly high. A second step has been to introduce privatisation and 'markets' for lifelong learning. However, the reliance on market forces alone has not been sufficient to improve cost-effectiveness. There have also been experiments with a number of devices for financing lifelong learning, each of which would have different effects in terms of encouraging a pattern of lifelong learning, leveraging resources from the partners, and promoting cost-effectiveness. These include government funding, educational entitlements, vouchers, the franchise model, 'auctioning' (where institutions bid for funded students), para-fiscal funds (all employers, private and public alike, would be subject to a training levy), single-employer financing (although this restricts training so that it becomes largely vocation-specific), and self-financing through tuition fees, as already touched upon (OECD 1996c). A careful analysis of these as well as other options is required. However, it is likely that, in developing an approach to financing lifelong learning that ensures inclusiveness and complementarity, a combination of mechanisms would represent the best approach.

Conclusions

Building an inclusive learning society is a long-term goal; achieving it will take major and sustained efforts over many years. New information and communications technologies are a necessary element in any framework for lifelong learning: issues of learning demand and supply, and the learning process itself, connect the two. But whether the potential role of such technologies in lifelong learning can be fully realised depends on whether the technologies will be stable, widely and easily accessible, and flexible in use. If there is widely varying access by different social or cultural groups, then lifelong learning will not be for all, but for the already privileged. New technologies and lifelong learning can be instruments of both exclusion and inclusion in a society. In seeking to reduce the exclusive tendencies in lifelong learning and the globalised techno-economy, governments will need to be prepared to intervene, not only in the markets for education and learning but also in the markets for technology and information.

Accordingly, because of the need for market intervention, there can be no single, unified and hierarchically structured 'system' of lifelong learning infrastructure that suits all countries. Lifelong learning will need to build upon specific national and cultural heritages, and policies modified to suit particular technological, social, and economic conditions and needs. Moreover, questions about which strategic directions to aim for do not apply to the education sector or to governments alone.

Three elements will need to be taken into account. First, a 'system' of lifelong learning cannot be imposed; it must depend and thrive on a great variety of initiatives taken by different actors in many spheres of life and work. Second, the role of government is not to 'invent', manage, and pay for a 'system' of lifelong learning opportunities, but rather to monitor and steer developments and redistribute resources so that the supply of learning opportunities is equitable, flexible, efficient, and cost-effective. Third, the very nature of lifelong learning – diverse, pluralistic, and undertaken over a lifetime – calls for a convergence of policy interests among many sectors, macro-economic as well as structural. Because information and communications technologies can help in widening access, improving flexibility and efficiency, and reducing or controlling costs, decision-makers will need to reflect in particular on the connections between technology policy and education policy.

References

Bélanger, P. and Tuijnman, A. C. (1997) 'The "silent" explosion of adult learning', in Bélanger, P. and Tuijnman, A. C. (eds), *New Patterns of Adult Learning: A Six-country Comparative Study*, Oxford: Pergamon Press.

Colecchia, A. and Papaconstantinou, G. (1996) 'The evolution of skills in OECD countries and the role of technology', STI Working Papers 1996/8, Paris: OECD.

OECD (1994) *The OECD Jobs Study: Facts, Analyses, Strategies*, Paris: OECD.

OECD (1995) *Employment Outlook, June 1995*, Paris: OECD.

OECD (1996a) *Education at a Glance: Indicators. 1996 Edition*, Paris: OECD.

OECD (1996b) *Employment Outlook, June 1996*, Paris: OECD.

OECD (1996c) *Lifelong Learning for All: Meeting of the Education Committee at Ministerial Level, 16–17 January 1996*, Paris: OECD.

OECD (1996d) *Measuring What People Know: Human Capital Accounting for the Knowledge Economy*, Paris: OECD.

OECD (1996e) *Adult Learning in a New Technological Era*, Paris: OECD.

OECD (1996f) *Adult Learning and Technology in OECD Countries,* Paris: OECD.

OECD (1997) *Education Policy Analysis*, Paris: OECD.

OECD and Statistics Canada (1995) *Literacy, Economy, and Society: Results of the First International Adult Literacy Survey*, Paris: Organisation for Economic Co-operation and Development, and Ottawa: Minister of Industry.

11

A non-European counterpoint

PRODUCTIVE TWO-WAY COLLABORATION BETWEEN TECHNOLOGICALLY DEVELOPED AND DEVELOPING COUNTRIES IN NEW TECHNOLOGIES FOR EDUCATION

Peter E. Kinyanjui

While modern information and communications technologies (ICTs) pose a number of challenges and constraints for developing countries, they also open up many opportunities for meaningful and productive collaboration between the technologically developed and the developing countries or regions. But this will not happen automatically or as a matter of natural process. It will call for careful planning, purposeful implementation, and systematic evaluation at every stage in the process. Indeed, there will have to be demonstrable benefits to be derived from any technological venture involving two or more partners, and, needless to say, the benefits will have to be mutual and complementary. The traditional view of media and technologies flowing in one direction is no longer tenable in the context of a 'borderless' educational environment offering new learning opportunities.

It is imperative that developing countries should move in the direction of modern information and communication technologies. They cannot afford not to experiment with new media and technologies. By borrowing from the experiences of industrially developed countries, developing countries will be able to tap the potential of information and communications technologies, applying them in modified forms to suit their own needs and circumstances. One of the difficulties in attempting to develop ICT is knowing where to start. There is one cardinal rule to follow: start where the chances of success are best. We need to identify and develop the key growth areas in ICT in any particular country or region, the 'critical points in growth' (Culpin 1996). We also need to train a critical mass of people with specific competencies to be able to make a difference in ICT. If developing countries are to be able to leap-frog technologies, we must start with the human capital and develop it. The biggest comparative advantage for any country is the quality of its people and their skills.

Developing countries might even find viable short-cuts in solving their human resource development problems and constraints. To this end, international collaboration is critical for the stabilisation and revitalisation of education and training. In order to make the best choices, people must be made aware of the implications and costs of the various alternatives. We must establish viable and affordable short-cuts for developing countries to follow in adopting and adapting ICT. One alternative might be found in the provision of hybrid ICTs, ranging from the simple to the complex, from the modest to the sophisticated. But time is not on our side, and action is needed now. There is an old African story, well told by Jeffrey Sachs, the Director of the Harvard Institute for International Development:

> A peasant farmer goes to the priest for advice on how to save his dying chickens. The priest recommends prayer, but the chickens continue to die. The priest then recommends music for the chicken coop, but the deaths continue unabated. Pondering again, the priest recommends painting the chicken coop in bright colours. Finally all the chickens die. 'What a shame', the priest tells the peasant. 'I had so many more good ideas!'

Modern technologies can enable, and indeed accelerate, human resource development by helping to increase access to, and improving the quality and range of, basic education, vocational and technical training, and associated job creation opportunities, which are possible only through well-developed infrastructures and services. I envisage in the new millennium the establishment of an integrated system of linked national, regional, and local learning centres and resource databases to support open learning and distance education. Such a network would ensure that teaching and learning systems are effectively implemented, and that the learners will have easy and affordable access to the necessary support services. In the words of the Expert Group on Commonwealth Cooperation in Distance Education and Open Learning, 'Our long-term aim is that any learner, anywhere, shall be able to study any distance-teaching programme available from any *bona fide* college or university' (Commonwealth Secretariat 1987).

What are the minimum requirements?

A number of conditions will need to be met if cooperation through technology is to lead to meaningful and sustainable development in the developing countries of the world. While there is no general agreement as to what constitutes the minimum package of requirements for technological take-off, the following conditions are considered essential:

- Access to quality information on a continuing basis.
- Access to the skills and tools required to make rational policy decisions regarding technology.
- Analytical and management capacities to utilise technology.
- Sustainable structures and resources to support technology.
- Evaluation skills to modify technology to suit development goals.

Capacity building and capacity development are the two key strategies, implied in each of these conditions, that will ensure that technology transfer takes place, and that it is effective and sustainable over a long period. Failure to apply these strategies will lead at worst to disaster, and at best to mere rhetoric about cooperation.

Possible growth areas

Judging from the growth of multiple accreditation systems already operating in Europe, there seems to be considerable prospect of extending these systems to regional partners motivated by existing trade agreements. An example would be a linkage between the European Union and the Africa–Caribbean–Pacific (ACP) states under the Lomé IV Convention. In addition, there are prospects for intra-ACP regional cooperation where two or more states would be involved. In the area of higher education, an interesting venture by the UK Open University is already under way through the planned delivery of a Masters programme in Development Management involving a number of South African intermediaries. This linkage offers an opportunity for capacity building through the open learning approach. There is an even greater opportunity in the delivery of a programme on Development Studies originating from South Africa and being offered by the UK Open University. Once the necessary infrastructures are established, there is no limit to the number and range of courses that could be delivered in *both* directions.

Another example would be the possible joint development of university-level courses such as those currently being planned by the newly established Open University of Tanzania, in the areas of environment, technology, and development, to be taken by all enrolled students. It would seem that collaboration between two or three universities in developing countries might yield enormous benefits in terms of time, cost, and quality.

The role of the Commonwealth of Learning

As an international, inter-governmental organisation dedicated to open learning and distance education, the Commonwealth of Learning (COL) is actively involved in the development of information and communications technologies in support of education. COL is helping to increase the capacity of developing countries to meet the demands for improved access to quality education and training by establishing new partnerships and networks. It has concentrated strategic initiatives on three dominant educational technologies.

First, COL has assisted in the establishment of *telecommunications links* to enhance the effectiveness of inter-institutional cooperation in areas such as administration, planning, and research. In this context, COL recently undertook a comprehensive economic and technical study, aimed at examining the feasibility of a regional telecommunications network for distance education in the Asia-Pacific region. Such a regional shared-user network will provide the basis for the delivery of teaching and learning systems, as well as providing a model for other regions, such as Africa and the Caribbean.

Second, COL has taken some steps to improve *access for developing countries to computerised information networks* operating internationally, such as the Internet, to which COL's headquarters is itself linked. With the rapid growth and popularity of the Internet, computer networking has become a particularly valuable means of linking educators and institutions for a whole range of purposes, ranging from teaching and research to advisory and consultative services.

Third, COL has been involved in the establishment of *programming cooperatives* among educators and broadcasters, an example being the Commonwealth Educational Media Cooperative for Asia (CEMCA) based in Delhi, India. The central idea is to provide a mechanism for pooling educational programming and re-distribution to member organisations.

Issues for further discussion

New technologies for education open up many opportunities for collaboration between technologically developed and developing regions. They also open up a whole new research area on educational, institutional and social effects of technical change. What effects would a 'borderless' educational environment have on teaching and learning opportunities? How will the quality of teaching, learning, assessment, and research be affected? What mechanisms will be put in place with regard to quality assurance, recognition, and transfer of qualifications? What additional roles will the conventional institutions have (for example, as brokers or franchisers)? What will be the relationships between education, business, and industry? How will the issues of policy, costs, and ownership be resolved? What mechanisms can be established to facilitate a wider sharing of the best practices in open learning and distance education? These are only few of the many questions students, educational institutions, planners and the educational industry need an answer to and the international research community may wish to address.

References

Commonwealth Secretariat (1987) *Towards a Commonwealth of Learning*, London: Commonwealth Secretariat.

Culpin, I. (1996) 'The Importance of Telework for European Employment and Business in a Global Context', paper presented at the International Workshop *Europe and the Developing World in the Globalised Information Society: Employment, Education, and Trade Implications*, Maastricht, 17–19 October.

12

TESTING TECHNOLOGY FOR TELE-EDUCATION: PILOT PROJECTS AT KPN IN THE NETHERLANDS

Eline de Kleine

Present trends in information technology, telecommunications, and electronics are driving the growth of a worldwide infrastructure interconnecting people in their homes, schools, and companies. We expect that, within five years, employees and trainees will be able to follow training courses, instruction sessions, and professionalisation programmes on their own workstations at home or in the office through some form of tele-education, tele-learning, or tele-working. People will be able to determine for themselves when they wish to learn. Tele-learning – the use of telecommunications in the learning process – may emerge in different forms, but it will always involve interaction between 'tele-coaches', trainees (either in working groups or as individuals), and remote databanks.

Numerous communication technologies already available can be used in tele-learning settings. These include audio conferencing (between two people or with several people at different locations), video conferencing (between two people or two small groups at different locations), chat boxes, screen sharing, e-mail, video-mail/audio-mail, news groups, bulletin board system (bbs), computer conferencing, shared filing systems/file transfer, and databanks/worldwide information systems. This list is by no means exhaustive, but it does give an idea of the technologies attracting most interest at present. There are various reasons for this interest. For example, some technologies can already be used by means of a 'cheap' Internet subscription and are thus accessible to large groups of people. Standard products (tools) are available on the market for almost all of the technologies listed above, often with a choice of different types varying in price and quality.

The fact that these and other technologies are not yet being used on a large scale for education and training is due to a variety of circumstances.

Each training institute will probably be able to cite its own particular reasons, such as the high costs for trainee and institute, the inflexibility of the education system (it is a fact that innovation in education is a very slow process), the lack of a theoretical background, or the lack of experience in designing a tele-learning setting from a didactic point of view. To get more experience with the practical aspects of tele-learning, the research branch of the PTT of The Netherlands (KPN), which has been involved in developing the technological aspects of advanced telecommunications-based services for tele-learning in The Netherlands, has undertaken a number of tele-learning projects over the past few years. Three projects that have advanced to the pilot stage are discussed here: ECOLE (European Collaborative Open Learning Environment); Electronic Forum (a combination of interactive television and computer conferencing); and the International Summer School.

ECOLE (European Collaborative Open Learning Environment)

The ECOLE project took place between 1992 and 1994. Six PTT organisations, IBM, Siemens, and Bull participated in this EC project. The first step was to design and develop the ECOLE environment, which contained a number of ISDN-based applications and services developed especially for use in telecommunications-based distance education. In 1994, a field trial was carried out to test the ECOLE environment, using three different courses, in Germany, France, The Netherlands, and Switzerland. Here we describe the combined Dutch–Swiss field trial of a cross-cultural co-operation course that took place in 1993.

The main objective of the ECOLE field trials was to test the package of ISDN-based services developed for tele-learning. Special attention was paid to the effects of this means of delivery on participants' perceptions of the learning experience; to its efficiency; to user attitudes toward the course; and to its costs.. The target audience for the course consisted of telecommunications managers who operate in cross-cultural contexts.

The course was designed for at least sixteen and at most thirty-two participants; the field trial involved four employees of PTT Telecom Netherlands and four from Swiss PTT Telecom.

The course had been originally organised in the traditional format of a classroom environment. The ECOLE version was developed in 1993. Table 12.1 shows the major differences between the two versions.

In the ECOLE version, roughly one-third of the original course devoted to lectures was replaced by a mixture of reading and group discussion by means of computer conferencing. Role-playing exercises in the original course were replaced by a management game. A tutor and a course manager were active in the ECOLE version. The tutor was responsible

Table 12.1 Comparison between classroom course and its ECOLE version

	Original course	ECOLE course
Time spent on course	20 hours (plus reading time after classes)	20 hours (plus reading time between modules)
Running time	2 days	4 weeks
Scheduling	Strictly scheduled within 2-day period	Pre-scheduled per week, but left open to the learner within the week
Teaching strategies	• lectures	• self-study • group discussion through computer conferencing
	• elaboration and presentation of assignments	• elaboration and presentation of assignments in audio conference with shared screens
	• role playing	• computer-based management simulation in multicultural groups
	• watching and criticising video	• watching and criticising digitised video fragments

for the content of the course and gave feedback to the students about their assignments. The course manager handled the technical and organisational aspects of the course. She organised the introduction to the ECOLE system, ran the help desk, monitored progress, and acted as an inter-mediary between students and tutor.

The course took place over a four-week period, within which work was divided into four modules of five hours each.[1] During each module, parti-cipants studied with printed material (book and syllabus) and worked on assignments, either individually or with a partner (in the other country). Participants were required to achieve a weekly target or accomplish a defined task. Participants were more or less free to fit their cooperation sessions into their weekly five-hour schedules.

The following ECOLE services were used in the field trial: *ECOLE shell* (an interface between users and the ECOLE system); *login and naming service* (for user identification and as a tool for the address book); *address book* and *electronic mail* (for communication with the tutor and among participants); *computer conferencing* (for one-to-many communication); *screen sharing* (for real-time video and audio communication among learners by simultaneous access to the same screen from different locations, participants taking turns at adding or altering text); and *file transfer* (between server and workstations).

As for system architecture, ECOLE adopts the client–server model. The server is based on a Pentium PC running UNIX SCO ODT 3.0. The client is based on 486 PCs running DOS 5.0–Windows 3.1. Communication links between clients and server are based on (Euro) ISDN and Ethernet. The communication protocol is TCP/IP and data management is performed by Oracle. The server was a Pentium 66 MHz, 16 MB RAM, 510 MB HD, SCSI 2, 3.5″ 1.44 MB floppy disk drive, with CD-ROM drive, a tape streamer, ISDN: BINTEC board, and Ethernet adapter (3COM). The workstations for tutor and students were 486 PCs with 33 MHz or 50 MHz, 8 MB RAM, and 525 MB HD, 3.5″ 1.44 MB floppy disk drive, audio board, ISDN: Stollmann Tina-ds V7 Ethernet adapter (for the tutor workstation). In addition to the various ECOLE applications, it was necessary to install the following extra software on the server and the workstations: UNIX SCO ODT 3.0 (including TCP/IP protocol), Development Kit for UNIX SCO (only during installation procedure), Oracle 6.0, Windows 3.1, ISDN driver, Ethernet driver, DOS 5.0, Windows 3.1, Word, TCP/IP, ODBC driver for Oracle, SQLNet 1.1.75, SQLPlus 3.0.10.1.4, W-Windows emulator (eXceed/W) 3.3, ToolBook Run-time, ISDN NDIS driver, and Ethernet driver (tutor workstation).

Before discussing the results of the field trial, it is important to mention that a number of less-than-ideal circumstances, which may have affected these results, must be taken into account. The profile of some of the ECOLE participants did not fit the target group definition – several participants had no international and/or management experience. In Switzerland, the distance between the ECOLE system and the participants' place of work might be the reason why they logged in less than required. Initial start-up and other subsequent technical problems (initiating screen sharing, loss of data) negatively affected participants' motivation. Lack of previous experience with Windows forced some participants to spend considerable time just learning how to operate the system.

In spite of these technical problems and less-than-ideal circumstances, most students declared themselves satisfied with the course. All of them enjoyed the subject and working together with a partner in another country. They also felt they had achieved the goals of the course, at least to some extent. In this respect, perceived learning effects of the ECOLE version are comparable to those of the original course, which was perceived only slightly more positively.

The cost analysis indicates that, when time away from work and travelling expenses of trainees are major factors in the training situation, costs of a distance course are considerably lower than those of a regular one. In the present case, the original course was more than twice as expensive as the ECOLE version, due almost entirely to time away from work and travelling expenses. Compared to a traditional classroom course where travelling costs are low or non-existent (e.g., for an attendance of local participants), expenditure for distance training is about 25 per cent lower than for regular classroom training. In addition to the cost differential, the advantages of tele-training *vis-à-vis* classroom training stem from: minimising 'lost opportunity cost'; productive use of 'lost hours' by filling them in with training activities; and reduction of time spent in student–tutor contacts. It is also necessary to consider initial and running costs of hardware and software. These may not be a significant hindrance to tele-training because of the trend in declining hardware prices and the fact that increasing numbers of companies have already incurred the costs of setting up their computer networks.

One of the main strengths of the ECOLE course was the flexibility of the learning process. Most of the learning could be planned by the students themselves. The weekly screen-sharing sessions with a partner stimulated progress and structured the workload. The negative side of flexibility became visible when priorities had to be set. Often the course got a lower priority than daily work. In addition, some students missed the social interaction of the original course. Yet, the possibilities for such interactions embedded in the system and in the ECOLE course were hardly used by the students. Almost all assignments in the ECOLE course involved the same partners.

Participants in previous runs of the original course had asked for organised course-related activities to be undertaken after the conclusion of the course. This proved to be unfeasible. In contrast, the ECOLE system allowed students to keep contacting each other after the conclusion of the trial, exchanging course-related experiences.

It is not clear what effects the absence of direct interaction between tutor and students might have had on learning results; this is a topic that needs more research. However, the ECOLE system itself contains elements that can be mobilised to minimise this problem; discussion sections between tutors and small groups of students supported by video conferencing may compensate for this lack of interaction.

Participation in computer conferences was far below the expectations of the designers of the course. The only place where the computer conference really worked was during the management game, where conferencing is an explicit part of the assignment. Even then, results were less than satisfactory. A successful conference requires that each user log in at least three or four times a week. It is impossible for a course manager or moderator to stimulate discussions if participants do not read their mail regularly.

A good course guide proved to be absolutely essential for this version of the course. The guide must be clearly written, and must be as accurate as possible. It should describe clearly what precisely is expected of the students module-by-module and step-by-step. The introduction to the system proved to be an essential part of the course. It is during the introduction that participants should be offered ample opportunity to practice with all the applications. Special attention must be devoted to manuals, help functions, and technical support.

Screen-sharing sessions are very demanding on participants. It requires considerable organisation and concentration to be able to formulate ideas while sharing a screen. Designers of tele-training courses should develop more efficient screen-sharing sessions. The field trial experience suggests that better results could be achieved if participants limited themselves to discussing their solutions to assignments and drafting notes for later elaboration.

Finally, it must be stressed that in distance-learning courses with systems like ECOLE, it is important to plan and reserve time for introducing the participants to the system well in advance of the start of the course.

Conclusion

The technologies used in the ECOLE system have a lot to offer in at least two ways. First, they enable the provision of some of the classroom interaction that is, by definition, absent in distance education. Second, they are able to enrich self-tuition by giving learners the opportunity to cooperate with other learners and/or the tutor at different locations at any point they chose. These technologies allow distance education to evolve toward open learning.

There are three essential requirements to be met in the development of a tele-training environment using different applications:

1   A user-friendly interface and applications are one of the most critical success factors; a viable environment is one in which applications can be used intuitively by non-computer literates.
2   Special attention must be devoted to the role of the moderator, and protocols for communication between users should be designed and conveyed clearly to them.
3   Learners should meet, with or without the tutor, before their first distance cooperation takes place. If meeting face-to-face is impossible, an 'electronic café' supported by videoconferencing might be an alternative.

Electronic forum

One department of PTT Telecom Netherlands started a professionalisation programme for the company's application managers in 1994. It was designed to try out a communication concept (interactive television and an electronic forum) developed to support 'learning by experience'. A television programme was broadcast at a fixed time for a number of weeks by means of a live satellite link. Participants were able to interact with the broadcasters by telephone during the programme, and to continue the discussion in an electronic forum.

The professionalisation programme aimed to increase the exchange of practical experience and information between functional managers in order to raise their level of professionalism and lower the need to enlist the services of external personnel. It also aimed at disseminating important developments concerning computer systems, and at raising the degree of involvement of the target group in matters and problems encountered within the company. The pilot project tested the communication concept in relation to possible necessary alterations, results achieved, and their relation to costs.

Members of the target group worked in the functional management of applications used by several departments of PTT Telecom to support a large number of processes (everything from the production of offerings for customers to the invoicing process). The job of functional application manager is positioned between the central development and management department (i.e., the software house of PTT Telecom) and the decentralised users of the applications (such as salespersons and clerical staff). The pilot project was organised for roughly seventy participants – functional managers from five departments and their immediate superiors.

The pilot project ran for eleven weeks. The broadcast programmes dealt with matters which were informative for the target group, such as changes in the organisation and work processes, the need to be customer-oriented, how another company works, and complaints from customers. The programmes were designed to provoke discussions, which took place during the broadcast and, following it, in an electronic forum. A moderator entered the pilot project later.

Broadcasting was done from a commercial TV studio where discussions and interviews were recorded. Recordings were also made on location and shown during the broadcasts. Transmitting equipment was installed at the studio to allow the satellite link with the participants' locations, where reception involved a dish antenna, special cables, a connecting point, and a television set. At each location participants had contact with the studio by telephone. For the electronic forum, the participants had access to a separate PC with a network connection and a selected application (Lotus Notes).

The pilot project was evaluated by means of written questionnaires (before and after), a group interview, some individual interviews, content analysis of discussions in the electronic forum, and cost analysis. The main results are summarised below.

Electronic forum

The main results of the pilot test of the use of the electronic forum were that (a) only 25 per cent of the target group participated actively by making written contributions to the discussions with some degree of regularity during the total period of the pilot project, and (b) contributions decreased as the project progressed.

Participants and their superiors cited many reasons for reduced participation: pressure of work, other priorities, unattractive content of the discussions, the possibility of communication by other channels, such as e-mail, the fact that satellite broadcasts were held too soon after each other, the possibility of similar discussions to be held in a small group immediately after the satellite broadcast, and the circumstance that Lotus Notes was not installed on the PC at the participants' places of work, thus making it necessary to start up a different PC. It also emerged that about half of the employees who wrote a contribution did not receive any response, and those who did were dissatisfied with its content. The target group showed higher appreciation for discussions about subjects closer to each participant's own work.

Interactive television

The main results in this area can be summarised as follows. While the 30-minute duration of the satellite broadcast was considered adequate, some subjects were experienced as not having been dealt with sufficiently. In a work setting, people apparently expect of a dedicated broadcast greater depth of debate and information than they do of standard television programmes. Participants preferred programmes to be broadcast every two weeks instead of every week to allow proper discussion of issues brought up by the broadcast. Participants did not spontaneously make use of the possibility of using the telephone to participate live during the satellite broadcast, even though they declared themselves pleased with this possibility. Their reluctance may be due to unfamiliarity with the medium and general setting in which they were required to act. Participants disapproved of the way in which subjects were approached in the programmes, which they saw as inducing a negative attitude rather than a constructive one. On the technical side, the pilot experiment went well. Only a few departments had problems in getting the satellite broadcasts up and running.

Costs

Approximately 90 per cent of the costs of the pilot project were incurred for the satellite broadcasts (rental of a studio and development expenses with the editorial team, production, and directors). Approximately 6 per cent of the total costs were incurred for the electronic forum. A substantial part of these costs concerned technical support (installation and help desk) and acquisition of a licence for Lotus Notes. Other costs involved the rental of PCs and of the network. Labour costs during the pilot project amounted to about 3 per cent of the total, and referred to lost income rather than costs actually incurred.

The cost analysis reveals areas where savings may be possible without greatly impairing the effectiveness of the concept. Particular attention was devoted to alternatives to live satellite broadcasts, which accounted for the highest costs. One such alternative is the broadcasting of previously recorded programmes; but this would not allow for the immediate and direct involvement of participants. Another alternative is satellite broadcasting devoted entirely to studio discussions rather than reports produced on location. Video tapes could also replace live broadcasting, though also at the expense of interactivity. An entirely different approach would consist of several live broadcasts on one and the same day, for different target groups, with several locations and several participants at each location. This would increase total cost, but reduce costs per broadcast per participant (or location). Finally, training could also be delivered through other communication media, such as video conferencing for the discussions and ISDN lines for the transmission of images.

Conclusion

The use of interactive television combined with an electronic forum may very well be an effective (and cost-effective) way of training large groups of employees and bringing about company-wide debate. It may also be an effective tool to induce a change in behaviour, depending on the content. However, it is important to realise that a change in behaviour is most often brought about by means of direct communication and feedback between the parties who wish to stimulate the change and those who are required to change.

A computer conference is a medium used on an entirely voluntary basis. Special attention has to be given to matters that increase the motivation of participants and give them fewer reasons to pull out. The content of the discussion must appeal to the target group, must have an added value to them. If it does not, participants will be quickly inclined to give priority to other matters. Discussions must be moderated, and the target group's level of knowledge and linguistic ability must be taken into consideration. The medium should offer a unique opportunity for exchanging information on a subject with the relevant people. It is important for the purpose of management of the training activity to determine the optimum number of participants. While about forty active participants seems to be a rule of thumb, the optimum number depends very much on the subject of the discussion.

Internationl Summer School

The 1996 NICE Summer School in Advanced Broadband Communications (ABC96) was a pilot testing of a distributed educational environment. Advanced broadband communication was both the content of the course and the subject of technological development and research. ABC96 was held from 9–12 July 1996 as part of an international conference. Fourteen different locations,[2] mostly European, were interconnected by means of ATM (asynchronous transfer mode) technology. Participants were able to remotely follow the presentations and lectures of international speakers. There was also the possibility of asking lecturers questions directly.

The aim of the Summer School was to provide participants with a distributed educational environment (tele-classroom). For KPN Research, the main objective was to gain more experience with tele-education using an advanced broadband infrastructure. Other questions to be addressed in the pilot study were: What training must employees receive for the rollout of advanced broadband communications? Can ABC researchers be trained using new communications technologies within a distance education framework? Can Centres of Excellence in advanced broadband communications be used for training ABC engineers? An additional but equally important objective was to drum up enthusiasm among participants for a career at KPN Research.

The target group was defined as young engineers with a background in IT who wanted to move towards telecommunications, or young engineers with a background in telecommunications who needed to update their knowledge of current software engineering. It also included technical managers with responsibility for projects, products, and services that incorporate telecommunications and information technology components. About 1,000 participants were involved in ABC96.

The Dutch group at KPN Research consisted exclusively of students of IT or telecommunications at selected universities in The Netherlands.

The presentation structure followed conference style, with invited speakers or discussants addressing the subject matter in their own terms.[3] For the 1996 Summer School, however, the planning committee decided that instead of using the 'conference' model, it would use the 'book of selected readings' model, which also lends itself to a distributed educational environment. Each presentational slot consists of a prefatory commentary, previously scripted, which introduces not so much the speaker as the topic to be presented, explains why it is important, and points out the particular aspects to be presented. There may also be a closing commentary, scripted in outline but modified in light of audience reactions.

Table 12.2 shows the schedule for ABC96 at KPN Research.

The first three days consisted of international and local presentations

182

Table 12.2 Schedule for ABC96 at KPN Research

Time	9 July	10 July	11 July	12 July
Morning	Opening and international presentations	International presentations and debates	International presentations and debates	Telecommunications game
Afternoon	Local presentations and debates	International panel discussion; Local presentations and demonstrations of research activities	Local presentations and forum with employees of KPN Research	Telecommunications game
Evening	Barbecue with employees of KPN Research	Dinner and boat-game	Start of telecommunications game	

and debates. In the morning sessions, advanced broadband communication tools were used for participation in international sessions. In the afternoon there was a shadow programme, mostly filled in with local presentations by KPN Research employees, followed by an international panel and some demonstrations of multimedia applications.

A telecommunications game was played on the last day. The game was developed by KPN Research for its own target population, especially for this Summer School. The theme was to prepare a plan for using a fictitious polder called 'Markerwaard' as a pilot area for the electronic highway.[4] The group of forty students was divided into eight groups, each representing imaginary companies in telecommunications networks, information technology, telecommunications and IT products, or telecommunications services. The first assignment in the game was to find combinations of companies capable of working together. These larger, collaborative ventures then had to design the plan. Groups communicated with each other by e-mail, telephone, shared file space, video conferencing (point-to-point and multi-point), PC application (Picturetel with ISDN), MS-Word, and MS-PowerPoint.

The multimedia application used at the Summer School is called ISABEL, a distributed multimedia computer-supported cooperative work (CSCW) application, designed to support the interconnection of audiences, not individuals, with full interaction. It supports N to N bi-directional communication for all the media exchanged and includes integrated event management to facilitate operation of large distributed events (tele-education and tele-working). ISABEL V3 runs on UNIX and includes the following application support functions (ASFs): multi-point audio conference, multi-point video conference, World Wide Web (high speed), tele-pointer, application sharing, shared blackboard, shared editor, and application management. Other support functions such as video archive retrieval and presentation manager can also be run in parallel with ISABEL as UNIX programs.

Different types of sites typically participate in a distributed event. *Interactive Sites* (IS) are prepared to exchange (send and receive) audio/video/data using ISABEL. Within interactive sites, *main sites* are those where there is a paying audience and lectures and presentations are given; *secondary sites* are those with a free audience, no lecturers, but still with the facility of sending questions and an occasional speech. Main sites provide back-up equipment (including back-up power supply), access to a back-up network, and a quality conference room with good audio-visual equipment. *Watch Points* (WP) can only receive audio/video/data sent from the interactive sites. *Control Site* (CS) controls remotely the configuration of all ISABEL applications located at the interactive sites. *Network Nodes* (NN) aggregate traffic from the 'leaves' towards the 'root' and perform traffic broadcast from the 'root' to the 'leaves'.[5]

Table 12.3 describes the hardware and software requirements of each type of site.

The main results and conclusions are summarized below. They refer only to content and teleconferencing tools as they were perceived and used at KPN Research in The Netherlands.

As regards to content, participants were extremely satisfied with the programme of the Summer School, and with the organisation, particularly its flexibility. Presentations and discussions were considered informative, instructive, and fairly innovative. Generally speaking, presentations by KPN Research employees received a slightly higher appreciation than the international presentations because they were made in the Dutch language, which increased the possibilities of interaction. In international presentations, it is sometimes difficult to follow speakers with a limited knowledge of the English language. In addition, the audio quality was sometimes less than perfect. Participants enjoyed the telecommunications game and considered it a good way of closing the training activities. Most students

Table 12.3 Hardware and software requirements in distributed event

Interactive site:	A, B, C, D, E, G, I, J
Watch point:	A, B, C, D, E, G (E recommended)
Control site:	E
Network node:	F, G, H, I

Notes

A ISABEL application. The most recent version must be used. It can be retrieved from a site on the Internet.

B ISABEL Workstation: SPARCstation 10/40 32 Mbytes RAM, with 300 Mbytes of free disk. A multicast SUNOS kernel with inter-process memory communication and other standard features is required.

C Parallax board with hardware M-JPEG compression. Models: Power video or XV-24SVC.

D Parallax software drivers for the parallax board and X.11 (recommended) or Openwin server software.

E Control Terminal: Any X-terminal that can display windows from the ISABEL WS. It is used to display the control windows of the ISABEL application. The purpose of this is not to display control windows in the screen of the ISABEL WS, because it is typically projected for the audience to see.

F Router ATM with Classical IP encapsulation over AAL5, high-performance multicast, sub-interface capability, DVMRP, PIM and some other features. (Typically Cisco 7000 with AIP and SSP cards.)

G ATM adapter card with drivers for SUNOS, multicast, traffic-shaping, multiple VCs, and other features. (Typically FORE SBA-200, with version 3.0 drivers. The physical interface should match the ATM network access available at each site.)

H Multicasting Equipment: SPARCstation 10/40, 32 Mbytes RAM, with 100 Mbytes of free disk. SUN-OS 4.1.3 with IP multicast support kernel. Additionally, multicasting capabilities in the ATM local switch (equipment I) at the site are required.

I ATM switch capable of switching to/from VPI = 0.

J Multiple audio-visual equipment (professional microphones, video cameras, screen projectors, audio mixers, audio amplifiers, etc.).

had no problems with the electronic media, except multi-point video conferencing.

In relation to the use of a teleconferencing tool such as ISABEL and other telecommunications tools, the main results can be summarised as follows. The quality and stability of audio and video links were apparently good enough to follow the elements of the course, but need improvement. Video and audio links in ISABEL were of a reasonable quality. Pictures were fairly sharp, images of the blackboards were good, but those of the sites in other countries were not very clear. This did not prevent participants from following what was going on. Audio quality was also reasonable, although a few faults were considered rather annoying.

Participants' opinions about duration varied very considerably, as did their reasons for the assessment. Complaints about long presentations were associated with subjects that did not appeal to the participant, difficulties in following the speaker, technology failure, and insufficient interaction between the group and the speaker. It is tiring to look at a screen for an hour, especially if you have a seat at the back of the classroom.

Possibilities for interaction were reasonably good in ISABEL, and participants found ISABEL a suitable presentation medium for training courses and instruction sessions. Similarly, the Summer School design was considered suitable to other courses. It was hardly surprising that familiar facilities, such as the telephone, e-mail, and the interchange of documents in MS-Word and MS-PowerPoint received this positive assessment. Less familiar facilities, such as video conferencing (point to point), audio conferencing, application sharing, databanks, and worldwide information systems such as the Internet, were also considered highly suitable.

Multi-point video conferencing was found an extremely difficult facility to operate. Unfamiliarity with the application, the level of noise in the room where the conferencing set-up was installed, and the variety of alternative methods for the participants to communicate with each other made the facility almost impossible to operate, even by relatively experienced and fairly technology-oriented students.

Summing up, a video conferencing application such as ISABEL is suitable, in principle, for use in tele-training activities. It is, however, essential that the technology be stabilised and the audio and video quality improved. It is also essential to give sufficient time for participants to familiarise themselves with sophisticated applications, and to ensure that the environment is isolated from distractions and disruptions.

Concluding remarks

Only a few projects developed at KPN Research were described in this chapter. Presently, new projects are being carried out to explore, for example, tele-education and the Internet, the use of Intranets for just-in-time learning, and the possibilities of ATM for tele-education, tele-cooperation, and tele-consultation. Experimentation with pilot projects like those described here usually produces considerable knowledge about tele-education. Based on these pilot studies, better and more efficient tele-education projects will be designed.

There is presently great interest in tele-education, not only in our company, but in the whole society. In my opinion, this is due to our increased experience with the utilisation of tele-education, the continuous technological improvement of networks and applications, and the reduction in the costs of tele-education, which puts it in reach of most people and institutions.

The interest in tele-education will grow even more in the coming years. This will not only lead to a modernisation of education as we have known it so far; it will also bring about totally new forms of education. The time is closer than we might think when class instruction and large group presentations will partly be replaced by private study at home or at the workstation. Project-based learning and group learning will soon be used in many teaching institutions. The role of the teacher will change from lecturing to coaching, and the learner him/herself will take more responsibility for the learning process. The possibilities for learning will increase and diversify in such a way that learning will take place independent of time and place. This means that in the future the possibilities of giving and receiving education will no longer be limited by organisation or country borders. People in all countries of the world can and should take advantage of these new possibilities. The time has come for more widespread use of tele-education.

Notes

1 Module 1: introduction of learners to each other (audio and/or computer conferencing) and to the general topic of the course (self-study and computer conferencing). Start of management game and the integration assignment. Module 2: theories about cultural difference (self-study, lectures, and computer conference). Module 3: participants write collaboratively a short presentation about their own cultures, to be presented and discussed in small mixed-culture groups. Module 4: collaborative assignments about specific aspects of cross-cultural cooperation. Closure: video conference with all participants and tutors; discussion of the course content and evaluation.

2 Switzerland (ASCOM and CERN), Belgium (Belgacom and the EU national host), France (CNET), Italy (CRIAI, Politecnico di Torino, and CSELT), Netherlands (KPN), Iceland (PTI), Sweden (SICS), Spain (Telefonica I+D and DIT-UPM), Germany (DeteBerKom), Norway (Telenor), Portugal (ET), Greece (Demokritos), Austria (Linz), and Canada (CRC).

3 In 1993, when there were only two sites, it was possible to supplement the presented material with tutorial sessions at each of the sites, and a continuing case study was designed that enabled the students to integrate the knowledge presented by the lecturers into a larger context. In 1994 and 1995, the case study

approach could not be used because the concept of small tutored groups could not be scaled up for a large number of sites, and an adequate substitute was not found.

4 Part of the Ijsselmeer in The Netherlands is now called 'Markermeer'. The area covered by still water had been considered in the past as one to be reclaimed. There were plans to use the newly recovered land for agriculture. These plans were scrapped, however, and the polder has never been drained.

5 In any distributed event, there is a single control site, typically between one and three network nodes, and as many interactive sites and watch points as desired. It is possible that a single institution may act as several sites (e.g., Telefónica could be an interactive site *and* a network node). An organisation may change its role from/to interactive site to/from watch point during the event. This is because it runs counter to ergonomic principles to have too many interactive sites at any one time (the maximum is about nine), but more than nine sites may want to participate interactively in the event.

13

A non-European counterpoint

THE BRAZILIAN 'TELECURSO 2000'

An experience with applications of communications technologies to vocational and continuous education

Arlete Azevedo de Paula Guibert

The educational panorama

The status of education in Brazil is not significantly different from that of other developing countries of similar average income. Three and a half million children from seven to fourteen years of age still do not have access to fundamental education (IBGE 1991). Only 40 per cent of the part of this age group that *are* enrolled finish the four initial grades, and less than 25 per cent do it without one or more failures. As a consequence, the average schooling of the population is low, leading to difficulties in social and economic performance. The statistics show that of the 17.7 million formal illiterates older than 15, only 4.1 million have a proper job (Ministerio do Trabalho 1992). And even among the employed, the lack of schooling is a matter of concern: 18 million have scarcely four years of schooling. In the richer state of São Paulo, 31 per cent of the formally employed had completed the eight years of fundamental education in 1992; only 14 per cent had managed to finish secondary education. Data for the industrial sector are only slightly better: in 1992 38 per cent of the industrial workers of the state of São Paulo had left school in the course of their secondary education.

Fundamental education and most of secondary education are the responsibility of the municipalities and the state governments, while most university education is either provided by the federal government or is in private hands. Public expenditure on education has reflected the country's financial difficulties and a lack of sustained political commitment. The

Cardoso government is making a strong effort at facing the nation's educational problems and mobilising alternative modalities of education, such as distance education, with this purpose in mind. Distance education, at present, is receiving great attention from the government. One of the privileged initiatives is the project called 'TV Escola'. This project consists in providing public schools with more than 100 students with a parabolic antenna, a television set, a videotape recorder, and tapes. This programme began in March 1996. The television programmes are transmitted by satellite from Rio de Janeiro and are complemented by a bimonthly magazine and handouts. The intention is to have state-produced programmes, from universities and other educational institutions, adequate to the local needs and culture. By July 1997, 120 kits had been distributed.

Vocational education is also considered a strategic matter for development. Formally an activity of the Ministry of Education, its responsibility is being divided with the Ministry of Labor by means of a National Professional Education Plan. The main objective of this plan is a flexible and democratic policy to enable access to vocational education.

Distance education in Brazil

Distance education began in Brazil in 1939 with the foundation of the Instituto Radio Técnico Monitor, which had the objective of preparing professionals for the assembling, repair, and installation of radio equipment. In 1943, the Serviço de Radio Educativo (Educational Radio Service) started operations, offering cultural and instructional programmes. There is no record of any evaluation of the penetration or results of these programmes. Project Minerva is a basic education programme that has been broadcast by 1,100 commercial radio stations in Brazil since 1970, and is reported to have reached about 120,000 students, enrolled in hundreds of 'telepostos' scattered all over the country. In spite of its expected usefulness, however, educational results were not monitored.

The use of television for educational purposes was first promoted by Roquete Pinto in 1952, soon after the inauguration of the first two TV broadcasting stations in São Paulo and Rio de Janeiro. Since then, state-owned or supported channels and commercial television have been used to broadcast various educational programmes. In the early 1960s, commercial television was used to broadcast a course that prepared candidates for an exam ('madureza') that gives equivalency diplomas for primary and secondary education. At the end of that decade, the first public-owned educational TV channel was inaugurated in Recife, in the North-eastern region, closely followed by TV Cultura from São Paulo. Five other public-owned educational TV channels started to operate with some success. The most striking example was the project of Fundação Maranhense de TV

Educativa (Educational TV Foundation of the State of Maranhao), developed in 1969 and still in operation, which consists of dedicated broadcasts for grades 5 to 8 designed to cover the lack of well-prepared teachers. Other projects by public entities for the exploration of TV as an instructional medium are: SACI (Advanced System for Interdisciplinary Communication) of the Brazilian National Space Agency, a feasibility study of satellite applications to basic education and teacher training; NUTES (Centre for Educational Technology in the Health Sciences), of the Department of Biophysics of the Federal University of Rio de Janeiro, which produced in the early 1970s instructional material for health education at university level; and LOGOS II, self-instructional modules for training in-service primary school teachers.

An innovative experiment in communications techniques for adult basic education through TV was first made in 1974 by the educational TV system of the Brazilian Ministry of Education with the project 'Joao da Silva', an educational soap opera. This series tells the story of a young man from a poor background in the north of Brazil who moves to Rio de Janeiro to make a living, and a housemaid who also wants to improve her lot. Between them, they have many adventures, which revolve around deficiencies in their education (e.g., he has to make a phone call but does not know how to use the telephone directory). These problems are only too familiar to the majority of Brazilian TV viewers, who pay close attention to the solutions. The episodes are frequently interrupted, not for commercials, as usual with TV programmes in Brazil, but for short, practical teaching units. The 'Joao da Silva' project, together with 'TELECURSO 2° grau' and 'Reading and Interpretation of Mechanical Drawing', described below, laid the basis for TELECURSO 2000.

'TELECURSO 2° grau' was a programme sponsored and broadcast by a private network teaching the disciplines of secondary education formal courses. The programme explored new ways of using video, and exemplified the difference that management can make in the production of a dynamic instructional broadcast, including the correct choice of market and the innovative production of accompanying printed materials.

'Reading and Interpretation of Mechanical Drawing' was a course prepared jointly by the privately funded National Service for Industrial Apprenticeship (SENAI) and the publicly owned Educational Television Channel of São Paulo to improve industrial workers' ability to interpret technical drawings. The target audience included workers in the mechanical and metallurgic industries and students in vocational education courses, including SENAI students. Television broadcasts and written materials were used by students and specially trained teachers called 'learning tutors'.

The first series of broadcasts took place from 2 August to 18 December 1978. Each television programme, corresponding to one lesson, lasted fifteen minutes and was accompanied by printed material containing the concepts of the lesson, activities, exercises, and questions for self-evaluation. The reception was organised in classrooms, called 'telessalas', twice a week, where the students watched the television lessons, performed group activities, and clarified their doubts with the learning tutors. The course was divided into four modules. At the end of each module, the student had a test to evaluate his progress. If needed, remedial instruction was provided. To evaluate the instructional materials, the performance of the participants, and the role of the tutors, an evaluation project was designed. The results were very encouraging: the drop-out rate, a very important issue in distance education, was only 17.5 per cent. As for the achievement of learning objectives, 92.3 per cent of the students scored above 70 per cent. The evaluation led to corrections in the instructional materials. The course had five additional presentations, achieving an audience of more than 20,000 students. (The course is still being used with only the printed materials.)

The efforts of tele-education in Brazil have been described as ambitious, impressive, and creative on many counts. However, Oliveira (1980) states that more concern was devoted to planning than to implementation; that the costs were neither a main worry nor a reason to continue or stop such projects; that few serious evaluations were attempted and the ones made were not read by the competent authorities; that no major pedagogic innovation was present, except in the media characteristics.

TELECURSO 2000

In December 1992, the Federation of Industries in the State of São Paulo (FIESP), the most industrialised centre of the country, and the Roberto Marinho Foundation, a private institution dedicated to social and educational projects, joined efforts to study the possibility of a large national project aimed at the cultural, educational, and professional needs of the country. The two institutions justified their initiative in a traditionally governmental field on the basis of their social responsibility as generators of the production, employment, and economic dynamism in the country. At the end of 1993, a contract was signed by both institutions for the implementation of TELECURSO 2000, a distance education project directed to the working world, using multimedia (television, printed materials, tutoring) to provide basic, secondary, and vocational education to young people and adults who lack basic education or who drop out from formal education. The field of study of metal-mechanics was selected for the vocational segment because it covers about 70 per cent of all the occupations in Brazilian industries, and thus has a very high potential of immediate application.

192

Pedagogical basis

Labour productivity is no longer assessed by the worker's ability to perform tasks but by his/her ability to receive, hold, and transfer knowledge in a continuous learning context. The worker's competence is thus determined by the capacity to relate and integrate knowledge and work. In this context, education is also a means to learn how to avoid waste, to reduce the rates of working accidents, and to increase awareness of rights and obligations, the importance of good health and safety, and the value of permanent education.

TELECURSO 2000 was designed especially for young people and adults already in the labour market. Taking into consideration characteristics determined by previous research, the project offers basic education equivalent to the last six years of the formal system, and secondary education corresponding to the three years of the regular courses. Besides the teaching of basic content, the didactic materials seek to expose the students to situations drawn from real life, which makes the use, comprehension, and transfer of knowledge easy and enables students to build and consolidate citizenship attitudes that are essential to the development of both the individual and society. The curricula are based on a choice of relevant contents, use appropriate media and adequate pedagogical treatment, and include provisions for continuous evaluation of the student's learning.

The skills that are considered basic for life in a society vary according to time and place. Today it is not enough to know how to read, write, or solve simple arithmetic problems; one must also have the ability to solve more complex problems, to be creative, to know how to 'read' and interpret different communications media, to understand a foreign language in which the manuals of new machines are written, to be aware of economic and quality control techniques to avoid waste, and to develop the ability for dialogue and learning with others.

The citizen acquires through education the means to perform political, productive, and cultural functions. Some of these functions are the subjects of TELECURSO 2000. They include recognition of the value of school, family, public property; respect for the elderly, every religion, the neighbours, individual differences, human rights; opposition to violence, prejudice, waste, and destruction of the environment; and responsibility for cultural roots, the democratic processes of community organisation, and self-determination, either political or cultural.

The intended audience

TELECURSO 2000 is directed to workers in the formal and informal sectors, either employed or unemployed, in need of professional development or learning a new occupation; students in the formal system, either public or private, enrolled in professional or non-professional schools, seeking an opportunity of improving their knowledge; teachers from professional schools, either public or private, who want to update their knowledge; and the general public.

The selected media

Television programmes, printed books, and the assistance of a special tutor were the media selected to convey the information, to motivate, and to interact with the students. In the preparation of the basic and secondary education courses, selected university teachers from each discipline planned the curricula, chose the relevant information to be presented, wrote the books, and discussed the television scripts. The vocational education course was the responsibility of the National Service for Industrial Apprenticeship, Regional Department of São Paulo (SENAI-DR/SP), which has a long and proven experience in the field. It selected the contents, planned the production of the written materials, and oriented the production of television programmes, involving more than a hundred persons in these activities. Television programmes were recorded in many SENAI schools, and many SENAI instructors performed as actors. SENAI is presently working on the establishment of the special classrooms ('telessalas') and on the training of tutors for basic, secondary, and vocational education courses. Since the institution must certify the TELECURSO 2000 basic and secondary courses, a group of professionals is working on the evaluation process.

The television programmes were designed to motivate and to make concepts more concrete. They are based on specially created characters, played mostly by professional actors. The centre of interest is always a real situation chosen to shorten the usual gap between curriculum content and reality. Each programme lasts fifteen minutes and corresponds to one lesson. They are broadcast by a very powerful commercial television channel, covering the whole country. Individual viewers are encouraged to videotape the programmes for further study.

Books complement the television programmes and contain the essentials of each discipline. Careful attention has been given to the language used, the illustrations, and the didactic approach. In addition, an overall pattern was developed giving visual identity to the printed materials. Each lesson presents activities and exercises to reinforce and test the concepts learned. Answers to the exercises are offered in the same book, providing for self-evaluation. The books present a selected bibliography for those who want to deepen their study. The books are available at newsagents all over the country.

Tutorial support is given to those enrolled in a 'telessala'. The tutor is not a teacher, but a person specially trained to help the students with their difficulties. He/she provides extra exercises, promotes group activities, and integrates the different media. A good tutor is a very important element in the system – the telessala work gives feedback to the specialists responsible for the planning and production of the courses.

Structure of the courses

The basic education course (Table 13.1) requires that the student know how to read and write, and is equivalent to the last six years of the basic school system. It has a duration of eighteen months (three semesters), with a total of 360 TV classes (120 each semester).

The secondary education course (Table 13.2) is equivalent to three years in the formal education system. It also takes eighteen months, with a total of 420 TV classes, 140 classes per semester.

The vocational education course has different features (Table 13.3). It takes a modular approach, comprising 'families' of technological information.

Table 13.1 TELECURSO 2000: basic education

First phase		Second phase		Third phase		Subtotal
Disciplines	TV classes	Disciplines	TV classes	Disciplines	TV classes	
Portuguese	40	Portuguese	50	–	–	90
Mathematics	40	Mathematics	20	Mathematics	20	80
History	40	–	–	–	–	40
–	–	Science	50	Science	20	70
–	–	–	–	Geography	50	50
–	–	–	–	English	30	30
Totals	120	–	120	–	120	360

Table 13.2 TELECURSO 2000: secondary education

First phase		Second phase		Third phase		Subtotal
Disciplines	TV classes	Disciplines	TV classes	Disciplines	TV classes	
Portuguese	40	Portuguese	40	–	–	80
Mathematics	30	Mathematics	40	–	–	70
–	–	–	–	History	40	40
–	–	–	–	Geography	40	40
Physics	20	Physics	30	–	–	50
–	–	Chemistry	30	Chemistry	20	50
Biology	50	–	–	–	–	50
–	–	–	–	English	40	40
Total	140	–	140	–	140	420

Table 13.3 TELECURSO 2000: vocational course

Modules	TV classrooms	Books
Introductory class	1	
The world of mechanics	5	
Standards	4	1
Job organisation	5	
Technical mathematics	15	1
Reading and interpretation of mechanical drawing	30	3
Materials	20	
Machine elements	55	2
Hygiene and safety	5	
Quality	5	1
Environmental quality	5	
Metrology	30	1
Tests of material properties	25	1
Heat treatment	10	1
Surface treatment	10	
Manufacturing processes	80	4
Mechatronics	20	1
Maintenance	35	2
Total	360	18

There are seventeen modules, each with a varied number of lessons, depending upon the complexity and volume of information to be conveyed. The course structure is quite flexible, allowing alternative sequences and uses. Practical courses/activities can be planned whenever possible. The total number of television programmes is 360, with fifteen minutes for each programme. Complementing the information, eighteen books were written. The course contents were planned under four general titles:

- *Introduction.* An overview of the possibilities represented by the world of mechanics in the industrial area.
- *Basic technology.* Six modules present the processes of mechanical production: materials, their properties, the treatments they undergo, and the final products.
- *Instrumental knowledge.* Six modules give support to the Basic Technology course with information on how to read and interpret blueprints, metrology, technical calculations, maintenance, and automation.
- *Complementary information.* Deals with hygiene and safety, quality, environment, and work organisation.

Implementation

There are three modalities of access to the course. The first is *organised reception*, in which the students enrol in a telessala either in schools, associations, trade unions, or community centres. The group meets every day for about two hours. Under the coordination of the tutor, the participants watch the television programme, read and do the exercises of the corresponding lesson in the book, clear up doubts, exchange experiences, and participate in group activities (research, production of bulletin boards, group discussion, etc.), depending on the tutor's creativity. The telessala is equipped with the television set, reference books, magazines, and other materials.

The second modality of access is *controlled reception*, in which the participant watches the television classes alone or in small groups and enrols in a control centre where he/she goes once a week to meet the tutor, clarify doubts, receive exercises, and be evaluated. Each tutor is expected to deal with around one hundred students.

Finally, in the modality of *free reception*, the student watches the television programmes and studies alone. All students, whatever the modality of access to TELECURSO 2000, are eligible to take the official tests of basic and secondary education and, if successful, receive the official certificate.

Evaluation and certification

TELECURSO 2000 has a built-in evaluation process through the many exercises presented in the books and also through the work of the tutors. This kind of evaluation follows the student's progress and allows remedial help. For basic and secondary courses, a final evaluation leads to a formal certificate, required for enrolment in further studies. Only bodies certified by the State Council of Education may give this officially recognised certificate. As for the vocational education course, students are evaluated after each module by means of a test given by the tutor. SENAI is accredited to certify students' achievements.

The TELECURSO 2000 basic education course began in January 1995, the secondary education course in May, and the vocational education course in September of the same year. According to the last statistics (January 1997), there were 3,264 telessalas in operation in the whole country, serving a population of 80,028 students. Students and telessalas are highly concentrated in the basic education course. The vocational education course still has a limited number of telessalas but it is expected that this will change quickly due to the interest of industry in obtaining the services of better qualified personnel as soon as possible. Because of the modular character of the course and the absence of prerequisites, industries can use the instructional materials as training, according to their needs, without the establishment of a formal telessala.

Final examinations for the certificate of adult basic and secondary education are public and are taken by people with different backgrounds, not only by students from TELECURSO 2000. Many students, though unprepared, 'take a chance' on this final examination. They are organised by the state Secretaries of Education and by authorised institutions. The examinations occur periodically and the participants may take them by discipline. The minimum grade for approval is 5 (five), in a zero-to-ten scale. When approved in all the disciplines of a course, the student receives a certificate.

Until December 1996, tests were given in the states of São Paulo, Mato Grosso do Sul, and Alagoas. The total number of candidates was 47,679 for the basic disciplines. For the secondary course, the number of students being tested was 17,511. These totals include students from the telessalas, students in unorganised reception, and students not linked to the TELECURSO 2000 project. In the basic education course, Portuguese Language was the discipline with more candidates (18,208), and with a percentage of approval of around 45 per cent. Only 4,210 students took the test for English Language, an optional discipline, with 17 per cent approval, a poor result. The Mathematics test was taken by 15,726 students, with 32 per cent approval.

Grades in the secondary education course were quite low. About 15 per cent passed in Portuguese Language and 5 per cent in Mathematics. The best results were in Chemistry: 40 per cent of the 10,753 students were approved. These results do not differ much from other distance education projects or from regular adult schools maintained by the Education Secretary in the state of São Paulo.

It is perhaps too early to assess TELECURSO 2000. Presentation of the courses via broadcast television have not finished yet, and a special methodology would have to be devised to distinguish the achievement of TELECURSO 2000 students in the national examinations. The lessons that the experimental stage of TELECURSO 2000 can already teach us are the need to strengthen support to students through stronger orientation to tutors, and for the preparation of a very careful evaluation of the project as a whole in order to detect and correct the weak points and to reinforce the strong ones. Presently, tutors in the modality of organised reception receive only a three-day training course. The Roberto Marinho Foundation, SENAI, and Social Service for Industry all have courses with this purpose, which can be used to strengthen the support structure of TELECURSO 2000.

Cost

The total production cost of the project was US$43.4 million. FIESP contributed US$16.7 million, corresponding to the production of all the didactic materials. The balance of US$26.7 million was incurred by the Roberto Marinho Foundation, which was responsible for the pedagogical orientation, and for the marketing and exhibition of the programmes through Rede Globo, the largest television channel of the country. Firms, communities, trade unions, and others wanting to use the programmes, can get the support either of SENAI or SESI by means of a contract. All costs involved with the set-up of the telessala, its equipment, the videotapes of the programmes, and the payment of the tutor are the responsibility of the interested party. Each videotape, with eight programmes, costs about US\$16.00. The books are usually bought by the students. Each book costs around US\$5.50. The students also pay around US\$5.00 for each test they take. This is a very low price, which covers the expenses of preparation of the tests, the printed material, the applications, and the correction.

Conclusion

TELECURSO 2000 is not expected to solve all the educational problems of Brazil. Nevertheless, all the institutions involved are working hard to establish the project in the whole country. Every effort counts in the direction of wider coverage and better education for Brazilians. This new partnership for basic, secondary, and vocational education feeds the hope that Brazil will be able to move in the direction implied by Gro Harlem Brundtland, Prime Minister of Norway, in her Broady Lecture (the keynote address) at the Fourteenth World Conference on Distance Education, organised by the International Council for Distance Education (ICDE) in Oslo, 6 August 1988:

If society is to develop and prosper as we approach the next millennium, it will be necessary to devise a policy of knowledge. The value of specific, advanced, and updated knowledge will increase with the growing sophistication of society and the increasing complexity of national and international relations. The ability of organizations and nations to acquire and develop such knowledge will become a decisive factor determining the level of competitiveness and the potential for economic and social development.

References

FIESP and FRM (1994) 'Fundamentos pedagógicos do TC 200', unpublished, basic documents of the projects, Rio de Janeiro: FRM.

SENAI (1994) 'TC 2000 – Mecânica', unpublished, basic documents of the projects, São Paulo: SENAI.

Guaranys, L. R. and Castro, C. M. (1979) O ensino por correspondência: uma estratégia de desenvolvimento educacional no Brasil, Brasília: IPEA.

Guibert, A. P. and Romiszowski, A. (1980) 'Educational Technology in Vocational Training in Brazil', in Programmed Learning & Educational Technology, Journal of AETT, 17, 4.

IBGE (1991) *Censo Demografico do Brasil 1990*, Rio de Janeiro: IBGE.

Ministério da Educação e do Desporto (1993) *Plano Decenal de Educação para Todos*, Brasília: MEC.

Ministério da Educação e do Desporto (1996) *Reforma do Ensino Técnico*, Secretaria da Educação Média e Tecnológica, Brasília: MEC.

Ministério do Trabalho (1992) *Relação Anual de Informações Sociais*, Brasília.

Ministério do Trabalho (1996) *Plano Nacional de Educação Profissional*, Secretaria de Formação e Desenvolvimento Profissional, Brasília.

Oliveira, J. B. A. (1980) 'Novos rumos da formação profissional', unpublished paper presented at the Seminário Internacional 'Novos rumos da formação profissional', Minas Gerais.

Silva Filho, R. L. (1995) 'O financiamento da educação e a situação no Brasil', unpublished paper presented at the Seminário Internacional 'Novos rumos da formação profissional', Minas Gerais.

14

TECHNOLOGIES FOR DISTANCE EDUCATION IN DEVELOPING COUNTRIES

Wolfram Laaser

This chapter aims at reviewing critically the experience with distance education technology in developing countries and at identifying the potential for future development. A question in the background of the current debate on this issue introduces this chapter: should developing countries necessarily follow the same historical steps that distance education went through in industrialised countries? In order to get a more detailed picture of the variety and nature of the educational problems developing countries face, a short assessment of pressing actual and future educational needs is presented. The picture is complemented by three case studies that show completely different approaches to distance education in developing countries. Against this background, characteristic problem areas in the implementation of educational technology are identified. In light of this discussion, the initially posed question of the inevitability of a certain trajectory of development as opposed to possible leaps in the application of technology is reconsidered, and the possible contribution of donor countries is investigated. The chapter concludes with some policy recommendations that respect the experience of past development and at the same time leave sufficient options open for future extended use of sophisticated educational technologies.

The modernising bias of the 'generations' approach to distance education

The current discussion of technological change in distance education echoes in some respects modernisation theories of development. This can be identified in the way the development of distance education is explained as an unfolding of technological 'generations'. Nipper and others have discussed a model of three or four generations (Nipper 1989; Ishikawa

1996), starting with correspondence education via printed text (until World War II), followed by a second generation dominated by the diversification of media into mail, phone, and fax (1960 to 1980), and a third generation in which digitisation integrated the formerly separated media via multimedia software (1980–1990). With the development of new electronic modalities of communications, such as e-mail, computer conferencing, and video conferencing, a fourth generation is said to be emerging to characterise the present stage of distance education. This is the stage, sometimes called the virtual campus or virtual school, in which administrative functions and literature searches, as well as production, distribution, and tutoring, are provided via electronic networks.

In my view, this 'generation approach' shares some of the characteristics of Rostowian development stages, and falls prey to some of the same pitfalls. First, each generation is not homogeneous; even in the more advanced distance education systems, elements of what is considered characteristic of earlier development stages still dominate. Second, the generation concept takes as a generalised paradigm simplified observations of patterns of development of distance education prevalent in industrialised countries. Third, it implies an acritical, optimistic view that the whole world is converging to a global classroom with equal learning opportunities for all. As a consequence, policy implications are clear: development efforts in the area of education should be concentrated on capital investments in the telecommunications infrastructure to allow the connection of third world countries to the educational system of the first world.

The history of economic development showed that Rostow's deterministic, unilinear conception did not hold. Similarly, I am convinced that the 'generation approach' to the development of distance education is not helpful as a source of valid explanation or policy prescription for developing countries.

Pressing educational needs of developing countries

World population growth poses a tremendous challenge for the ideal of education for all. Even in the year 2025 about 100 million children will remain out of school. In the year 2000 the young age dependency ratio (population aged 0–14 as a proportion of the population aged 15–64) in developing countries will be 56 per cent, compared to 31 per cent in developed countries. The respective old age dependency ratios (population aged 65 or more as a proportion of the population aged 15–64) will be 8.3 per cent compared to 20 per cent.

The youthfulness of the population in developing countries has significant implications for the demand for teachers, who are needed whatever the modality of education, in the classroom or at a distance. These rather crude facts make it obvious that the priority of educational efforts in developing countries will be to incorporate young people in first- and second-level education, whereas age structure in industrialised countries explains their interest in improving and extending adult education.

Resources available in the developing world to meet the economic challenges of broadening educational opportunities are extremely limited. In the least developed countries overall public current expenditure per pupil declined from US$50 in 1980 to US$45 in 1988, while increasing from US$1,862 to US$2,888 in developed countries and from US$106 to US$219 in developing countries generally (UNESCO 1991: 37).

In the less developed world the pressure of increasing enrolment has led to the over-burdening of teachers. At the same time, declining real income in many countries has undermined teachers' morale, encouraging absenteeism and the search for supplementary sources of earnings and support. Widely prevailing shortages of textbooks and learning materials worsened as funds for their purchase dried up. In addition, the whole infrastructure of support services deteriorated. Furthermore, internal migration from rural to urban areas in Africa, Asia, and Latin America has overwhelmed the provision of education. Moving available resources from first to second and third levels of education, which added to the economic pressure on education budgets, was justified by pupil/teacher ratios and teacher remuneration, which are higher at more advanced educational levels. An additional burden is high school drop-out rates. In developing countries nearly one-third of the children who start the first grade are estimated to drop out before completing grade four (UNESCO 1991: 31).

From these facts we can conclude that the educational challenges of developing countries are lack of funding, lack of qualified teachers, and lack of adequate learning materials. Educational problems are reinforced by deficient infrastructure and inequality within the educational sector. Thus it is not surprising that many developing countries have looked at distance education as a low-cost alternative for mass education. However, the concepts of distance education developed in the industrialised countries for adult education match only in part the educational needs, availability of resources, and learner characteristics of developing countries.

While correspondence education has been used in Australia and Europe from the beginning of the century, distance teaching reached developing countries only after World War II. Several programmes were based on radio broadcasting supported by printed material. Later on, full-fledged distance teaching institutions were set up, as can be seen from the list below:

- University of Nairobi Correspondence and Mass Media Unit, Kenya (1968)
- Tanzanian National Correspondence Institute (1970)

- Mauritius College on the Air (1972)
- Free University of Iran (1973)
- Everyman University, Israel (1974)
- Allama Iqbal Open University, Pakistan (1974)
- Universidad Estatal a Distancia, Costa Rica (1977)
- Universidad Nacional Abierta, Venezuela (1977)
- Sukothai Thammathirat Open University, Thailand (1978)
- China Central Radio and TV University (1978)
- Andhra Pradesh Open University, India (1982)

This list is certainly not exhaustive. Distance teaching institutions at university and non-university levels can be found today in nearly every country of the world, either as autonomous distance teaching institutions (e.g., Open University in Great Britain, Fern-Universität in Germany) or as departments of external studies of traditional educational institutions (e.g., in the former communist countries and in Australia). More recently, distance education systems have also emerged as network systems that connect a variety of providers of teaching material (e.g., National Technological University in the US).

Selected examples of distance education in developing countries

China Central Radio and TV University

The China Central Radio and TV University was established in 1978 basically to train primary and secondary school teachers. From 1979 to 1986 the university enrolled over 1,700,000 students (Yun 1988: 3). Nearly every second Chinese graduate comes from this university. Programmes are distributed by satellite to local educational TV stations, which broadcast them to local audiences. Local governments are responsible for the setting-up of local TV stations and study centres with playback facilities. In 1991 there were about 700 local TV stations and around 50,000 study centres. Students complete most of their course work after viewing the tele-classes at the local study centres. The workload consists of additional readings and face-to-face lectures. The curriculum is unified and administered by the Provincial Radio and TV University. Examinations are prepared centrally. The answer-sheets, however, are marked by local teachers.

The new China Educational TV (CETV) now broadcasts on two channels, offering 31 hours of programmes. Over the last twelve years CETV published printed material for more than 300 courses, with a total sale of 150 million volumes (Chunjie 1992), plus 20,000 hours of audio-visual material. The speed of training primary and secondary school teachers has been significantly accelerated by this mode of training. Today, preparation of teaching materials has become dominantly geared to continuing education.

In the late 1980s, each graduate from CETV cost about 2,000 yuan, about one-third of the cost of graduates from conventional universities (Yun 1988: 7). So far, the Chinese teacher training programme is considered a success. Unfortunately, there is little detailed evaluation to serve as an empirical basis for this assessment. One indication of the reality (which does not diminish the significance of the effort nor the achievements so far) is the drop-out rate, which is not negligible in China, around 50 per cent in the late 1980s (Yun 1988: 14). As for the quality of material, broadcast TV lectures are generally of a poor didactic quality, and printed materials actually seem not to be adequate for self-study. In addition, the actual ratio of self-study to watching TV programmes is 2:1, which seems rather low. The effect of these features on the learning process is unknown. Because of limited transmission capacities, videotapes and audiocassettes are expected to be more widely distributed. Preparation of materials of higher didactic quality, including the printed material, constitutes one of the challenges for CETV.

The system is characterised by top-down teaching and may be somewhat comparable to the one-way correspondence model, using TV instead of print and with less focus on individual self-study (Bates 1991). A positive feature of the system is that it addresses specific educational deficits and the deficient transport and communications infrastructure. Use of TV for mass distance education seems to be not easily transferable to other developing countries. In non-socialist developing countries TV broadcasting is a private business, and broadcasting time is nearly out of reach for public educational institutions.

Correspondence education in Papua New Guinea

Papua New Guinea is a small, sparsely populated island nation with about four million people. Major distance education institutions are the College of Distance Education (CODE) and the Institute of Distance and Continuing Education (IDCE) of the University of Papua New Guinea. CODE provides secondary correspondence courses for grades 7 to 10 and in 1987 enrolled about 10,000 students (Kealey 1987: 21). By 1993 enrolment had grown to 44,000 (Markowitz 1994a: 2). IDCE is a dual-mode institution, offering both traditional and distance education courses. Enrolment at IDCE increased from 855 students in 1985 to 14,000 in 1995 (IDCE 1996: 24). IDCE offers review courses, courses at the secondary level (grades 11 and 12), and a growing programme at university level.

Instruction at both institutions is mainly delivered by print, with some additional audiocassettes (Arger 1990: 14). The correspondence material is supplemented by face-to-face sessions at local study centres where students register, receive their study materials, and submit their assignments for grading. Only a few centres have qualified tutors available.

From their inception, distance education programmes in Papua New Guinea aimed at:

- Offering more equal educational opportunities to people who have not had the chance of full-time study, especially those doing important work in remote areas.
- Improving educational standards of professionals without serious loss of work time.
- Offering a cost-efficient alternative to the formal educational system.

By the mid-1980s, these aims were far from being attained. Due to relatively low student numbers, media other than print were not seen as viable. The college operated more like a handicraft shop than a mass production industry. There was no evidence that courses were cost-effective. At the university level, the Department of Extension Studies was teaching distance education students as external students, without a specially designed curriculum or teaching materials. Conventional university lecturers prepared and conducted distance education courses with some central administrative support. Only after 1994, when IDCE was established, was more emphasis given to the development of special correspondence courses and centralised academic services (Markowitz 1994a). Since then, the system has shown rapid growth. However, new problems have been added to the already existing ones: students have to wait months for their courses to arrive (Markowitz 1994a), there is tremendous under-staffing, and incentives for authors of course material are lacking. Allocation of financial resources in the dual-mode IDCE seems to heavily favour the traditional part of the university (Pena 1993). To serve better the growing student population, educational broadcasts via satellite are being considered, but scarcity of qualified human resources may be a hindrance (Markowitz 1994b: 8).

Radio-based distance education in Latin America and Africa

A survey made by the Organisation of American States in the early 1980s identified fifteen radio education projects directed toward the formal basic education curriculum and thirty-two for out-of-school adult learners (Nielsen 1991: 129). Radio programmes in the basic education projects involved an idea of interactivity absent from the projects directed to out-of-school adult learners.

Radio programmes developed to improve classroom teaching at primary school level combined daily radio lessons with 15–30 minutes of teacher-led activity and some home study with printed worksheets. The radio programmes tried for interactivity, requiring a student's response every few seconds, even though this response was not broadcast or transmitted back to the radio speaker.

Radio programmes for out-of-school learners typically consisted of one or more hours of transmission, followed by group work led by project facilitators. Groups gathered at homes, community centres, or school buildings during evening hours. Short printed information materials were also used to supplement radio lessons. Programmes promoted basic literacy, numeracy, and livelihood skills and covered the basic education curriculum required for a formal certificate. Project facilitators usually received only a few days' training.

'Interactive' radio has been used in various Latin American countries, such as Nicaragua, Honduras, Bolivia, Costa Rica, and Ecuador. Radio programmes for out-of-school learners are used in Mexico, the Dominican Republic, Colombia (ACPO), and Argentina (INCUPO). They have also been used in some African and Asian countries. Some of these programmes aim at a basic education curriculum while others are more directed toward political and social mobilisation or at reinforcing local social or productive activities.

Evaluation of several 'interactive' radio projects shows that they were highly effective, particularly in rural areas, and that there were lower drop-out rates than in conventional education. 'Interactive' radio programmes seem also to be cost-effective for widespread and quicker improvement in education of a large population, compared to alternative strategies of textbook distribution or massive teacher training. The Radio-Assisted Community Basic Education (RADECO) project in the Dominican Republic claims that, with just a one-hour daily broadcast and some discussions and exercises, children's achievement levels matched those of students of regular schools (Nielsen 1991).

One can conclude, based on these experiences with radio-based distance education, that:

- Printed material plays a supportive role, audio information being the central instruction media.
- Group learning is fundamental, while individual study at home is much less decisive. Incentives for group action are a built-in feature of this modality of distance education.
- Tutors play the role of facilitators, for which less demanding and less formalised training is needed.
- Direct feedback from participants to facilitators is more important than feedback through assessment papers or written comments.
- The one-way character of radio transmission is adaptable to stimulate student participation and provide some sort of interactivity.

- Projects often address local needs of participants instead of merely repeating the content of formal school curricula.

Radio-based distance education clearly has some limitations. One is that students have to listen to radio at fixed hours. (This limitation can be mitigated by the flexibility of audiocassettes.) Interactive features can be included in this one-way medium only to a very limited extent. A true interactive dialogue with learners is costly and, for larger groups, almost impossible. In addition, sound information imposes severe limits to the learning of subjects in which the visual component is significant. In this case, printed information is a more adequate medium and has to receive stronger emphasis. As for content, programmes are sometimes hardly distinguishable from conventional education, simply making use of a different communications medium. Finally, the low qualification of tutors may backfire and hinder learning outcomes, particularly when a formal certificate is aimed at.

Summing up, the projects discussed above demonstrate a low-cost approach to mass education that requires relatively little emphasis on individual study and uses a communications medium that provides students a learning environment with some degree of participation and interaction.

Problems in implementing distance education in developing countries

I do not aim at constructing a complete picture of developing countries' experiences with distance education. The examples given above were meant only to illustrate the nature of some of the far-reaching distance education projects addressing the most urgent educational issues in developing countries, and the kind of problems these countries have faced in their implementation. I did not report on the full range of institutional settings, particularly the various types of open universities modelled after European distance education systems. With this caveat, I want to draw attention to what in my view are the prevalent characteristics of most distance education projects in developing countries: the dominant use of printed material, combined with the support of some mass communications media, generally with low interactivity; little and weak tutorial counselling; and the use of traditional textbooks instead of self-sustained modules. These characteristics must be reconsidered if distance education is to contribute to meeting some of the educational needs of developing countries.

It is important to recall the foundations on which distance education was based in the form in which it was introduced in industrialised countries to make my point clear. Distance education as we know it in the developed world is based on a highly individualistic concept of learning and on the primacy of the written word. While this mode of education flourished in the Anglo-Saxon cultural environment, it needs sweeping adaptations to produce the expected results in cultures that emphasise communalism and the spoken word. Cultural features of many regions and communities of Africa and Latin America, for instance, contrast sharply with the assumptions of distance education in the industrialised countries. In the former, education has to rely more significantly on group learning, face-to-face tutorials, and audio or audiovisual information. This is even more the case when the focus of education moves toward learners with little learning experience and low entrance qualifications. Such cultural aspects impose restrictions on the home study component of distance education, and if the means to re-create them for each individual learner are to be provided, this will usually result in a significant increase in costs. This is not to say that distance education is inapplicable in such cultural environments, but that it will have to be carefully designed, including the choice of communications media, to account for these special characteristics.

Distance education in developed as well as developing countries still has to struggle to gain the social acceptance and prestige of conventional education. The high enrolment figures of distance education systems, sometimes higher than those of conventional education, are not matched by similar quality assessments. Comparability with the conventional system is expected to be ensured by the adoption of virtually the same curricula. But this can, in fact, hinder innovative approaches that could make distance education, with its ability to cater for specific target groups, a characteristic that stems from its modular structure and superior flexibility in mobilising expertise, invaluable.

The educational systems of many developing countries, often inherited from the colonial powers, are characterised by centralised, authoritarian, and rigid structures. These characteristics have favoured in some countries the development of huge, autonomous, open universities which, by their 'industrial' mode of education production and delivery, have reinforced authoritarian structures. This kind of institutional context hinders the emergence of participatory approaches to distance education. In a study of the Institute of Distance Education in Papua New Guinea, Guy writes:

> The Institute effectively creates and defines the other through its practices of exclusion and authoritarianism. Students have to accommodate to this culture. There is little room, if any, for negotiation in a culture defined in terms of sameness, and it has resulted, generally, in a dependent student population that is open to control and manipulation.
>
> (Guy 1995: 80)

Furthermore, distance education systems need continuous restructuring and adaptation to changing curricular needs if they are to be effective. In order to gain the necessary flexibility, distance education institutions of industrialised countries draw substantially on the market to hire services and to contract personnel for a limited time. Such conditions often do not prevail in developing countries, which adds to the rigidity of their distance education institutions.

When distance education systems do not cater to local needs but instead rely on traditional, standardised, formal curricula, they may promote instead of reduce migration from disadvantaged areas to the crowded urban areas. An illustration can be taken from the Mexican TeleSecundaria (secondary education through TV). According to Palavicini, 'if Tele-Secundaria is to be effective in promoting the development of the Mexican countryside, to fill present educational needs, and to decrease urban migration, then this system should consider the introduction of a more rural-oriented secondary school curriculum' (Palavicini 1985: 136).

Many distance education systems in developing countries received initial aid for infrastructure and, occasionally, for course development. Frequently they face difficulties in covering recurrent costs after initiation of activities. As they cannot count on fees from young, usually unemployed people, they become generally dependent on public funding, for which they have to compete with politically stronger conventional institutions. Consequently, distance education institutions have to lower their recurrent costs by cutting down teaching staff, by offering relatively poor tutorial and counselling services, and by not investing in the quality of the learning material. Increases in drop-out rates follow, and the efficiency of the system drops.

Are leaps in technology possible?

It is argued that modern telecommunications applications in education can overcome some of the obstacles that the educational systems of developing countries are facing. These applications offer access (e.g., WWW, File Transfer Protocol) to external resources for learning, powerful tools (e.g., video conferencing and audio conferencing) for oral communications, and facilities for cooperative work in multiple locations (e.g., electronic mail, computer conferencing).

At face value nobody could deny the significant potential contributions of such applications. It is, however, essential to also consider negative impacts and possible threats. One possible outcome of accessing educational resources and teachers on the Internet is the constitution of a free market for education. Without compensatory action, many teachers and educational institutions in developing countries will not be competitive, and will probably become redundant. In this scenario, even if these countries specialise in some small niche of the educational market, they will become fundamentally consumers instead of providers of educational services to their own population. Their students will be taught by foreign teachers, with foreign material, about foreign issues.

Access to the Internet is in any case relatively costly in transition economies and developing countries. (In a current Russia/US joint project for course development through e-mail, the rather nominal connection fee of US$20 on the Russian side was considered extremely high by participants and probably will lead to the end of the entire project.) Thus, its potential benefits will be available only to the economically privileged, who can afford the investment in equipment and connection costs. The inequality within the educational sector of developing countries might increase. A countervailing measure could be to equip study centres, but this would only be viable if study centres provide sufficient workstations for a great number of individual learners. Open access thus may be more a myth than a reality. In addition, the required investments in telecommunications infrastructure will take substantial funds away from other social and educational uses. It is questionable whether the economic and social rates of return on this investment are really high.

As pointed out earlier, the most pressing problem of many developing countries is mass education. The solution implied by this 'fourth generation' model of distance education represents a switch from extensive to intensive growth. Tutoring via Internet is not labour-saving: it will increase the need for many highly qualified human resources. The use of video conferencing will reinforce this trend. Once again, this step in the development of distance education in developing countries reflects the situation of developed countries, rather than their own situation.

In my view a direct leap to modern telecommunications-based distance education is neither feasible nor desirable for most of the poorer developing countries. Even if the necessary investment in infrastructure is made, other components, such as operational services, adequate teaching, and tutoring, would still be deficient. The situation is somewhat more favourable in the middle-income and newly industrialised countries, which are capable of providing the necessary telecommunications infrastructure, are aware of the resulting operational costs, and are willing to tackle the problem of re-training human resources. The Latin American situation is described by Chacón in this volume:

> Distance education programs in Latin America have already taken a step toward the new ICTs, the main facilitating forces for this being governmental policies (in some countries), the experience accumulated in previous stages of development, and the existence of a relatively good infrastructure for electronic communications, including access to the Internet, for the whole continent [see page 230].

However, since public investment is not automatically accompanied by corresponding investment in private home computers, the trickle-down of the benefits of this investment to the grass-roots level, that is, to private homes, the basic study site for students at a distance, will still take years.

Short- and medium-term strategies for developing countries to bridge the gap

It is often recommended that countries translate or even directly use foreign course material as a fast and cheap solution until their own resources are sufficiently developed. This approach often disregards the fact that the transfer of course material can only be successful if a set of complementary conditions is fulfilled. Content and learning objectives, characteristics of students and trainees, educational functions and didactic concepts, characteristics of media, the learning situation, and economic conditions should widely correspond in the original and the intended transfer situation (Wickham 1993).

Another medium-term strategy would be to train students directly in foreign distance education systems. It is well known that a certain quota for foreign students in the traditional university system has always existed, and has certainly contributed to mitigate gaps in the educational systems of developing countries. However, it has been a source of considerable brain drain as well. Distance education today offers a relatively cheaper way of enrolling students of third world countries while reducing the risks of brain drain. Nevertheless, the full range of services, such as study centres or summer schools, is not usually available to the foreign student and may impair learning efficiency and lead to drop-out.

Therefore, both strategies – use of ready-made foreign material and access of students to foreign distance education services – may only serve to meet very urgent, immediate needs, not to provide viable solutions to major educational problems in developing countries.

Donor strategies

Distance education in the third world has been heavily influenced by donor countries. Nearly every project received some sort of funding, at least in the beginning, and every donor agency propagated its own model with some local adaptation.

The model of the British Open University was replicated in similar institutions in India, Pakistan, Thailand, Indonesia, and Hong Kong. These institutions follow the autonomous centralised pattern, with some tutorial services at local study centres. The International Extension College established a series of correspondence schools in Africa (Dodds 1985). The two large Latin American distance teaching universities in Costa Rica and Venezuela were modelled after European open universities.

The US Agency for International Development (USAID) favoured interactive radio schools, but the World Bank did not put much emphasis on distance education for many years (Haddad *et al.* 1990). Up to the end of the 1970s, educational priorities at the World Bank were given to formal secondary education and to vocational training, even though early investigations demonstrated that social rates of return on investment in education decline at higher educational levels (Jones 1990: 20). Now the World Bank is supporting some initiatives in tele-communications applications to education in developing countries through INFODEV.

Attempts to save costs in distance education, especially in course development, by coordinated international development policy, are numerous, but little cooperation is found at national or regional levels in developing countries themselves. International cooperation all too often follows a pattern that can be described as follows: First a network among participating educational institutions is established in a consider-able number of meetings. The network is highly donor-oriented, and other existing networks are ignored. Then common course development and exchange of information is initiated, using high-standard telecommunica-tions facilities sponsored by the donor. Data banks for mutual information exchange are established, but contain mostly research results and course materials developed in the donor countries. Once funding comes to an end, the network ceases to exist.

That this scenario, although somewhat exaggerated, is not completely unrealistic is demonstrated by the history of the Commonwealth of Learn-ing project. The nearly ten years of discussions meant to establish a multilaterally operated Commonwealth Higher Education Programme, including the harnessing of distance education and modern communica-tions and information technologies to support and accelerate development in countries that have neither the experience nor the resources to do it alone, have been described by Christodoulou:

> The Commonwealth is fast evolving into two camps: those who need and hope to receive, but are constantly frustrated; and those who have and give – but what they give and how they give is influenced primarily by their own trade and international political interests and their determination to control their own funds. For the present and as far as I can see into the future, Commonwealth co-operation, if not an outright sham, is an undernourished and sickly infant, and I join with those who predict perhaps irrepar-able damage to the Commonwealth connection.
>
> (Christodoulou 1992: 29)

Distance education played practically no role in German donor organisation strategies. Emphasis was given to the establishment of vocational training centres in developing countries and to exporting the German dual system of vocational training. One of the few attempts at supporting distance education projects is that of the German Foundation for International Development. The project addressed training of writers of material for basic distance education. Workshops were held over several years for audiences composed of external and local experts. This initiative was successful in improving the quality of learning materials in many ongoing projects. Organisational difficulties in local educational institutions (e.g., allocation of time for writers, delays in printing, and rapid turnover of staff) reduced the outcomes of a project that otherwise could be seen as a complete success.

Some lessons for international cooperation learned from past donor policies may be summarised as follows:

- Support should be given mainly to ongoing national projects, and administrative and organisational support should be supplied over a considerable time.
- Local staff should be trained to develop their own teaching materials instead of translating foreign course material.
- Projects that address local educational needs and are related to labour market demand should be favoured for international support and co-operation.
- Low-cost technology approaches such as audiocassettes supplemented by print should preferably be used. Mass media might serve to give motivational support and publicity.
- Expensive telecommunications links, if considered really indispensable, should be used strictly for discussion and not for delivery of the basic content.
- Projects should emphasise self-organised group learning and respect cultural styles of learning.
- Cooperation and specialisation among local distance teaching institutions as well as cooperation with local conventional institutions should be fostered.

Perspectives for future development

Geographic extent, population growth, and lack of qualified teachers are strong reasons for the wider use of distance education in developing countries. Visions of the world becoming a global classroom with equal opportunities for all are, however, misleading and hide the interest of industrialised countries to sell high-powered telecommunications and computer equipment. Pelton's words are revealing: 'in the light of the tremendous needs for both the developed and the developing world, tele-education may be the only means for long-term human survival' (Pelton 1991: 3); and (some pages later): 'From a management viewpoint, creating one or even two global production centres for tele-education to serve the entire world would be highly efficient and desirable, especially distribution, billing, scheduling, and marketing' (Pelton 1991: 8). Some initiatives in the US, such as the Global University or the University of the World, are already institutional incarnations of these ideas.

Advanced telecommunications and computer technologies are already spreading quickly to developing countries and will probably accelerate in the future. In the short run, their main application in education might be in the production of printed material, administrative support, and evaluation rather than in technically mediated tutoring or on-line distribution of teaching material. However, once the material is processed and stored in digital form, all options for future electronic distribution remain open (Laaser 1996: 258). New technologies have to be incorporated stepwise, and only after gaining experience with simpler methods of distribution and delivery. Often the main deficits are not of equipment or funds but of qualified human resources for teaching and management. The deficits will not be overcome in an efficient manner by merely adopting a system designed for the special purposes of industrialised countries. Although distance education will not solve all the educational problems of developed or developing countries, it can make a very important contribution if it is carefully applied and tailored to the specific needs and economic potential of each country.

References

Arger, G. (1990) 'Distance Education in the Third World: Critical Analysis on the Promise and Reality', *Open Learning*, June: 9–18.

Bates, A. (1991) 'Third Generation Distance Education: The Challenge of New Technology', *Research in Distance Education* 3, 2: 10–15.

Christodolou, A. (1992) 'Commonwealth Co-operation, Reality or Myth?', Broady Lecture, ICDE Conference, Bangkok.

Chunjie, X. (1992) 'An Overview and Prospect of Satellite Television Education', Proceedings of the ICDE Conference, Bangkok.

Dodds, T. (1985) 'The Development of Distance Teaching: A Historical Perspective', *Pakistan Journal of Distance Education* 2, 2, reprinted in Jenkins, J. and Koul, N. B. (eds), *Distance Education*, Cambridge: International Extension College, 1991: 6–12.

Guy, R. (1995) 'Contesting Borders: Knowledge, Power, and Pedagogy in Distance Education in Papua New Guinea', in Nouwens, F. (ed.), *Distance Education: Crossing Frontiers*, Proceedings of the 12th Biennial Forum of the ODLA of Australia, Rockhampton: Central Queensland University, Distance Education Unit.

Haddad, W. D., Carnoy, M., Rinaldi, R. and Regel, O. (1990) 'Education and Employment', Washington, DC: World Bank Discussion Papers No. 95.

IDCE (1996) *Institute of Distance and Continuing Education, Annual Report 1995*, University of Papua New Guinea, 1996.

Ishikawa, A. (1996) 'Virtual University and Classroom', in *Proceedings of the Second International Conference on Distance Education in Russia*, Moscow: Association for International Education, pp. 8–9.

Jones, G. W. (1990) 'Population Dynamics and Education and Health Planning', World Employment Programme, Paper No. 8, ILO, Geneva.

Kealey, G. S. (1987) 'The Impact of Distance Education in Papua New Guinea', in *ICDE Bulletin*, May: 18–35.

Laaser, W. (1996) 'How to Distribute Printed Course Material Electronically', in *Proceedings of the Second International Conference on Distance Education in Russia*, Moscow: Association for International Education, pp. 258–61.

Markowitz, H. (1994a) 'Management of Rapid Growth in Distance Education in Papua New Guinea', in *Structure and Management of Open Learning Systems*, New Delhi: Indira Gandhi National Open University, pp. 232–44.

Markowitz, H. (1994b) 'Prospects for Improving Distance Education at the University of Papua New Guinea through Telecommunications', paper presented at the Conference on Pacific Distance Education Networks, Suva, Fiji, March 1994.

Nielsen, D. (1991) 'Using Distance Education to Extend and Improve Teaching in Developing Countries', in *Perspectives on Education for All*, Ottawa: IDRC.

Nipper, S. (1989) 'Third Generation Distance Learning and Computer Conferencing', in Mason, R. and Kaye, A. (eds), *Mindweave: Communication, Computers, and Distance Education*, Oxford: Pergamon.

Palavicini, J. (1982) 'A System Analysis of a Mexican Educational System: Telesecundaria', Ph.D. dissertation, Concordia University, Montreal, Canada.

Pelton, J. N. (1991) 'Technology and Education: Friend or Foe?' *Research in Distance Education* 3, 2: 2–9.

Pena, P. M. (1993) 'Critical Challenges Facing Distance Education in Papua New Guinea: The Case of the Extension Studies Department', paper presented at the 1993 Conference of the Distance Education Association of New Zealand, Palmerston North, New Zealand, Massey University, College of Education.

UNESCO (1991) *World Development Report.*

Wickham, A. (1993) 'Transnational Co-operation in Course Development', Background Paper, European Association of Distance Education (EADTU) Conference, Heerlen.

Yun, Shen Qi (1988) 'Broadcasting Higher Education in China', Working Paper 002 E 88, NIME, Chiba, Japan.

216

15

KIDLINK – A GLOBAL
NETWORK FOR YOUTH

Claus Berg

What is KIDLINK?

KIDLINK is a global dialogue project for children aged 10 to 15, their teachers, parents, and other adults involved in education. Class participation begins at the fifth grade level. More than 90,000 children from 105 countries in all continents have participated since 1990, when the project was launched. KIDLINK is run by the KIDLINK Society, a non-profit organisation with headquarters in Norway. Most of the dialogue is based on electronic mail, but other means of communication (including the traditional post) and conferencing are also being used. KIDLINK runs a Web-site and a private IRC system, which will be explained below.

All children are required to answer the following questions as a starting point for participation in the global dialogue:

1   Who am I?
2   What do I want to be when I grow up?
3   How do I want the world to be better when I grow up?
4   What can I do now to make this happen?

Answers are submitted by e-mail to the RESPONSE mailing list, or through the automatic form included in a Web-page on the KIDLINK server.

The RESPONSE archive contains all the presentation messages from children throughout the years and is a very valuable resource within the project. Classrooms can do social studies and demographic surveys on different issues, comparing similarities and differences in the answers from children of all participating countries. Some children also use the RESPONSE 'database' to look for future electronic pen friends.

After joining KIDLINK through their RESPONSE messages, participants have several places to choose to go. Currently, we operate the following mail lists for youth dialogue. Adults are allowed to read the lists, but only children aged 10 to 15 can 'talk' here.

1   Open e-mail discussion:

>   KIDCAFE-INDIVIDUAL
>   KIDCAFE-SCHOOL
>   KIDCAFE-TOPICS
>   KIDCAFE-QUERY

2   Language-specific KIDLINK dialogue:

>   KIDCAFE-PORTUGUESE
>   KIDCAFE-SPANISH
>   KIDCAFE-JAPANESE
>   KIDCAFE-NORDIC

KIDCAFE-HEBREW, KIDCAFE-TURKISH, and KIDCAFE-ÍSLENSKA (Icelandic) are in different stages of development, but not yet open to youth dialogue, though the first two are already open to teachers and other adults.

3   Organised discussion:

>   KIDFORUM (involving classroom groups of students)
>   KIDPROJ (for long- and short-term projects)

4   Real-time chat on a private system:

>   KIDIRC

5   Gallery of computer art:

>   KIDART

Several KIDCAFES

When KIDLINK began in 1990, we had one conference called KIDCAFE being run from a computer in Toronto, Canada. When we moved our operations to the Internet in October of that year, KIDCAFE changed into a mailing list. In those early days, everything was simple – except the number of messages per day! We tried to find ways of making things easier for participants to deal with the amount of correspondence in their mail boxes, but the growth in the number of messages just would not stop. Eventually, KIDCAFE split into many mailing lists, each with a different purpose. Today, there is no single KIDCAFE, but instead all the KIDCAFEs listed above.

While we invite dialogue in any language on the first four of these lists, most of the discussions happen to be in English. Some may think that we consider them to be a KIDCAFE-ENGLISH group. Wrong! We think of them as part of a KIDCAFE-MULTIPLE: all languages are accepted. In the KIDCAFE-MULTIPLE domain, participants from countries other than the US are becoming more active, writing many messages. Sometimes there are messages in Spanish, Portuguese, Japanese, and German. Messages from Asian and African nations are also growing, which makes us feel very happy and pleased. KIDLINK is really reaching children all over the world! In addition to English, children now have a choice of languages in which to dialogue. This facilitates communication with children that share the same language and widens the possibilities of training in the knowledge of foreign languages.

KIDCAFE-SCHOOL now has over 300 schools registered. It is a non-moderated list where schools can participate in planned activities. This non-moderated method is much easier for teachers to manage. KIDCAFE-TOPICS is used for debates. Some examples of recent topics discussed include 'band practice' and 'about being a jerk or a nerd'.

KIDFORUM – a global classroom

This is our offering for classrooms to participate in planned/scheduled global on-line activities. Each topic is usually discussed for about six weeks, and includes a number of different opportunities to interact and learn from each other.

'Blue Print Earth' was one of the projects developed in the 1996/97 school year. It took place in the period from 1 January to 28 February 1996. The children discussed our environment, and tried to identify earth's major problems and possible solutions to them. Children designed equipment and goods whose consumption would contribute to solving the problems, planned marketing of these products, and arranged a week of auctioning. Some children also published essays on this topic. Moderators Indu Varma (Canada) and Tor Arne Richvoldsen (Norway) worked with children from twenty-six countries. Participants who answered all parts of the project received a diploma. Other KIDFORUM topics in the 1996/97 school year included 'Our Water' (1 March to 30 April), 'Friends and Families' (1 September to 31 October), and 'International Engineering and Robotics' (1 November to 23 December). For details on upcoming KIDFORUM topics, visit http://www.kidlink.org/KIDFORUM

'Virtual China': an example of a KIDPROJECT

In 1995 and again in 1996 we had a very special activity in the KIDPROJ list: the 'Virtual China' project. Students around the world were glued to their computer screens while students from Hong Kong International School reported their exploratory trips into mainland China.

The Hong Kong students were split into two groups. The first group made a one-week bicycle trip in rural southern China. The other group made a week-long trip to Xi'an, home of the famous terracotta soldiers. Both trips offered the opportunity to create memories to last a lifetime. The students posted their daily writings on KIDPROJ under the subject heading 'Virtual China'. All groups brought a digital camera and a laptop computer to capture digital images. KIDPROJ students from around the world 'travelled along', and asked e-mail questions to the groups throughout their journey.

'Virtual Sumatra', 'How People Live', 'I Have a Dream', 'Word Food', 'Money Project', 'Legends, Poems, Prose, and Stories Around the World', 'Hunt for Famous Explorers', and 'My Hero and Me' are some of the twenty-three projects developed in the 1996/1997 school year. Another fantastic opportunity to get a better knowledge of other cultures, is the KIDPROJ Multi-Cultural Calendar, which contains descriptions of national holidays written by participants from a great number of countries. See it at http://www.kidlink.org/KIDPROJ

KIDART

As children communicate not only in text, some are now mastering the ability to use electronic means to create beautiful pictures. The KIDART activities give them an opportunity to get a deeper experience with both their own and other children's artwork. The first KIDLINK Computer Art Exhibition was in 1995, showing work of children from Brazil, Denmark, Egypt, The Netherlands, Russia, Slovenia, Sweden, Uruguay, the UK, and the US. The 1996 KIDLINK Worldwide Computer Art Exhibition was a joint project of KIDART, Stephan de Haas, and the Botkyrka Friskola in Stockholm. It accepted contributions from 2–4 May and showed pictures made by children from Canada, Denmark, England, Japan, Russia, Slovenia, Spain, Sweden, and the US. The pictures of both exhibitions can still be seen (and downloaded for educational purposes) from http://www.kidlink.org/KIDART

KIDIRC

There is much interest in the Internet Relay Chat (IRC), but there is also confusion and suspicion. The IRC environment is very different from conferencing by electronic mail because it is a multi-user, multi-session, real-time screen chat option. The global IRC is indeed not a very safe place for children to go, and it is usually not regarded as a proper learning environment. KIDLINK has its own private IRC, where only registered participants can chat. It is used for formal educational purposes, distance education, on-line discussions, and just for cosy chatting between pen friends. KIDIRC is being used mostly in integration with planned/ structured activities. Read more about KIDLINK IRC service at http:// www.kidlink.org/KIDIRC

Meeting rooms for the adults in KIDLINK

All these activities could not possibly take place if adults (teachers and parents) did not have meeting rooms where they could discuss ongoing debates, plan new activities, and monitor the whole set of projects. KIDLINK currently operates the following coordinated forums for adults: KIDCAFE-COORD, KIDART-COORD, KIDFORUM-COORD, KIDIRC-COORD, KIDPROJ-COORD, KIDLEADER, KIDLEADER-PORTUGUESE, KIDLEADER-JAPANESE, KIDLEADER-SPANISH, KIDLEADER-NORDIC, KIDLEADER-HEBREW, KIDLEADER-GERMAN, and KIDLEADER-TURKISH. Most of these forums have their own pages on the KIDLINK Web server, directly accessible from links under the home page.

KIDLINK Research Institute

The KIDLINK Research Institute, created in 1997, is composed of two departments. The Research Department encourages research in education, human, and social sciences based on KIDLINK archives. The Educational Department offers formal training on KIDLINK for teachers, parents, universities and colleges, practitioners, and others. Information can be obtained from Marisa Lucena (mwlucena@ax.ibase.org), Research Department, and Lara Stefansdottir (lara@ismennet.is), Educational Department.

A girl from Brazil

Finally, I pass the floor to Michelle Lerner Melamed (11 years old), who gave a touching speech on how important KIDLINK became in her life, during a KIDLINK workshop in Rio de Janeiro, November 1996:

> Good afternoon! Well, the first time I used the Internet, although I already had a good relationship with computers, I have to say it was not easy. I was anxious to answer the four questions and take part in the KIDLINK group. I had prepared a message and then the problems started. The first one was to send the message. That was only possible on the second day of attempts, when I decided to do a step-by-step procedure with Marisa Lucena, by phone. Maybe this difficulty was due to the fact that I am used to programs with a more friendly interface by means of icons, as

in Windows, WinWord, or even Print Shop Deluxe. After sending the message, my expectations were very high. On that day I opened the mail about twenty times waiting for new messages. Soon, greetings started to arrive. I share the mail with my mother and when there is not even a small message for me it is quite a disappointment. The KIDLINK space was very important to me, because there young people from all over the world describe their experiences, all of them aiming at the same thing: new friendships. Something good that had happened was taking part in a recipe book, not only with Brazilian recipes, but also from many different parts of the world. In this project it was clear that neither the distance nor the language had served as any kind of obstacles to the work. We have also received messages about Timor, a place that I had never heard of before. I had to look up on maps to be able to find it, but the information that Timor was a colony that had achieved its independence from Portugal in 1974, and in 1975 was invaded by Indonesia for economic and political reasons, was something I learned through KIDLINK. This shows the power of the circulation of information through the KIDLINK net. Finally, I would like to say that undoubtedly through the KIDLINK net we can meet people and visit places that we would hardly have the opportunity to know personally.

KIDLINK builds bridges with curriculum-based projects and free dialogue between different cultures, across geographic borders and language barriers. In my opinion, the opportunity for new generations to use information technology to build their own global personal networks is one of the most important ways to prepare them to live and take responsibility in the global information society.

Notes

Information about KIDLINK is available on KIDLINK interactive information servers: World Wide Web address (http://www.kidlink.org), gopher://gopher. kidlink.org, gopher.kidlink.org All our public mail lists are run on a LISTSERV server. The full e-mail address to this resource is LISTSERV@LISTSERV.NODAK. EDU To receive an information file on KIDLINK by e-mail, send an e-mail message to: LISTSERV@LISTSERV.NODAK.EDU
Put the following command in the body of the message: GET KIDLINK. GENERAL
You can also write to our local contact persons around the world for information about how to join and more. Retrieve the file KIDLINK.CONTACTS for a list of addresses. KIDLINK has local representatives in Argentina, Australia, Bolivia, Brazil, Canada, Chile, China, Colombia, Costa Rica, Denmark, Estonia, Finland, Germany, Guatemala, Honduras, Hong Kong, Iceland, Ireland, Israel, Italy, Japan,

New Zealand, Norway, Peru, Poland, Russia, Saudi Arabia, Slovenia, Sweden, The Netherlands, Thailand, the UK, Uruguay, and the US. Finally, you can also write to KIDLINK, 4815 Saltrod, Norway.

The KIDLINK name and logo are service marks of the KIDLINK Society.

16

A non-European counterpoint

DISTANCE EDUCATION IN LATIN AMERICA AT THE TECHNOLOGY CROSS-ROADS

Fabio José Chacón Duque

Increasing *educational coverage* and *educational equity* have been permanent goals of distance education institutions in Latin America. Another important goal has been to improve the *quality* of education through innovation in technologies and methods. If one looks back sixty years, having in mind what is now called distance education, the obvious conclusion is that there has been an evolution in several stages, under the influence of shifts in technology.

From 1946 to 1966, correspondence and radio programs were used in adult basic education to raise the basic life skills of rural and underprivileged urban populations. The main content areas were literacy, numeracy, hygiene, agriculture, and crafts. These programs existed in almost all countries of the region. During this period, correspondence schools of the US and Canada established branches in Latin America.

An era of mass education followed (1967–76), this time characterised by the pre-eminence of television as a medium of mass education. There was an intense exchange between many Latin American academic centres and universities in North America and Europe, with the purpose of training personnel in all skills associated with the design, production, and delivery of educational television. Many TV centres were created in universities and ministries of education. There were serious attempts to establish continental tele-education programs (e.g., *Proyecto Andrés Bello* and *Proyecto SERLA*), but they stalled in the political decision phase.

The period between 1977 and 1989 is what might be called the stage of maturity. The leading event during this period was the creation and further consolidation of Open Universities or Open External Programs in Latin

America. These were modelled after the successful British Open University. Latin American open universities were created to respond to the strong demand for higher education of a growing young population. They also respond to the need of many adults for re-entry into the formal educational system in order to improve their qualifications for a more competitive society. Finally, and more defining of this stage, they share a model of distance education based on *multimedia instruction*, which combines print, tutorials, audio and video recordings, experiential activities, and other media for defined learning purposes. Other programs aimed at vocational and continuing education were also created under the influence of this higher-education model.

The 1990s are witnessing a paradigm shift in Latin American distance education with the emergence of open interactive learning systems. This is the current situation, in which information and communications technology (ICT) applications are being slowly introduced and experimented with in distance education programs. Some may dispute the very existence of this new stage because it is not widespread, but this is exactly how the previous stages started: some advanced institutions adopted a technology, demonstrated it to others, and triggered an emulation effort. I identify the beginning of this new period to be, symbolically, in 1990, the year of the Fifteenth World Conference of Distance Education in Caracas, a meeting that attracted more than 1,200 delegates. New ICTs and their applications were presented and discussed at this event, with many educational leaders and practitioners of the region in attendance. For many, this was their first contact with ICT.

The history of distance education in Latin America shows that there is no complete substitution of technologies, but rather a dominance of certain models during periods whose limits are blurred.

The current status

Distance education has been adopted in almost all countries in Latin America, but the countries where it has achieved larger coverage in terms of students and knowledge areas are Argentina, Brazil, Colombia, Costa Rica, Mexico, and Venezuela. Table 16.1 shows representative data about distance education programs in these countries, collected by direct observation and from interviews with educators. It must be mentioned that, while not ranking among the larger distance education user countries, Bolivia, Chile, Cuba, Ecuador, Guatemala, and Nicaragua also have important programs of distance education, whose numbers of students range from a few hundred to a few thousand.

The information in Table 16.1 indicates that the number of students in distance education is not very large, compared to the enrolment in traditional systems. Distance education students, however, are usually

Table 16.1 Descriptive data of distance education programs in Latin America

Country	Number of distance education institutions	Number of distance education associations	Approximate student population	Programs using ICT	Stated mission of programs
Mexico	51	1	200,000	4	Undergraduate, Graduate, Vocational, Continuing, Secondary, Basic
Costa Rica	2	0	15,000	1	Undergraduate, Graduate, Continuing, Secondary
Colombia	37	1	150,000	3	Undergraduate, Graduate, Vocational, Military, Secondary, Basic
Venezuela	5	1	100,000	3	Undergraduate, Graduate, Vocational, Continuing, Basic
Brazil	85	3	250,000	8	Undergraduate, Graduate, Vocational, Continuing, Secondary
Argentina	23	2	46,000	3	Undergraduate, Graduate, Continuing, Secondary

economically active adults who have a larger potential influence on social behaviour, particularly those training in professions such as basic and secondary education, pre-school education, business administration, public administration, and agriculture, which are the programs with the largest enrolment in most institutions. The existence of professional associations indicates a certain maturity of institutions. The introduction of new ICT applications is still at an incipient stage.

The low rate of adoption of ICT applications will certainly be reversed in the next few years due to two processes already in motion. One is the creation of graduate programs for training distance education staff in and with the new technologies, which started in 1994. Such programs exist in Argentina, Brazil, Chile, Costa Rica, Mexico, and Venezuela, and are delivered electronically within the countries or even internationally. The second process consists of large investments in ICT, particularly in public, but also in private, education sectors. Investments by public universities and schools are part of governmental policies for innovation in education, justified on the basis of the acknowledged importance of the incorporation of ICT for increased participation in the information society, more efficient methods of teaching, and the development of superior thinking skills. Following these policies, the national governments of Mexico, Brazil, Costa Rica, Chile, Cuba, Colombia, and Venezuela have made large investments in computers and networks for public schools. It is expected that other countries will follow soon. The deployment of these new systems is accompanied by intensive training programs for teachers, which, in turn, create demand for more specialised education. Private institutions are also expected to use ICT for innovative education. This is the case, for instance, of the Instituto Tecnológico y de Studios Superiores de Monterrey (Mexico), which has enabled its twenty-six campuses to interact via satellite using modern facilities for teleconferencing, computer communications, and distributed facsimile. Non-educational organisations such as the Galaxy Corporation and Televisa of Mexico have announced plans to offer courses via interactive TV.

Cooperative learning in Latin American schools: the *Quorum* network

A theme frequently mentioned in connection with the revolution of ICT in education is the use of distributed environments or virtual spaces for the purpose of collaborative learning. Learning may take place within the formal premises of the school or in an informal setting, such as the home, a café, or an electronic museum. The *Kidlink* network is an excellent example of informal collaborative learning, with teachers acting as mediators. Kidlink has gained so much acceptance in some Latin American countries since the Spanish and Portuguese clubs were created that Latin American students constitute, in fact, the majority of children participating in the project.

A similar, more formalised experience in collaborative learning that was designed and implemented in Latin America is the *Quorum* network, which originated in the pioneering work of some researchers in the school system of Costa Rica. This work was transformed into a large international project with support from IBM and West Florida University. *Quorum* involved a number of public and private schools in ten Latin American countries.

Quorum is a complementary tool for learning academic subjects in the schools. It provides computing and communications tools to teachers and students with a view to upgrading the quality of school learning by co-operation and development of curriculum materials. The core of *Quorum* is a set of computer applications termed *Thinkware,* which includes CMapEdit, Logo-Writer, Micro Mundos, and SuperLink. Students and teachers interact via e-mail in a controlled environment, although they can send and receive messages from the Internet. They can also search the Internet through a Proxy Server, which is set by the system operator to rule out sites considered improper. A special e-mail program allows each teacher and student to have a personal address, although their external connection is under one single Internet address for each school. Internal e-mail is used to announce activities, share text materials, and for free interaction.

CMapEdit is a tool for generating conceptual maps that allows input from many users. Children and teachers choose an important concept in any area of knowledge and start generating properties and relations for that concept. When a property or relation is mentioned by several users, it may be included in the concept map. In this way, children are stimulated to think and search on key concepts of science, language, and technology. *Logo-Writer* and *Micro Mundos* are two derivations of the Logo language used to create applications for drawing, illustration of principles, language games, etc. *SuperLink* is a multimedia authoring program that is very easy to use. It enables teachers and students to create presentations and instructional materials. The products are shared as attachments to e-mail messages.

The new educational methods in
Latin American distance education

One of the most evident effects of ICT is to introduce new ways of producing and distributing distance education. The ones most extensively used in Latin America are the enriched modular package, teleconferencing, individual multimedia, and on-line education.

The *enriched modular package*, used by Universidad Estatal a Distancia in Costa Rica and by the Sistema de Universidad Abierta of the Autonomous University of Mexico, results from the combination of text as major medium, with access to remote databases and web pages, and tutoring through e-mail or electronic lists. *Teleconferencing* is a leading tool in the Virtual University of Instituto Tecnológico y de Studios Superiores de Monterrey (Mexico) and in the Universidad del Valle in Cali (Colombia) for the delivery of expert lectures through audio or video communication devices that allow interaction with students. *Individual multimedia* is a central medium used by the University of Colima in Mexico, which has produced entire college-level and research courses in CD-ROM. *On-line education*, entirely delivered by means of computer networking, was first used in 1997 by the Universidad Nacional Abierta of Venezuela, for an International Specialisation Program on Informatics and Telematics for Distance Education. The program used the electronic network for briefings, discussions, forums, interviews with experts, communication within project teams, and debates. It is expected that new methods and educational principles will enable distance education programs in Latin America to overcome some of the inherited problems associated with this mode of education: high drop-out rates, low interaction between students and advisers, obsolescence of learning materials, scarce resources for staff development, and the low social status of distance education students and teachers.

International cooperation for distance education in Latin America

All this movement of renewal in Latin American education, both at a distance and in the classroom, could decline in a few years if there is not a mechanism in place for exchange of experiences among programs that stimulate users to share, emulate, and nourish from external sources. Fortunately, these links already exist, and it is foreseeable that they will widen and deepen in the future. The most important agencies of international cooperation dealing with distance education and its technological innovation in the region are named below.

AIESAD (Asociación Iberoamericana de Educación Superior a Distancia) was formed by the rectors of distance education universities or programs. The coordinating office is in UNED of Spain. *CREAD* (Consorcio-Red de Educación a Distancia) is a professional and institutional association that coordinates exchanges between North and South in the Americas. Its headquarters are at Pennsylvania State University (US). *RIBIE* (Rede Iberoamericana de Informatica na Educação), formed by twenty-one countries, deals mostly with informatics and telematics applied to education and promotes conferences every two years. The coordination function rotates among the countries. *IESAD* (Proyecto de Innovación en Educación Superior a Distancia), sponsored by UNESCO, provides staff development programs to all countries in Latin America. The coordination function is at Universidad Nacional Abierta, Venezuela. *GENESIS* is the network that supports the *Quorum* program. It can be accessed through any IBM branch in the Americas.

Conclusions

Distance education programs in Latin America have already taken a step toward the new ICTs, the main facilitating forces for this being governmental policies (in some countries), the experience accumulated in previous stages of development, and the existence of a relatively good infrastructure for electronic communications, including access to the Internet, for the whole continent. In spite of policy inconsistencies and the general scarcity of financial resources, this change has already had important results in the modernisation of instruction. Programs applying ICT to education are now increasing their performance indicators in terms of achievement and retention of students. Changes in distance education programs toward the new paradigm are desirable because they will reduce, and in some cases eliminate, the major flaws of these programs.

One beneficiary of improved distance education will be the public education system, because of the greater number of better-prepared teachers that will come out of the modernised programs. These teachers, already familiar with the new working environments, will be major agents of innovation in the two modalities of education.

Since the goal of a computer plus communications facilities for each student is not feasible in the current situation of the region, distance education institutions and public schools must provide local facilities that can be shared by several students and use the new ICTs in combination with printed text, audiocassettes, and television broadcasts. At the same time, institutions must connect with computer and telecommunications companies in order to provide facilities for those students who would like to communicate from their homes. Lending systems for machines, preferential rates for connection, leased machines with option of purchase, and retail shops for used machines are among possible solutions.

A number of recommendations are in order for the European Union (EU), which has been and will be involved in many cooperation efforts dealing with distance education and ICT in Latin America. The European Commission can provide its expertise in the management of telecommunications systems and the creation of effective links among countries. It can also extend its cooperation for staff development in distance education, sharing its extraordinary experience with the most successful and enduring distance education institutions in the world. The already existing staff development programs in Latin America can be supplemented with European courses, and some new ones can be created. A catalogue of

EC programs for development of distance education staff is an ultimate necessity.

Finally, part of EC aid to Latin America could be assigned to countries that still do not have distance education, or have a very poor communications infrastructure. Continuity of aid could be conditioned on improvements in performance indicators, such as student retention, grade averages, and reduction of completion times.

CONCLUSIONS

Despite their diversity in experience and approach, the authors of this volume attempt to identify the opportunities for, and the limits to, a rewarding economic partnership between Europe and the developing world. As they argue, it is the emerging forms of organisational and knowledge networking that set the parameters of cooperation and competition between two, albeit unequal, economic blocs. For Europe, the transformative power of the ICT revolution makes it possible to locate new markets and to secure appropriate skills in the developing parts of the world (see chapters by Djeflat and Kaplan in this volume). In the face of the declining demographic trend and the scarcity and expense of cognitive skills in Europe, the advantages of relocating information-intensive work to countries with surplus knowledge workers prove rewarding for the efficiency of the European corporate sector (see chapters by Mitter and Efendioglu, Huws, and Basrur and Chawla). The spur that such relocation provides leads also to an expanding market for Europe, particularly in telecommunications infrastructure and equipment. The examples are satellite and radio technologies, as well as mobile hand phone systems (see chapter by Davies). The authors demonstrate the new market possibilities such expansion presents for Europe. They also point out the business strategies that will make Europe more attractive as a trading partner to the developing world *vis-à-vis* Japan or the United States (see chapters by Bastos, Djeflat and Kaplan). The role of telematics-mediated distance education is placed in the context of such a strategic vision by the contributors.

The increase in information intensity of the production process of the service and manufacturing sectors facilitates the trade in telematics-related goods and services. It also leads to alterations in the requirements for skills and to a need for continuing technological education. The possibility of dispersing employment with the use of ICT, from the core urban areas to peripheral regions of Europe or to offshore countries in Asia and Latin America, has opened up new opportunities to excluded regions and, at times, to traditionally disadvantaged groups, such as women, in these areas (see chapters by Richardson and Reardon). Yet, the gains may be short-term unless the employees are assured of life-long training and career paths.

In the face of automation and rapid changes in skills requirements, it becomes important that employees have access to continuing education and training. In the absence of such facilities, as some of the authors argue, such relocated work may represent the information age analogue of branch plant manufacturing (see chapters by Richardson, and Mitter and Efendioglu).

The need for flexible and lifelong training, necessary for securing and maintaining a niche in the global information economy (see chapter by Tuijnman), makes the case of telematics-mediated distance education a special one, especially in the context of an evolving relationship between Europe and the developing world. The phenomenon of 'brain drain' from the developing world has become a vexed question among Europe's trading partners (see chapters by Djeflat and Kaplan). Europe itself looks at the question of immigration with a certain unease in the face of rising un-employment (see chapters by Huws and Laaser). The possibility of deliver-ing technical and professional education through new electronic modes of communication, from Europe to the developing world (see chapter by Laaser), to a certain extent mitigates the tension around this question of the global mobility of labour and its consequences.

European educational packages marketed in the developing world need not be geared to delivering training that caters to the needs of Europe alone. The material produced by relevant institutions in Europe could also meet the skills requirements of domestic markets in the developing world. Such trading links could go far beyond the domain of English-speaking nations. The multiple linguistic and cultural links between Europe and the developing world could be a source of a new form of trade, in electronically transmitted educational materials (see chapter by Bastos).

The papers elucidate the possibilities of mutually beneficial trade, but they also emphasise the challenges that the internationalisation of the production process and educational materials pose for the trading partners. Inadequacies of infrastructure are only one of the major handicaps that most partners in the developing world encounter. Inadequate literacy, numeracy and computer skills make it difficult for the developing world to absorb either the relocated work or the facilities of distance education and training. The limited capacity of the developing world thus limits the market potential of European companies. Here, researchers and practi-tioners of distance education give readers a timely warning against the notion of a 'technical fix'. The experience of using the electronic mode of distance education in Europe (see chapter by De Kleine) is acknowledged to be of importance to the developing world (see chapter by Kinyanjui), but the experience, the contributors argue, should be replicated with proper modification.

Using case studies from a wide range of developing countries, a number of the authors alert us to the importance of respecting the educational and cultural traditions of the non-European countries before adopting the European model of distance education (see chapters by Laaser and Guibert).

In teletrade, as well as in telematics-mediated education and training, some developing countries are making innovative experiments for human development, social cohesion and sustainable development. Such experiments are of significance both to Europe and to developing nations. The example of Tata Consultancy Services (TCS) of India in carving out a market niche in the software trade highlights the business and market strategies that a company can successfully deploy (see chapter by Basrur and Chawla), be these in Europe or elsewhere. The Latin American experiments with new modes of distance education could likewise provide models of basic and professional training for disadvantaged regions and groups in Europe (see chapters by Chacón and Guibert).

In mediating a rewarding economic relationship in the emerging information society, the text and the context of the contributors in this volume thus call for a new partnership in the research agenda, extending to academic institutions, the corporate sector, trade unions and government bodies.

There is a potential for collaboration and cooperation, to mutual advantage, between Europe and the developing world. Rigorous research in the relevant areas is likely to pave the way to identify strategies that will make this potential an achievable goal.

INDEX

Note: Entries in **bold** text show contributions to this volume. Page numbers in **bold** indicate figures or tables. These are only given where there is no textual reference on the page.

Abbreviations used in subheadings

ATMs automated teller machines
CoPS complex product systems
EU European Union
ICT information and communications technology
IT information technology
MNCs multinational corporations
NIT new information technology
PSTN publicly switched telecommunications network
TCS Tata Consultancy Services

DATE DUE

MAY 1 2 2001

MAY 0 1

NOV 2 0 2002

NOV 3 0 REC'D

BOWLING GREEN STATE UNIVERSITY
DISCARDED
LIBRARY

GAYLORD

PRINTED IN U.S.A.

HE 8084 .E96 1999

Europe and developing
countries in the globalised